Selling
and
Communication Skills
For Lawyers

A Fresh Approach to Marketing Your Practice

JOEY ASHER

2005

ALM Publishing
New York, New York

Cover Design: *Ehren Seeland*

Interior Page Design & Production: *Amparo Graf*

Library of Congress Cataloging-in-Publication Data

Asher, Joey, 1961-
    Selling and communication skills for lawyers: a fresh approach to marketing your Practice / Joey Asher.
        p. cm.
    Includes bibliographical references and index.
    ISBN 1-58852-130-3 (alk. paper)
1. Lawyers—United States—Marketing. 2. Advertising—Lawyers—United States. 3. Practice of law—United States. I. Title.

KF316.5.A97 2005
340'.068'8—dc22

2005007608

DEDICATION

For Johanna

ACKNOWLEDGMENTS

This book is the result of years of helping hundreds of lawyers at dozens of firms. I am grateful to all of them for their help in providing me with their experiences and stories. I am particularly grateful to those terrific lawyers and marketing professionals who generously agreed to be interviewed for this book, including Bruce Richards, Steve Whitehead, Mike McGuire, Jim Stokes, John Yates, Bob Pile, Scott Petty, Brett Lockwood, Jocelyn Hunter, Michael Golden, Kenneth Glazer, and Ed Schechter.

Thanks also to my former law professor Tim Terrell for his help in reviewing my analysis of the ethics rules. As he did when I was in law school, he found the flaws in my legal analysis.

I also want to thank Richard Gard, former editor of *The Fulton County Daily Report,* for his initial encouragement and support of this project. Thanks also to Caroline Sorokoff of American Lawyer Media for her continuing support throughout this effort.

Finally, thank you to my terrific editor Dory Green. Dory did what fine editors should do: push the writer forward, question choices, suggest improvements, and provide encouragement.

Contents

PART TWO

COMMUNICATION SKILLS

INTRODUCTION:
IT'S ALL ABOUT HELPING
BUSINESSES SUCCEED

This book is about how to win clients and how to make them love you. To do this, lawyers must be more than great technical lawyers. They need to build relationships and communicate in terms of the client's business value.

Contrary to what many lawyers will tell you, the best way to win business is not simply by being a "great lawyer." Many great lawyers generate no new business for their firms. The best way to win business is to make a prospect believe that you can add value to that client's business.

And you don't keep clients happy by always getting the "right answer." Great technical lawyers get fired all the time. You keep clients happy by communicating in a way that builds relationships and guides the client toward business success.

I'm always amazed at how many lawyers fail to grasp the idea that businesses love lawyers primarily when they generate business value, not when they provide "great legal work." Even the greatest lawyers at the nation's most prestigious firms forget this fundamental concept.

I was doing a workshop recently for a group of litigators at a very prestigious New York law firm. The billing rates of the lawyers in the room tended toward $500 to $600 an hour. And their clients happily paid those fees.

We were gathered in a very high-profile midtown university club in a beautiful old, wood-paneled conference room. I was standing at the front of the room with a marker and a flip chart. And I asked the following question: "Why do you think that a business would select any of you as their lawyer over another lawyer from another firm further down Sixth Avenue?"

For a moment there was a pause. Then a hand went up.

"They pick us because we're the best lawyers in the city," said this fantastic trial lawyer.

"They pick us because of our experience," said another truly wonderful attorney.

"Expertise."

"Quality of our work."

"We're just great lawyers."

And I wrote down all of these answers until we had a list of ten possibilities, all of which related to the perceived high quality of the legal expertise of the attorneys in the room.

I then paused and surveyed the group.

"None of these is the correct answer," I said. "I've asked this same question of general counsels and business owners many times. And even though great legal work is important, it's not the primary reason why businesses hire one lawyer rather than another. Over and over they tell me that they want lawyers who understand their business, are focused on helping them achieve business goals, and can speak to them about the law in terms of how it can help them achieve their business goals."

And these litigators sat in silence for a few moments until one of them nodded and admitted that her best client, one that she had been helping for many years, loved her because she understood the business and was focused on its success.

This book will help you succeed in generating and keeping clients by making sure that you're always focused primarily on understanding and communicating about helping the business succeed.

BEING A GREAT LAWYER IS A "TABLE STAKE"

Let's be clear about something. I'm not saying that it's not important to be a good lawyer.

Of course it's important. But being a good lawyer in and of itself is no longer enough to succeed. Lawyers are technically better now than they've ever been. When I was hired at my former firm more than a decade ago, one of the partners told me, "I don't think I could get hired today at this firm. The bar has been raised too high. Every kid coming in here is too smart."

Being a good lawyer today is assumed. It's the price of admission to the game. In poker it would be called a "table stake." And businesses know it. "Great legal work and work product is assumed," one in-house lawyer told me recently. "We won't even speak to you if you're not a terrific attorney."

And this book can't help you unless you're already a terrific attorney. If you're not already a great lawyer, put down this book right now and go learn your craft because otherwise you're going to have a miserable career. There are too many great lawyers who will beat you every time. But assuming that you understand the law, this book will help you communicate about the law so that you connect with clients and potential clients. In other words, it will show you how to win business and how to keep business.

For example, you should read this book if you want to learn how to:

> Conduct a one-on-one sales meeting with the President of a $50 million aluminum fabricator and make him want you as his company's lawyer. (Some lawyers insist on calling these encounters "business development meetings" rather than something so untoward as a "sales meeting." Call them whatever you want. Just don't come back without the business.)

> Make real estate developers listen to your discussion of the Federal Tax Code (instead of rolling their eyes and thinking that you're a geek).

> Have utility employees care about an antitrust law presentation. (What's not to love?)

> Persuade a bank executive to take your advice and disclose troublesome information to regulators.

> Connect with human resource executives at a labor law conference (instead of hovering close to your partners or fellow associates and making no connections).

▶ Get a meeting with that theater chain CEO who happens to be your neighbor but whom you're a little nervous about calling to discuss business.

▶ Win the "beauty contest" being sponsored by the local gas company that has decided to consolidate all its legal work into only a few firms.

How Good Are You at Getting and Keeping Clients?

Without a doubt, the most important key to becoming a successful lawyer is being able to communicate effectively with clients and potential clients. Indeed, many unsuccessful lawyers have little problem dealing with the technical aspects of their jobs but fail in those jobs because they confuse clients or potential clients when they try to explain problems and remedies.

Want to see how you rate on the client communication scale? Take the Client Connection Assessment Test (CCAT) to see how well you connect with business people. Answer all questions by circling "yes" or "no."

(1) Whenever you speak to clients about the technical aspects of the law, before even mentioning Code provisions, you start by discussing how the law will impact their business. For example, you have never begun a conversation with a client with the words, "The Federal Tax Code says that. . . :" **Yes** **No**

(2) You have no problem calling up friends and "near friends" who own businesses and asking to meet with them to discuss the value that your firm can bring to their businesses. The mere thought of calling a fellow soccer dad does not prompt you to reach for your Prozac. **Yes** **No**

(3) When you meet with a prospective client, you know exactly how to conduct the meeting in order to ensure that he sees how your firm will be able to provide great value to his business. **Yes** **No**

(4) When you attend conferences and industry meetings, you know how to "work the rooms" so as to make as many

potential business contacts as possible. When it comes to schmoozing, you know how to do it tastefully, yet effectively. **Yes   No**

(5)   During "beauty contest" presentations, you know exactly how to present your firm so that you separate yourself from the other prestigious firms that are also in the competition. **Yes   No**

(6)   When someone asks you, "What do you do?" you have an answer that doesn't make people want to run away. (One answer that makes people flee is, "I'm a lawyer."). Rather, you have prepared and learned a simple answer that helps the questioner understand the value you provide to your clients. **Yes   No**

(7)   When someone asks you a complex legal question during a meeting, you don't get a "deer in the headlights look," but rather respond simply and in a way that connects with the real issue that is driving the question. **Yes   No**

(8)   You know how to conduct meetings with current clients where you seek out further ways that your firm can add value to the clients' businesses. **Yes   No**

(9)   When you speak at industry conferences, your presentations actually invigorate your colleagues rather than inducing deep REM sleep. **Yes   No**

(10)   When you give presentations educating your clients on how to comply with the law, your presentations focus on a few simple, practical issues rather than "black letter law." **Yes   No**

Total up the number of "yeses" and check your score below:

9 or 10 Yeses. "Superb Client Connector." You have a strong understanding of how to communicate about legal issues in a way that connects with executives and how they see their business. You speak simply and without too much "legal geek speak." You also know how to communicate with prospective clients in a way that makes them want to hire you. You should be making a lot of money. If you're not making a lot of money, you'd better go back and recheck your test.

5 to 8 Yeses. "Client Connection Potential." You have some skill at connecting with clients. I wouldn't doubt that you're a partner in a prestigious firm. But you still don't communicate with the clarity that characterizes the best lawyers. And you probably aren't close to maximizing your business development potential. To get to the next level, read on.

0 to 4 Yeses. "Legal Geek." You may be able to draft a humdinger of a "Complaint for Damages and Application for Temporary Restraining Order and Preliminary and Permanent Injunction." But your clients probably have no idea what you're talking about. And they may not love you as much as you think. Also, you probably have no idea how to bring in business. That's not to say that you can't learn. To do that you must read on.

RAINMAKING IS CLIENT-FOCUSED COMMUNICATION WITH GUTS

Why combine both rainmaking and client communication into one book? Because business development and great client communication utilize extremely similar skills sets. If you can make your existing clients love you, you can make prospective clients want to hire you.

Put another way, if you can effectively and simply communicate why your client should adopt a new tax strategy, you can almost certainly meet with a CEO and persuade her to hire you as her company's tax lawyer. In both cases, the key to success is understanding the client's perspective and being able to articulate simply the business value you provide.

To be sure, business development takes both planning and guts. To win the client, you must have a meeting with the CEO or General Counsel. That's not hard to do. But you also need to know what to say when you pick up the telephone to ask for such a meeting. Most important, you need the nerve or guts to actually pick up the telephone and dial. But if you know how to communicate effectively with existing clients, then you can make that telephone call successfully.

TWO STEPS TO SUCCESS

Great business lawyers know how to communicate with existing and prospective clients. This book shows you how to do both.

Prospective Clients

The first part of this book will show you how to win clients. That includes how to:

- ▶ Work a room at seminars and industry conferences.
- ▶ Create and deliver the kind of "elevator pitch" that makes executives interested in your practice.
- ▶ Set meetings with prospective clients by calling them on the telephone.
- ▶ Conduct effective meetings with prospective clients.
- ▶ Win beauty contest presentations.
- ▶ Conduct meetings with existing clients that make them want to give you more business in different practice areas.

Existing Clients

The second part of this book will show you how to make your existing clients love you. That includes how to:

- ▶ Deliver presentations that wow clients and colleagues.
- ▶ Develop a communication style that makes your clients like you as a person.
- ▶ Communicate effectively in meetings.
- ▶ Respond effectively and simply to client questions, no matter how complex they may be.

PART ONE

Selling

CHAPTER **1**

Overview of Selling Skills

INTRODUCTION
   This Ain't Your Father's Business Development Strategy
   You Can't Wait for the Telephone to Ring

A FORMULA FOR EFFECTIVE BUSINESS DEVELOPMENT
   Prospecting: Connecting with People Who Hire Lawyers
   Showing Value: What Most Lawyers Don't Understand

TIME: PLANNING AND FOLLOW-UP TO MAKE BUSINESS DEVELOPMENT HAPPEN
   Maintaining a Long-term Attitude

PERCEIVING AND FILLING NEEDS

INTRODUCTION

When you speak to seasoned lawyers in corporate law firms, you can get a lot of advice on how to generate business. I've heard senior lawyers advise junior lawyers to do all of the following to win new business:

- ▸ Just be a great lawyer. The business will come to you.
- ▸ Return all of your phone calls.
- ▸ Give speeches to colleagues about changes in the tax laws.
- ▸ Write articles on the changes in OSHA regulations for a national trade publication.
- ▸ Teach Sunday school at the local Methodist Church.

▶ Sign up for the Peach Bowl committee and sell more tickets than anyone else.
▶ Become a leader at your synagogue.
▶ Manage the campaign of your local congresswoman.
▶ Network with people on your block, or better yet, get involved in the Neighborhood Planning Unit.
▶ Raise money for Cornell University.
▶ Become President of the University of Maryland alumni association.
▶ Raise money for the American Cancer Society.

For the most part, this advice is highly misleading and not very helpful. How does raising money for your college lead to revenue for your law firm? Suppose I show up at the fundraiser and make calls for my college fundraiser. I get to know a few people in town. And then what? What's going to make my telephone ring? What's going to make a general counsel think of me when he has a legal problem? At what point do the rain clouds begin to gather? When does the money start to come my way?

Ask those questions and the senior lawyer will say something vague like, "Well, people will get to know you and eventually people will start to call you."

This is the "it happens by magic" theory of business development. You get to know people and, after a while, by magic, these people start to somehow believe that you can help them with their business problems.

The problem with the "it happens by magic" theory is that *it doesn't work*. People won't just "start to call you." Sure, they'll get to *know* you. But why will they call you for legal work? They're going to hire you to oversee a business merger because you are a heck of a fundraiser for your college? Gimme a break!

Let's face it. Networking with the local bar, selling Peach Bowl tickets, writing legal articles, and raising money for charity by themselves won't bring in business. Even being a great lawyer in and of itself doesn't bring in business consistently. Why not? Because none of these activities bear any relationship to *why businesses hire lawyers.*

If you don't have a strong grasp on why lawyers are hired, you will never consistently generate revenue for your firm.

This is not to say that selling Peach Bowl tickets might not help a *good business developer* get the contacts needed to *start* to win business. There are many things that lawyers can do that eventually lead to business if done properly. *But there is only one way that business people decide to hire lawyers.* And here it is:

> **Business people hire lawyers whom they believe will help their business succeed.**

That's it. At its most fundamental level, business development is no more complicated than applying the truth of that statement. *The more your business development activities are aimed at showing specific business people that you can help their business succeed, the more successful you will be.*

Of course, this principle's corollary is that if you don't show specific business people that you can add value to their business, they won't hire you. In fact, you can know more than a Yale Law professor, be the best friend of the general counsel, and be the godfather of the President's daughter. But if you don't show business people that you can add value to their business, they probably won't hire you as their lawyer. Nor should they.

That's not to say that if you ignore this business truth you will never generate business. Even blind pigs stumble across acorns once in a while. But if you want to consistently squirrel away the "acorns" of new business, you must *systematically do things* to spend time with business people and make them believe that you can add value to their specific business.

That's it. Nothing else works consistently.

Let me go even further. You can invest in clever advertisements that run in *The American Lawyer* and on your local public radio station. You can hire a graphic design firm to create beautiful brochures. You can hire an expensive consultant to tell you how to be innovative in billing your clients. Although those marketing devices have their own value, none of them cause business people to pick up the telephone, dial your number, and say, "Can you handle this transaction for our business?" That only happens when a business acknowledges that you understand its business and have value to offer.

This Ain't Your Father's Business Development Strategy

The ideas in this section are clearly contrary to the historical orthodoxy of growing a law practice. But the orthodoxy must be challenged because of the increasing commercialization and commodification of the big firm law practice.

To me that orthodoxy is represented by a wonderful lawyer whom I'll call Charlie. When I was practicing law, Charlie would regularly speak at CLE functions about business development. Keep in mind that Charlie was a legend, one of a handful of the most reputable lawyers in the city, a "go to guy" when your business was in trouble.

And when Charlie discussed business development, here is what he would say, as best I can recall. To hear Charlie tell it, business development boils down to two rules:

RULE 1: "The most important rule for developing business is to do great work. Be a great lawyer. You'll never get a following if you're not someone who reliably turns out a great result for your clients."

RULE 2: "Return all your telephone calls."

That was it.

Do good work and return telephone calls.

Charlie would talk for a full hour. But that was the sum of it. And all across the country, senior lawyers tell young associates the same thing about business development. Develop a great reputation and be responsive. The business will come.

But the fact is that is not enough. In retrospect, I want to stand up and shout to Charlie, "That's your business development advice? *Really? Truly?*"

Doing great work and returning telephone calls is certainly good general advice. And no doubt it worked for Charlie, who, as I mentioned was one of the top three or four lawyers in the city. His telephone rang off the hook because of a reputation developed over thirty years.

But for lawyers today, "Do good work and return phone calls" is ridiculously simplistic and misleading business development advice. I know dozens of lawyers who do wonderful, highly creative legal work and return every one of their telephone calls and yet have no clients of their own.

For example, I know a partner in a large firm—let's call him Jim—who is considered a truly brilliant brief writer and lawyer. He gets great results for his clients. And he returns all of his telephone calls.

Get this. He actually takes Charlie's advice one step further, doing better than "returning his calls." Sometimes, he actually answers his telephone! You know, just picks up the thing when it rings (which I suppose might be considered innovative business development activity by some standards).

The problem is that Jim's telephone never really "rings"—at least not in the way a good business developer's phone rings: with clients calling asking for legal help. All of Jim's clients were given to him by other partners, many of whom were not as good technical lawyers as Jim.

The reason for Jim's failure to develop business is that Jim apparently has taken the advice of lawyers like Charlie. Rather than finding ways to get in front of decision-makers who can hire him (be it new prospects or firm clients who could be cross-sold), Jim waits for his telephone to ring.

You Can't Wait for the Telephone to Ring

Waiting for your telephone to ring is terrible business development advice because today (apparently unlike the days when Charlie started practicing law), the telephone doesn't just ring. There are too many lawyers doing great legal work today. I know a managing partner of a large law firm who says, "Legal work in the top firms is a commodity." In other words, great lawyers are a dime a dozen.

What's more, the lawyers who bring in business are often not the best practitioners. I know another lawyer, let's call him Freddie, with a large firm in Washington, D.C. He is renowned as a great "rainmaker." But he's also known as only an average "technical lawyer." So whenever he brings in a nice piece of complex corporate finance work, the finance wonks whisper, "He's not actually going to do that work, is he?" And of course he doesn't. He just palms the work off on others and goes out to get the next piece of work.

Of course, the difference between Jim and Freddie is that Freddie ignores the advice of lawyers like Charlie. Freddie writes a newsletter on topical issues in corporate finance. He is constantly finding excuses to meet with firm clients and prospective clients. In those meetings, Freddie doesn't really talk much about himself or his legal qualifications. Rather, he focuses on understanding the business needs of the business leaders. And when he hears a need, he finds a way to solve the problem.

Doing great work is wonderful. But that's just a "table stake" in today's highly competitive world of law practice. Businesses won't look at you at all unless you do great legal work. Returning phone calls (and responding to faxes and e-mails) is nice too. It'll certainly keep your existing clients from hating you. But if you want to develop business, you're going to have to start positioning yourself with business leaders as someone who can understand business problems and solve those problems.

A FORMULA FOR EFFECTIVE BUSINESS DEVELOPMENT

The simple key to winning business is convincing specific business people that you can add value to their specific businesses. Our simple Business Development Formula for lawyers lays out a process that, if followed consistently, will bring you business by connecting with business people and showing them the value you can provide.

This Formula doesn't tell you exactly when the business will show up. And it doesn't tell you exactly which business will hire you. But it does create an environment for business development to occur. It convinces business people to believe that you can add value to their business.

Follow this formula and you'll develop business consistently. Ignore it and you won't. Here it is:

$$\frac{P + V}{T} = \$$$

P = "Prospecting"; V = "Value"; T = "Time"

In other words, Prospecting plus Value over Time equals business development.

Prospecting: Connecting with People Who Hire Lawyers

Prospecting *is the process of identifying and connecting with people* who can hire you. To develop business you have to put yourself in contact with business owners, general counsels, assistant general counsels, chief financial officers, Vice Presidents of Human Resources, etc. If you fail to connect with these "decision-makers," you'll never consistently generate business.

There are numerous ways to get to know decision-makers. You can work with your firm's existing clients to "cross-sell." You can meet with the business owner that you met at your daughter's soccer game. You can speak at industry functions and then follow up with attendees. You can call your friends who own or manage businesses. You can even cold-call business owners or general counsels. It doesn't really matter how you reach those decision-makers. But you have to reach them, meet with them, and convince them that you can add value to their businesses. Otherwise, you'll never become an effective business developer.

There are also several fundamental skills that will help you connect effectively:

> ▶ *Networking:* This is the fine art of engaging in conversations that begin to position you as someone who can add value to a business person's business.
>
> ▶ *Delivering an effective elevator pitch:* How you respond to the question "What do you do?" is critical for getting business people to start to see you as someone who provides value to business.
>
> ▶ *Understanding who your prospects are:* Too often I work with lawyers who have no clear sense of who their prospective clients should be. Great business developers know exactly when they're speaking to someone who is a target for their business.

▸ Cold-calling: This can be a very effective way to develop business for lawyers. And it can be very easy if it is done right. Don't dismiss this too quickly.

▸ Developing a prospect list: Many of the best business developers put together a "wish list" of clients and slowly start to work their way through the list, connecting with decision-makers and gradually winning business.

▸ Finding prospects on the firm's client list: This is the first step in cross-selling.

▸ Using events to develop prospects: One of the best ways to connect with prospects is creating and using events to make decision-makers come to you.

Don't be discouraged by the use of the sales word "prospecting." Since many lawyers hate to think of themselves as *"salespeople,"* you can call this concept *"connecting with decision-makers."* Still too sales-y? Then call it *"Getting in contact with people who can hire you."*

Call it whatever you want. But remember that in order to be a true business developer, you must make contact with the people who can choose you as their lawyer.

Showing Value: What Most Lawyers Don't Understand

Providing value is doing things that make a client's business more successful. In the business development context, *"showing value"* is taking the time to understand clients' businesses and what the clients need, and then demonstrating that you can help them succeed. Most lawyers fail at business development because they do not demonstrate that they can provide value to their contact's business.

Consider a managing partner of a nationwide labor firm, who came up to me during a program and told me the following story. He described a lawyer, let's call him "Jimmy," in one of his offices who, in his words, "Is the most connected person in town." He went to the local high school, was prominent in the state university's alumni association, and was one of the key figures in the largest church. "But he brings in virtually no business," he said.

When I met with Jimmy, I found something that is common among lawyers. Jimmy knew many people. But he made few efforts to get those contacts to understand how his legal work could add value to their specific businesses.

Indeed, many lawyers have enough contacts to start generating business. But few lawyers actively try to make those contacts see the value that they can provide to the businesses involved.

Showing the Prospect How His Firm Can Succeed

Remember that business people only hire people whom *"they believe will help their business succeed."* That's a loaded statement. It suggests that the lawyer takes the prospect on an intellectual journey, first showing an understanding of the prospect's business and then demonstrating how to help that business succeed.

Now think about what specific activities have to occur to take that business person on an intellectual journey:

▶ *A telephone call to get a meeting:* To convert contacts into business, you must meet with them to discuss their businesses. To meet with them, you have to pick up the telephone, dial their phone numbers, and ask for the meeting. If you know a person well enough, you can call him or her on the telephone and ask to meet. If you don't feel comfortable with a direct call, you can get an intermediary to set up the meeting for you.

▶ *The business development meeting:* When you meet with the contact, you must conduct the meeting so that you can learn what it is that the contact believes he or she needs in the business to be successful. (Note that the emphasis of this meeting is the contact's needs, *not* your qualifications.) Clients don't care about what you're qualified to do until they're convinced that you understand their needs.

Making phone calls to prospects and conducting effective business development meetings are the core skills that will enable you to succeed at business development. Whether you're cross-selling or calling on new prospects, you're still going to have to call up a decision-maker and ask for a meeting. Then you're going to have to conduct that meeting in a way that emphasizes the value you can offer the business.

TIME: PLANNING AND FOLLOW-UP TO MAKE BUSINESS DEVELOPMENT HAPPEN

In order to be a strong business developer, you first need a plan. There are many ways to plan for business development, but at the least, the plan should include the following:

▶ A list of your prospects
▶ Tactics for scheduling a meeting with the key decision-makers
▶ Tactics for following up

What happens all too often is that you fail to create and follow a plan. You summon up the courage to call your college roommate, who now owns a business. He meets with you and you do a nice job of discussing his business and learning what he needs for his business to succeed. But when nothing further happens, you get discouraged and conclude that business development is too hard for you, that it is only for slick "salesman" types.

This is the wrong attitude. *Of course nothing happens immediately.* This is business development. You can't make people hire you. All you can do is create an environment where people will want to hire you. You create that environment by compiling a Rolodex or e-mail address book of people who understand the value you can provide to their business. You encourage development of that environment by staying in touch through various means, always focusing on how you can provide value to their businesses.

If you've done a good job of showing enough people the value you can provide and you stay in touch with them, eventually people will hire you. I can't tell you which people. And I can't tell you when. But I guarantee that it will happen.

It just takes time.

Maintaining a Long-term Attitude

Good business developers have a long-term attitude. I worked with a labor lawyer who told me how he had hoped to obtain business from a large utility. This lawyer used a connection to contact and ultimately arrange a meeting with the CEO of the utility (that's *"prospecting"*). At the meeting, the lawyer spent a great deal of time listening to the CEO, trying to understand the company's business objectives. During the meeting, the lawyer briefly discussed how he might help further those objectives (that's *"showing value"*).

After the meeting, the lawyer stayed in touch with the CEO and others within the company. He provided newsletters, invited them to conferences, and sent personalized legal summaries. He was just staying in touch (that's *"over time"*), creating the environment for them to buy.

Two years later, someone in the human resources department called him and asked for help on a small project. He did a great job and was hired for another project. Now the utility has grown into a major client.

I asked this lawyer the following question: "At the time you first called on the CEO, what did you think your chances of getting the business were?"

"I thought we had about a 20% chance of getting something," he said. "But that's just business development. I figured if I got four more opportunities like that, we'd get something."

Now that's a true business developer. He understood that the process is about creating an environment for sales to happen. He did this by building the Rolodex, staying in touch, and waiting.

PERCEIVING AND FILLING NEEDS

For many lawyers, the business development process is shrouded in mystery. You're told to join organizations, become active in your church, run for a position on your school board. And all of those things can help you develop contacts.

Or worst of all, "Just be sure to be a great lawyer and return your phone calls."

The problem is that the telephone rarely rings. At least not with new clients calling and asking for legal advice.

If you're going to get that telephone to start ringing with new clients, you're going to have to start to go after business with a system. That system is simple:

(1) meet with people who can hire you,
(2) learn their needs, and
(3) show how you can fill those needs.

Do this enough times and the telephone will ring. And it won't be your mother calling to ask how you're feeling.

PROSPECTING: CONNECTING WITH PEOPLE WHO CAN BRING YOU BUSINESS

I f you want to develop business effectively, you're going to have to learn how to prospect for business. In other words, you need to learn how to connect with people who can hire you.

I know a business litigator whom I'll call Jack who built his own law firm in part because he is an excellent prospector for business. Everywhere he goes he seems to run into people who could potentially hire him. Indeed, sometimes it seems that he is incapable of going out into the world without coming back with business. It's amazing.

My favorite story about Jack occurred when he was swimming off his boat on Lake Lanier, north of Atlanta. While he was taking a break and sitting on the boat, Jack looked across the cove and saw another boat parked at a dock. It looked like a boat he might want to buy, so he swam over to take a look. When he climbed out of the water, Jack struck up a conversation with a man who was cleaning the boat. After chatting a bit, Jack asked the man, "What do you do for a living?"

The man replied that he owned a chain of dry cleaners in Atlanta. They talked some more and before long, Jack had learned quite a bit about the man's business, including that the man was interested in acquiring more dry cleaners. Jack took the man's business card, accepted a ride back to his own boat on board the entrepreneur's boat, and within a few weeks had a new client.

Now this might seem like a fluke. After all, what are the chances of swimming across a cove and meeting a client? But it's the kind of thing that happens to Jack all the time. Jack is a very good business developer in part because he's very good at connecting with people who can bring him business. He understands his target market: small business owners. He knows how to strike up conversations with people; he's a good schmoozer. And he knows how to quickly make people understand how he helps businesses succeed; he's got a great elevator pitch.

Of course, there are many other skills that Jack uses to succeed. He's a great lawyer too, and his clients love him. But as far as prospecting goes, Jack is a master with the total package.

So, let us ask, what is "prospecting"? It's simply connecting with people who can bring you business. And if you want to be a good business developer, you're going to have to learn how to prospect well. All the volunteer work and CLE speeches in the world won't bring you any business if you don't connect with the people who can actually hire you.

With that in mind, this section focuses on how to prospect. We will learn how to:

▸ Know a prospect when you see one, including a good cross-selling prospect,

▸ Create a prospect list to start your business development process,

▸ Start a conversation that helps position you for business, i.e., how to work a room,

▸ Answer the question, "What do you do?" in a manner to get decision-makers interested in you as a lawyer, and

▸ Leverage your firm's existing resources to connect with decision-makers.

CHAPTER **2**

Knowing Your Prospects and Defining Your Market

INTRODUCTION

Business development starts with having a very clear sense of who constitutes a decision-maker for your practice. Indeed, if you're going to generate revenue consistently, you must learn to spot a decision-maker when you see one.

You might take a lesson in prospecting from my dog Rocko. Rocko is a white West Highland Terrier—a "Westie." Westies are froofy little pooches that have been bred for hundreds of years to hunt and kill what the British euphemistically call "small game." Here in the U.S. "small game" means squirrels, chipmunks, and gophers.

As a result, being outdoors with Rocko presents an interesting lesson in prospect identification. Rocko is a very focused animal. When I jog with him, he pays no attention to other dogs. He doesn't get distracted by or start barking at cats. He doesn't bother with cars or passing children. But if, on our jogs, we happen to pass by a squirrel, Rocko goes berserk! He barks and growls wildly. If I'm not paying attention, he'll jerk the leash from my hand and bolt after his prey.

Rocko knows that, for him, squirrels are good prospects. Somehow, in his genetic make-up there is a very clear template of what his prey looks like. Whenever he sees that fluffy brown tail, the little ears, and big eyes on the side of the head, he thinks "That's what I want!"

Lawyers who are good business developers think in much the same way. They have a very clear sense of who they are after, who their prospects are.

Defining Your Market

Like Rocko, the best business developers have a very finely tuned sense of who their prospects are. John Yates is a great business developer with Morris Manning & Martin in Atlanta. He focuses his efforts on high-tech and fast-growth companies. Ask him who his target market is and he can tell you without pausing. "We're looking for early stage companies with a strong probability of being financed within six months," he says. His team also wants to make sure that the companies they pursue have a strong management team.

Like Rocko, Yates is always on the lookout for companies and entrepreneurs that match his criteria. As a result of that clear focus, he has been very successful at keeping his pipeline full of up-and-coming companies.

However, there are many lawyers who constantly miss good business development opportunities that are right in front of them. I worked with a lawyer for a large firm who lived down the street from me. When he told me that he had had little success developing business, I asked him who his target clients were. He gave me a vague answer about "businesses seeking to buy other businesses."

He and I worked to better define his focus based on the type of work he had done in the past and for which he felt most qualified. He zeroed in on software companies with up to $100 million in revenue. No sooner had we finished our conversation than we both remembered that one of our neighbors owned a software company. Here was a prospect living across the street on whom he had never focused. This is an example of how simply defining your prospects can help you actually find a prospect.

Preparing an Ideal Prospect Profile

The first step to defining your best prospects is simply to look at the clients you have now. What do they do? What is their revenue? Are they public or private? At what stage did you find that they needed you? Following is a worksheet to help you profile an ideal client.

Industry: _____

Type of Company (service, manufacturing, etc): _____

Annual Revenue: _____

Public or Private? _____

Number of Employees: _____

Regulatory Environment: _____

Type of Workforce (white collar, union, etc.): _____

Fill out the above worksheet, and then commit the characteristics of a good prospect to memory.

Focusing Your Marketing Makes Prospecting Easier

One of the best ways to boost your marketing skills has nothing to do with selling skills. It has to do with the focus of your practice. That is, you have to ask yourself, "What do I want to do with my life?"

Before answering that question, take the following quiz. Based solely on the descriptions below, can you guess which individuals are more likely to be the better business developers?

- General corporate lawyer vs. corporate lawyer who focuses on software companies
- General litigator vs. litigator who focuses on patent litigation
- General litigator vs. labor litigator
- Corporate lawyer vs. ERISA lawyer
- Corporate lawyer vs. real estate lawyer
- Corporate lawyer vs. intellectual property lawyer
- Intellectual property lawyer vs. patent lawyer

It shouldn't be a surprise that the more focused specialties are easier to market. Why? Because you can be more effective at learning the challenges of the decision-makers and speaking their language.

Focusing on a single market also makes it easier for you to position yourself as an expert in that market. If you're spending all your time marketing yourself to the HR professionals as an ERISA expert, it won't take long before you know most of the HR professionals in town, and they will associate you with ERISA. If you specialize in construction litigation, it won't take long before you know all the top construction firms in town and their decision-makers. Further, as a specialist in construction litigation, you can be far more effective than a generalist in learning how the decision-makers see their world. That can only make you a better marketer.

I know a corporate lawyer who has never had much luck developing business. That all changed, however, when he decided to focus his marketing efforts. A life-long car lover, he decided to focus his practice on businesses in the automobile industry. Now his clients include auto dealers, repair shops, and many of the other related businesses that comprise the automobile industry.

FOCUSING A LITIGATION PRACTICE

Certain practices are naturally focused. Bankruptcy lawyers must network with banks. Energy lawyers must get to know key players at energy companies. Real estate lawyers must become close to developers.

But what if you're a general litigator? One of the most common questions I get is from litigators who ask, "How can I network with people who are about to get sued?"

The solution is to create a focus to your practice. Although you cannot network with people who are about to be sued, you can network with firms in a particular industry niche. Just pick a niche that interests you and that has numerous businesses of a size that you'd like to represent. For example, many litigators focus their networking on high-tech companies. Other litigators network with financial services businesses.

Picking a niche doesn't mean that you only have to work in that niche. Like many litigators, you'll probably still undertake a broad range of work. But your marketing efforts will be more effective by virtue of your focus. I know a litigator who does a wide range of corporate litigation. But his marketing efforts are focused almost solely on media companies. After ten years, he has earned a good reputation representing media companies in a variety of matters.

REFERRAL SOURCES, LISTS, AND SELLING TO EXISTING CLIENTS

Your best prospects may not always be defined in terms of a company's characteristics. Your best prospects may simply be "Existing clients of the firm that don't use us for tax work." Following is a guide for finding your best sources of prospects.

Cross-Selling

For many lawyers with a narrow practice niche, the best source of clients can be your firm's existing client list. This is the classic cross-selling scenario. I worked with a patent litigator who got almost all of his business from his firm's existing patent clients. Once we understood this scenario, we emphasized to the client that his firm's patent clients constituted his prospect list. This list was substantial and had not yet been effectively targeted.

As another example, I know an ERISA lawyer who begins each year by getting a list of his firm's top 100 revenue-producing clients. He then picks ten clients from the list that he thinks would be good prospects for his work and calls on the relationship partners for those clients, seeking ways to add value.

A great first step for anyone trying to grow a practice is to obtain a list of his or her firm's existing clients.

Referral Sources

Criminal lawyers get almost all of their business from other lawyers who either can't handle a specific case or are conflicted out. But other types of business can come through referral sources as well. Corporate lawyers classically get referrals from accountants who get involved in big transactions.

I worked with a litigator who got a lot of business from forensic accountants. The accountants would be retained to investigate a problem and would call in this litigator to handle the litigation when it hit.

Pick a Prospect or Ten

A good strategy is simply to target ten companies that you think you could help. I know a lawyer at a large law firm in Atlanta who identified fifteen of the city's largest clients as his prospects and systematically went after them. After about ten years, he had done some work for about half of them.

Of course, don't bite off more than you can chew. If you don't think that your firm could adequately service the Fortune 100 client with a headquarters down the street, pick a smaller company that you think would be a better prospect.

Indeed, you should never underestimate the power of simply focusing on a key client. Several years ago, a labor group at a large Atlanta firm decided that it wanted a particular Fortune 500 company as a client. Working as a team, they brainstormed ways to make a connection with the law department. They decided to make a cold call to the Associate General Counsel in charge of Human Resources and invite him to speak at a firm conference on HR issues. He accepted the invitation. During the meeting, this associate general counsel hit it off with one of the lawyers at the firm, and soon they were playing golf together. Six months later, the firm had some business that eventually grew into more business. And this all resulted from simply picking the company as a target.

"Picking a prospect" might seem counterintuitive. How can you expect to get a client before you even know whether you have a contact there? But picking the prospect should then lead to finding ways to infiltrate the target. You can usually find your entrée into any prospective client if you try hard enough.

For example, recently I was working with a real estate lawyer who described a large multi-use real estate development as "the next deal we need to get." She then started writing down all the contacts she had with the deal and all the ones she didn't have yet. When this book was being written, that attorney had not yet gotten the deal. But she's working the phones to find the connection necessary to get chosen when the deal actually happens.

GOOGLING YOUR WAY IN THE DOOR

One of the most effective ways to build business is simply to pick five or six prospective customers that you want and systematically work your way into their good graces. Once you pick the client, the problem then becomes, how do you get your foot in the door?

Any good business developer should be able to get a meeting with the decision-makers at virtually any company. Some meetings take more time to schedule than others. But with a little hustle and some creativity, you should be able to do it.

Here are the steps:

STEP 1: *Call on anyone you know who works at the company.* I'm always amazed at how some lawyers are reluctant to call on their friends to get an introduction to a decision-maker. I was working with a litigator who wanted business from Georgia-Pacific. "I need to meet with the chief of litigation," he told me. "Do you know anyone who works there?" I asked. "Well there's one person. My cousin is in the law department." (Hmmmm!!) After he met with his cousin, she introduced him to the head of litigation.

STEP 2: *If you don't know anyone, ask your friends and colleagues if they know anyone.* This almost always works. We do workshops with law firms where we ask, "Someone name a dream client that you want but don't have now." Someone names a client like The Home Depot. I then write "The Home Depot" on the flip chart and say, "Anyone in this room know anyone who works at The Home Depot?" With ten to fifteen participants in the workshop, some hands almost always go up regardless of the company that is being targeted. Usually, someone in the room knows someone relatively highly placed in the company. If you really want to get your foot in the door of a company, you can do it if you ask around long enough. Guaranteed.

STEP 3. *Google your way in.* In other words, go online and do some research. Get a list of the key officers from the website. I know one lawyer who did this and found that an old friend was a senior vice president. But even if you don't know any of the key officers, pick a couple of key decision-makers and "Google" them on your favorite search engine. You'll find their social and business activities. If you really want to get to know them, start attending some of the same functions they attend. Does this sound like I'm suggesting you become a stalker? I guess it does. But do you want the business or not?

DEFINE YOUR MARKET AND GO GET THOSE SQUIRRELS

Before you can start prospecting, you must be very clear on identifying your prospects. With that in mind:

> ▶ Define your ideal prospects. That process may require you to focus your practice on a clearly marketable niche.
> ▶ Scan your firm's client list for prospects in your specialty.
> ▶ Pick some additional clients as prospects.

Before long you'll be seeing squirrels everywhere.

CHAPTER **3**

Schmoozing

INTRODUCTION

A SCHMOOZING TOOL
The Crazy Picture: A Mnemonic Conversation Device
The Five-Foot Rule

GOING BEYOND GOLF: QUALIFYING THE LEAD BY LEARNING ABOUT THE BUSINESS
May I Have Your Card?
May I Call You?

NETWORKING IS SHOWING INTEREST

INTRODUCTION

An embarrassed bankruptcy lawyer told me the following story.

During one Little League baseball season, this lawyer would sit in the stands every game next to a woman he knew as Janet. Over the course of a season, they spent quite a bit of time together, chatting about the games, commenting on who was playing well, and generally gossiping. It was only after the season that this lawyer read in a banking trade magazine that Janet was a high-level vice president at a major bank and probably could have been a source of business for him.

"During all that time, I had never asked her what she did," he said. "It was a missed opportunity."

Unfortunately, this kind of thing happens to lawyers all the time. Too many lawyers go to networking events or meet other people and chat away without ever capitalizing on opportunities.

Once you know who your prospects are, you're going to have to find ways to connect with decision-makers and start to learn about their business. And in the practice of law, the primary way that people connect with decision-makers is through networking.

When I speak of networking, I'm including any situation where you have to start a conversation with someone you don't know. It could be an industry conference, a cocktail party, a golf tournament. And yes, it could be at your child's baseball game. All of these situations require the same basic skill:

> *Being able to converse with a stranger and get a relationship started.*

A few lawyers are very good at this. They tend to be good business developers. But most lawyers (and most people, for that matter) are not especially competent at chatting with strangers because, I suspect, they consider this to be one of those unseemly "sales-y" skills.

One common misconception is that to be a great business developer you have to be a charismatic "salesman type"; another is that you have to be "smooth." Since neither is necessarily essential, what kind of conduct will in fact make you a successful business developer? Quite simply, *you must show interest in other people.* One of the great conversationalists of all time is TV news personality Barbara Walters. When she was asked about her secret for connecting with people she said, "The secret to being interest*ing* is to be interes*ted.*"

Of course, networking for business is more than just being interested. It's being interested *with a purpose.* "The key to networking is to figure out the specific needs of your target and to provide immediate personal attention to address those needs," says John Yates, a top-notch business developer at Morris Manning & Martin.

The goal is to build enough rapport with someone so that eventually you can ask the question, "What kind of business are you in?" or "What do you do?" After all, we don't network just to get to know people. We want business. If you are going to be an effective networker for business, you have to start probing about a prospect's business. To do that you're going to need a strategy for working a room: a strategy like a *"schmoozing tool."*

A Schmoozing Tool

If you're not good at working a room, then it can be helpful to have a little tool that will help. Here's what we do during our workshops to help people learn how to connect with other people. You'll need a pencil and a piece of paper.

(1) At the bottom of a piece of paper, draw a **doormat.**
(2) On top of the doormat draw a **globe of the world.**
(3) On top of the globe, draw a **house.**
(4) On the house draw windows with **people looking out.**
(5) Coming out of the chimney of the house, draw a **work glove.**
(6) Draw the work glove holding a **tennis racket.**
(7) Flying into the tennis racket, draw an **airplane.**
(8) Off the tail of the airplane, draw a **light bulb.**

This picture is a memory device that will enable you to always be able to start a conversation with any stranger. Indeed, if you did the drawing, you should be able to quickly recall the entire drawing because it is so strange. To test your memory, close your eyes and first picture the doormat. You should have no trouble recalling what was drawn on the mat, on the globe, and so on.

The Crazy Picture: A Mnemonic Conversation Device

Each part of these pictures represents a question that you can ask anyone to start a conversation. The goal isn't to work your way through every question. Nor should you grill your conversation partner like a crime suspect. Rather, you should be searching for some commonality as the starting point of a relationship. You're looking for a moment where a relationship becomes possible. It need not be anything profound. "You love golf? So do I!" usually works just fine.

Following is a breakdown of the significance of each part of the above mnemonic device:

Doormat: This is just a basic greeting. "Hi!" works well. You can also use "Hello," "How are you?" or "Howdy!" It's funny how these simple conversation beginners get things off to a good start. Unless gatherings of people make you really nervous, you probably don't need a mnemonic device for this one.

Globe: "Where are you from?" Don't underestimate the power of this simple question. I know a lawyer who asked an in-house lawyer, "Where are you from?" and they learned that they both were from Philadelphia. That connection led to a relationship that eventually led to some business for the lawyer.

House: "Where do you live?" If you're from the same city, it's always a potential conversation starter to discuss neighborhoods.

People looking from the windows: "Tell me about your family." This is usually not a great question to start with. Many people don't want to talk about their families too soon. "Do you have kids?" might seem invasive if you don't know a person too well. But once you feel like you've established rapport, most people love to talk about their kids.

Work glove: "What do you do?" *You have to ask this question!* You're not networking for your health. You're networking because you want to connect with people who can bring you business. You can't do that unless you learn what other people do for a living. Many lawyers won't ask this question because they will have to answer the same question themselves. And many lawyers don't like discussing their work. Get over it! We'll soon discuss how to answer "What do you do?" effectively.

Tennis racket: "What do you do for fun?" This is a great question. I recently met a senior attorney at a large, very traditional law firm who told me he drove Harley Davidson motorcycles and attended biker events. If you don't find that interesting, then there's something wrong with you.

Airplane: "Are you going anywhere interesting this summer?" There is a travel question for every season. "Did you do anything fun over the holidays?" "Are you planning a trip for the July 4th weekend?" "What are your plans for Labor Day?" etc.

Light bulb: This is a catch-all for current events. At any given time there is a news event that is center stage. These questions usually begin with, "What do you think . . . ?" For example, "What do you think of the mutual funds payoff mess?" Or "What do you think of the World Series?" Or "What is your opinion of the Acme merger?" Ask someone his or her opinion. Then listen. There are few better ways to build rapport.

The Five-Foot Rule

Schmoozing is not just for cocktail parties and industry conferences. Many good business developers practice the "five-foot rule," i.e.:

> ***Thou shalt say hello to anyone who is within five feet of you.***

The five-foot rule works because you never know who you're sitting next to. Here's a personal example. As an avid tennis player, I was waiting by my health club's courts for my partner. My partner failed to appear. Sitting beside me was another player who also seemed to be waiting for a missing partner.

"Is your partner ditching you too?" I said.

He looked at his watch and shook his head. "I think so. This has never happened before."

We struck up a conversation and eventually played a couple of sets of tennis and had a fine time. I learned that the other tennis player was a partner in a large firm. And he later helped me get a meeting with a key player at his firm. Eventually I got some business. And this is all thanks to the "five-foot rule."

I know a lawyer who never gets on an airplane without at least striking up a brief conversation with the person in the seat next to him. That's the five-foot rule in action.

Another lawyer I know who hangs out in Starbucks always says hello to his fellow coffee drinkers. That's the five-foot rule in action too.

Still another lawyer I know goes to the deli every Sunday for bagels and never leaves without speaking to someone in line. Once again, that's the five-foot rule.

I know that many of you will never do this. I don't always feel comfortable doing it myself. Like many lawyers, I'm not that outgoing. But you never know who you're standing next to in the checkout line.

Airplanes and the Five-Foot Rule

I think it's crazy not to at least say hello to the person sitting next to you in an airplane. If you're traveling on business during the week, chances are that you're sitting next to a fellow business person.

I admit that I don't always follow my own advice. But I'm often rewarded when I do. Here are just a few of the companies and executives whose *officers* I have met during airplane rides:

- ▶ UPS
- ▶ The Home Depot
- ▶ J. P. Morgan
- ▶ American Express
- ▶ The owner of a chain of auto dealerships
- ▶ The owner of a chain of movie theaters
- ▶ The owner of a chain of quick oil change dealers
- ▶ An attorney from a medium-sized software company

And I don't even travel that much. If you travel a lot and you don't at least say hello to your seatmate, you're probably missing out on numerous opportunities to connect with people who can help your business development efforts.

Five-Foot Rule Challenges on Airplanes

There are some challenges in applying the five-foot rule on airplanes. You don't want to strike up a conversation and then feel stuck in that conversation for the next two hours. The way to avoid this is simply to have a book or some work available that you can turn to when the conversation reaches a natural stopping point. Telling your seatmate "I've enjoyed speaking with you" is a perfectly acceptable way to signal that you have something else to do. Just say it nicely.

I've also had women tell me that they don't like to start conversations on airplanes because men tend to think that women are "hitting on them." That's a legitimate concern, and some women might not be comfortable with the practice.

But airline flights are great business development opportunities.

GOING BEYOND GOLF: QUALIFYING THE LEAD BY LEARNING ABOUT THE BUSINESS

Suppose you're at a networking event and you have a nice rapport with a man who, you learn, owns a business. You're a corporate lawyer who could probably help the business owner in many ways. What do you do now?

You must do something that in sales we call *"qualifying the lead."* In other words, you need to determine whether the prospect is someone who might be a good client for you. In particular, you should ask some questions about the prospect's business. Just about any "big picture" question will do.

Some good opening questions are:

> ▸ "So how did you get into that business?" People love to tell you their stories.
> ▸ "What does your business make?"
> ▸ "Tell me about the manufacturing process."
> ▸ "What service do you provide?"
> ▸ "Any new initiatives you're working on?" If the prospect loves his business, he'll be excited about his new venture and enjoy telling you about it.
> ▸ "How much competition do you have in that business?"

Ultimately, you must determine whether this business is the kind that needs lawyers like you. But that doesn't mean that if you're an environmental lawyer you initially ask, "Are you involved in the disposal of chemicals?" You might start with the question, "What kind of manufacturing do you do?" And then follow up with, "Tell me about the process involved."

Or perhaps you're a patent lawyer. You might first ask what the company manufactures. Then you might probe a little about the technology it uses in the manufacturing process.

The goal of qualifying the lead isn't to win a piece of business at that moment. Rather, the goal is to get a sense of whether you ought to follow up with this person in the future. A few big picture questions usually do the trick.

May I Have Your Card?

There's a famous automobile salesman who gives out as many business cards as possible. At football games, when something exciting happens, he tosses hundreds of cards into the air like confetti. Similarly, many lawyers will tell you that to get business, you must give out as many cards as possible.

I disagree.

I think you should do just the opposite: *obtain* as many cards as possible from prospects.

"May I have your card" is a magic phrase for starting a business relationship. It's magic because it's not a hard question to ask. It doesn't seem intrusive. And most of the time people will happily give you their card.

But the question also subtly says, "I want to have your name and business information because I'm interested in you and your business." And when someone gives you a card, this is assumed. After all, the purpose of a business card is to allow people ready access to the card owner and his or her business.

So if you think you've found someone who *might* be a good client for you, ask for a business card. If you've done a good job of listening and showing interest in the prospect, he or she is sure to like you and will be happy to give you a card.

And once you've gotten the card, you're perfectly positioned to follow up in a few days and contact the prospect to meet with you to discuss the prospect's business further.

May I Call You?

The goal of networking is to begin to build a business relationship. Once you've established contact through networking, the next step (as we will soon see) is to meet with the prospect. You probably won't get the prospect's business unless you start to learn about that business and begin to show him or her how you can add value to that business.

Hence, the ultimate networking question is, "May I call you?" No question better positions you for the critical next step in the business development process—a meeting with the prospect.

This question isn't one that you'll ask every person you meet. You'll have to use your judgment to determine whether rapport between you and the prospect has been created. And you want to make sure that the business prospect is a good one. But if the prospect seems interested in what you do, usually there's no harm in asking.

And there's a great advantage. If the prospect says "yes," then you've essentially been invited to speak more with the prospect about his business. That's a very valuable invitation. Indeed, most lawyers would pay for an invitation to meet with a business leader to discuss his business. You can get that opportunity for free. You just have to ask.

Networking Is Showing Interest

The key to networking is showing interest in other people. Just ask a few questions and listen. Once you find a common point of interest, you will be forming the beginning of a strong relationship. The key to turning that relationship into a business relationship is to make sure to ask about the business.

If the business is a good prospect for you, get the person's business card and ask if you might telephone the prospect. What do you have to lose?

CHAPTER **4**

The Elevator Pitch

INTRODUCTION

THE ELEVATOR PITCH DEFINED

THE ELEVATOR PITCH AS VOCAL CALLING CARD

ELEVATOR PITCHING: OUTSIDE THE BOX

THE ELEVATOR PITCH: A GOOD START

INTRODUCTION

I recently conducted a workshop with a group of lawyers, and when I got to the point where we were going to discuss the *"elevator pitch,"* an attorney raised her hand and said, "I never ask people what they do because I don't like answering the question myself."

I asked her what she typically said when someone asked her what she did.

"I say, 'I'm a lawyer,'" she told me.

No wonder she hates getting the question.

"I'm a lawyer" is accurate. But it's boring and does nothing to help you develop business.

A good "elevator pitch," however, should be a verbal "calling card" that begins to position you as a value provider and help you get business. It communicates the essence of your value proposition in just a few short sentences. Although traditionally elevator pitches occurred in that brief minute as two business people rode up (or down) in an elevator, they can actually be used anywhere, any time.

Remember that people hire lawyers whom they believe understand their business and can add value. Your elevator pitch therefore should be phrased to explain how you add value to businesses.

A good elevator pitch has two parts:

▸ First you indicate the value that you provide in the marketplace; and

▸ Then you describe an example of the kind of work you do.

THE ELEVATOR PITCH DEFINED

Value

Begin your answer by simply telling what you do to help companies. Such activities depend on your specialty. Examples include the following:

Employment lawyer: "I'm a lawyer with Smith and Williams. I help companies that have disputes with their employees."

Securities lawyer: "I'm a lawyer with Smith and Williams. I help companies comply with securities laws."

Mergers and acquisitions lawyer: "I'm a lawyer with Smith and Williams. I help companies buy and sell other companies."

Litigator: "I'm a lawyer with Smith and Williams. I help companies win disputes, informally or by mediation, arbitration, or at trial."

Patent lawyer: "I'm a lawyer with Smith and Williams. I help companies protect and maximize the value of their inventions."

Labor lawyer: "I'm a lawyer with Smith and Williams. I represent companies in their dealings with labor unions."

Real estate lawyer: "I'm a lawyer with Smith and Williams. I help developers with their real estate deals and transactions."

Immigration lawyer: "I'm a lawyer with Smith and Williams. I help companies and their employees comply with immigration laws."

Bankruptcy lawyer: "I'm a lawyer with Smith and Williams. I represent companies involved in bankruptcy proceedings."

Corporate lawyer: "I'm a lawyer with Smith
mid-sized companies in a range of transaction

Environmental lawyer: "I'm a lawyer with Smith
help companies comply with environmental laws."

Products liability lawyer: "I'm a lawyer with Smith and Williams.
I defend companies in product liability cases."

Intellectual property lawyer: "I'm a lawyer with Smith and
Williams. I help companies protect and maximize the value of their
intellectual property."

Examples

You should showcase the value you provide to companies with an
example. That is, you should be ready to tell a little story of how
you've helped a client recently. You need not relay the story right
away. But if a prospect has any interest in what you do, you should
be ready to give an example. Some samples are as follows:

Employment lawyer: "I'm a lawyer with Smith and Williams. I
help companies that have disputes with their employees. . . .
Recently, I had a client who wanted me to train his managers to avoid
sexual harassment lawsuits."

Securities lawyer: "I'm a lawyer with Smith and Williams. I help
companies comply with securities laws. . . . *Recently, I helped a
client get financing through a bond issue."*

Mergers and acquisitions lawyer: "I'm a lawyer with Smith and
Williams. I help companies buy and sell other companies. . . .
*Recently, I helped a small trucking company buy another trucking
company."*

Litigator: "I'm a lawyer with Smith and Williams. I help
companies win business disputes. . . . *Recently, I worked with a small
company to win a dispute with an employee who stole confidential
records and then took a job with a competitor. We won a $50,000
settlement."*

Patent lawyer: "I'm a lawyer with Smith and Williams. I help
companies protect and maximize the value of their inventions. . . .
*Recently, I helped a doctor get a patent on a new device for detecting
heart murmurs."*

Labor lawyer: "I'm a lawyer with Smith and Williams. I represent companies in their dealings with labor unions. . . . *Recently, I helped negotiate a labor contract between my airline client and a labor union.*"

Real estate lawyer: "I'm a lawyer with Smith and Williams. I help developers with their real estate deals and transactions. . . . *Recently, I helped a client close a deal to develop a mixed-use development in downtown Detroit.*"

Immigration lawyer: "I'm a lawyer with Smith and Williams. I help companies and their employees comply with immigration laws. . . . *Recently I worked with a software company to help it get work permits for a staff of software engineers from overseas.*"

Bankruptcy lawyer: "I'm a lawyer with Smith and Williams. I represent companies involved in bankruptcy proceedings. . . . *Recently, I helped a client collect on a large contract with a bankrupt airline.*"

Corporate lawyer: "I'm a lawyer with Smith and Williams. I help mid-sized companies in a range of corporate transactions. . . . *Recently, I helped a record company create an Internet subsidiary for selling its music online.*"

Environmental lawyer: "I'm a lawyer with Smith and Williams. I help companies comply with environmental laws. . . . *I recently worked with a company to create a safe way to dispose of chemicals involved in its manufacturing process.*"

Products liability lawyer: "I'm a lawyer with Smith and Williams. I defend companies in product liability cases. . . . *I recently defended a drug company in a lawsuit by a patient who claimed he was injured by one of the company's products.*"

Intellectual property lawyer: "I'm a lawyer with Smith and Williams. I help companies protect and maximize the value of their intellectual property. . . . *Recently, I worked with a large utility in helping it create guidelines to protect the use of its trademarks.*"

ELEVATOR PITCHING AS VOCAL CALLING CARD

Here's a typical conversation I have with my clients:

"How many of your friends and neighbors know what you do?"

"All of them know I'm a lawyer."

"But how many of them know you're a corporate lawyer who helps buy other small companies?"

"Most of them … I think."

The fact is that many lawyers could develop more business simply by ensuring that all their friends and acquaintances have a clear picture of what they do. By that, I mean making sure that they know how you help businesses succeed.

One of our clients, a labor lawyer, wanted to start developing business and made sure that everyone on his very social neighborhood block knew what he did. Within six months, one of the neighbors, a business owner, had hired him to handle an employment discrimination suit.

Your elevator pitch is like a vocal calling card. The more people who hear it, the better chance you have to get some business.

ELEVATOR PITCHING: OUTSIDE THE BOX

If you want to get someone's attention, trying creating an "outside the box" elevator pitch.

Ask one corporate lawyer whom I know what he does and he will say, "I'm a problem solver and dream facilitator."

Now that will get your attention. And that's why it's a great elevator pitch. It always draws a follow-up question such as, "What do you mean?" And suddenly he's involved in a discussion about his work as a lawyer and how he helps his clients achieve their goals.

This lawyer never tells people, "I'm an attorney." With that kind of answer, he says, "I'm stuck with whatever box they put attorneys and lawyers in. I don't have a chance to distinguish myself."

Of course, this kind of elevator pitch is not for everyone. But if you're willing to be a little bit "out there," then an outside-the-box elevator pitch might be right for you. It just might bring you some business.

THE ELEVATOR PITCH: A GOOD START

One of the biggest challenges that lawyers have is persuading their acquaintances to see them not just as friends, but as value providers. You can start to solve that problem by introducing yourself to others in terms of the value that you provide.

When people ask what you do, don't say "I'm a lawyer." Tell them that you're an attorney who helps businesses make lots of money. They probably won't hire you on the spot. But at least they'll know that you're someone who could potentially help their businesses.

If you want their business, that's a big plus.

CHAPTER **5**

Cold-Calling for Lawyers

WHAT IS COLD-CALLING FOR LAWYERS?

HOW TO MAKE A COLD CALL

EASY COLD CALLS THAT BUILD RELATIONSHIPS

THE ETHICS OF COLD-CALLING

PROSPECTING BY MAIL: MAKING THE COLD CALL EASIER

TRY COLD-CALLING: IT WORKS

When I suggest to lawyers that they consider making cold calls, most of them react as if I've just invited them to attend a human sacrifice. Their looks range from shock to disbelief to utter contempt.

Indeed, most lawyers dismiss the idea as preposterous and unethical.

I disagree. For lawyers, cold-calling works if it is both done right and done ethically. (And yes, it can be done well within the bounds of ethics.) What's more, many lawyers practice cold-calling and get business as a result.

So sniff if you want. But cold-calling has been used for decades because it is effective. The only challenge to making it work in the legal profession is being creative.

What Is Cold-Calling for Lawyers?

First, there is a significant misconception about what cold-calling actually is in a professional services context. Cold-calling is nothing more than calling up people you don't know already. But this doesn't necessarily mean calling them while they are eating dinner (as in "Hello, Mr. Asher, how would you like to save 50% on your next phone bill?") and asking them to hire you as their lawyer. Such activity would indeed be unethical under all the legal professional responsibility codes.

But there is no restriction on direct solicitation for the purpose of simply starting a relationship. For example, nothing in the rules of professional responsibility prohibits you from calling up prospects (1) to offer them something for free, (2) to invite them to a conference, or (3) to ask them to speak on a panel. In fact, such activity is perfectly ethical and can be a great way to start a relationship.

"You'd be surprised how willing we are to accept free stuff," one in-house lawyer at a large healthcare software firm told me. This lawyer said that he would certainly be interested, for example, in attending a free seminar on developments in healthcare law offered at his office by a well-respected firm, even if he doesn't know the presenting lawyer personally. And since the call to make the offer is not a business solicitation, there's nothing unethical about it.

I recently interviewed attorney Bruce Richards, former general counsel at Equifax and Certegy, who told me that after the Sarbanes-Oxley Act was enacted in 2002, he would have welcomed being sent a spreadsheet tool for organizing a review of his company's Sarbanes-Oxley issues—provision by provision. Such a spreadsheet tool could have included a tracking list to emphasize the steps his company should undertake to ensure compliance. Richards said that he might even have entertained a cold call from someone who was offering such a useful compliance tool. Instead, he received free summaries of the Act from dozens of firms, none of which, after the first one, were of much assistance to him or to his company.

And consider the Atlanta law firm that wanted to develop a relationship with a large Fortune 500 company based in Atlanta. Since the firm had no connection with the company's law department, one of the firm's lawyers made a cold call to an attorney in the law department. He did not ask for the company's business. But he did ask the company's attorney to speak at an in-house conference held by the firm. The in-house lawyer accepted and the firm eventually was able to build a relationship with the lawyer and get some business.

These are examples of cold calls where you're not soliciting business but are seeking to initiate a relationship. Certainly the hope is to get some business eventually. But that's not what the direct solicitation is for. Therefore, this is perfectly ethical. More important, it's an effective business development tactic.

How to Make a Cold Call

The problem with cold-calling is that the person on the other end of the line isn't waiting for your call. He doesn't know you. And he or she is usually inclined to reject you. In order to overcome this obstacle, you must quickly explain who you are and why your offer should be accepted.

Obviously, you need to initiate the call with a clear plan. And you need to keep it short.

With that in mind, there are generally three steps to a cold call:

(1) Identify yourself;
(2) Offer something of value; and
(3) Propose a call to action.

STEP 1: *Greeting and identification.* "Hello. This is Joey Asher. I'm a partner at the law firm of Jones and Howard." This ain't brain surgery. But this is a very important step. Remember that the person wasn't waiting for your call. Simply stating who you are is going to help orient the listener. I received a cold call recently from a business consultant who never told me the name of her firm or what she did. I had no idea why she was calling and only found out when I asked, "What does your company do?" Telling your name and that you work for a law firm avoids that problem.

STEP 2: *Transition to business/hook.* "The reason I'm calling is that I read that you are one of the leading experts in anti-trust litigation in the country. We're offering an in-house seminar next month on antias it applies to the Internet, and would like to invite you to participate in a panel of speakers we're putting together." Here you're offering the prospect something that is presumably of value to him: an opportunity to be seen as an industry expert. Finding a business hook is incredibly important. You have to address the "What's in it for me" for the prospect as clearly as possible.

STEP 3: *Call to action.* "The seminar is going to be held June 5th at 9 A.M. at our offices [at location]. Are you available?" You need to ask for the "order," i.e., telling him the time and place and putting the question to him simply and directly.

EASY COLD CALLS THAT BUILD RELATIONSHIPS

Business development takes a little creativity, and cold calls permit you to use your imagination. Just formulate something valuable that the prospect probably wants, and offer it to him or her. Then pick up the telephone.

Example 1: An invitation to an in-house seminar

STEP 1: "Hi. This is Joey Asher. I'm a partner at Smith and Howard."

STEP 2: "We're holding a seminar here at the firm next month on the topic of negotiating contracts with labor unions. I read in the newspaper that your firm will be negotiating with one of its labor unions within the next six months. We will be addressing some of the very issues your firm will likely be facing."

STEP 3: "The seminar is March 12th at 9 A.M. here at the firm. Are you interested?"

Example 2: An interview for an article

STEP 1: "Hi. This is Joey Asher. I'm a partner at Smith and Howard."

STEP 2: "I'm writing an article for the state bar journal on employee retention practices. I've read about your business's innovative employee practices and would love to learn more about them. I'd be interested in meeting with you to learn more as I prepare this article."

STEP 3: "Are you available next week for a meeting in your office?"

Example 3: Providing a free seminar at the prospect's office

Step 1: "Hello. This is Joey Asher. I'm a partner at Smith and Howard."

Step 2: "I'm calling you about a seminar that we're offering to companies about compliance with new healthcare regulations. Since your company sells specialized healthcare software, we thought you might find it interesting. We're available to come to your office and give our seminar to up to fifteen people."

Step 3: "We're available to deliver the program next month. Would your firm be interested?"

Example 4: Meeting at a conference where you're speaking

Step 1: "Hello. This is Joey Asher. I'm a partner at Smith and Howard, and I've noticed that, at next month's tax issues conference, you are signed up to hear the session in which I am speaking."

Step 2: "I want to make sure that my remarks are relevant, and would love to hear about your firm's challenges before I give my presentations."

Step 3: "There is a dinner on the opening night of the conference. Do you mind if we sit together at that dinner?"

Example 5: Offering a Sarbanes-Oxley compliance tool

Step 1: "Hello. This is Joey Asher. I'm a partner at Smith and Howard."

Step 2: "I'm calling to tell you about a Sarbanes-Oxley compliance spreadsheet that we've developed and are offering for free. It's a simple spreadsheet that you can use to ensure complete compliance with the new statute."

Step 3: "I'd love to drop off the spreadsheet at your office and explain how it works. Are you interested?"

THE ETHICS OF COLD-CALLING

Whenever I mention cold-calling in my workshops and seminars, one of the first issues that comes up is ethics. "Doesn't cold-calling violate bar rules?"

The answer is, "Not if it is done right."

Certainly it is not ethical to call up a prospective layperson when you know he needs a lawyer and offer your services. The ABA Model Rule of Professional Conduct 7.3(a) reads as follows:

"A lawyer shall not by in-person, live telephone or real-time electronic contact solicit professional employment from a prospective client when a significant motive for a lawyer's doing so is the lawyer's pecuniary gain, unless the person contacted:

"(1) is a lawyer; or

"(2) has a family, close personal, or prior professional relationship with the lawyer."[1]

So no, you shouldn't call up prospective clients and ask them to hire you as their lawyer.

But notice that there are some pretty big exceptions that allow for some very effective cold-calling if you want to do it. The rule only prohibits calls to "solicit professional employment." In other words, you should feel free to contact prospective clients for reasons other than to "solicit professional employment." For example, you can invite a prospective client to a free seminar. You can call prospects and offer them a free newsletter on a business topic. You can contact prospects and ask them to join an organization. You can call in-house counsel and invite them to speak at your seminar. None of these calls would be to "solicit professional employment."

Notice also that the rule allows calling anyone with whom you have a "family, close personal, or prior professional relationship." In other words, there is no restriction on making calls to family, friends, and especially to former clients. This latter group can be pretty large. Most firms have significant backlists of clients that are inactive. However, be careful not to call a previous client that was dissatisfied with the legal work done by your firm. But most of the time, the client stopped being a client simply because the project was completed. There might well be a need for additional legal services arising soon.

---

[1] ABA Model Rules of Professional Conduct (2002 edition).

Calls That Directly Solicit Business from In-House Lawyers

Historically, one of the clearest ethical "no-no's" has been direct solicitation of business. By that, I mean calling someone up and directly asking him to hire you as his lawyer. The idea behind such a rule was to prohibit "ambulance chasing." And most of us agree that laypersons should be protected from the sharp tactics of scurrilous lawyers.

But the "ambulance chaser" rule makes little sense when a lawyer directly solicits an in-house counsel of a business. In-house counsels are presumably sophisticated enough about legal matters to protect their interests.

With that in mind, the ABA Model Rule of Professional Conduct 7.3, adopted in 2002, explicitly allowed soliciting from other lawyers. As noted before, the rule prohibits direct solicitation "unless the person contacted . . . is a lawyer. . . ." In other words, if and when your state adopts this rule, you should feel free to call in-house lawyers and ask them if you could meet with them to talk about their business.

Regardless of whether direct solicitation of lawyers violates ethics rules, the more practical question is whether the practice works.

In my experience, sometimes the practice works. And sometimes it doesn't.

Regardless of the rule, lawyers have been directly soliciting in-house lawyers for years. As I researched this book, in-house counsels told me that they regularly receive cold calls directly soliciting business. None mentioned any ethical qualms about receiving the calls. But most of those same in-house lawyers did tell me that they don't think the cold calls that they receive are particularly effective in getting their business.

The fact is that companies don't hire lawyers in the same way that homeowners buy long-distance telephone service. I heard of one hungry associate at a large law firm who cold-called all of the general counsels in the Fortune 200. He didn't get a single piece of business.[2]

---

[2] I learned this story from fellow associates who were mocking their colleague. I give the cold-calling associate credit for taking the initiative. That's what it takes

But just because this practice doesn't *always* work, does not mean it can't work. In fact, some general counsels have told me that they don't mind the occasional cold call. Steven Whitehead, general counsel of Randstad North America, said that he would not mind receiving a call from someone who was solely interested in learning his business. "What would impress me is a lawyer who did not have my business who came to me and said, 'I want to learn your business,'" he said. "I appreciate the fact that someone has the *chutzpah* to do that."

And in the right circumstances, directly soliciting business through cold-calling *can work*.

I know an attorney at a prestigious Atlanta firm who had developed expertise in working with media companies. He made an unsolicited cold call to the general counsel of a Georgia newspaper he thought might need his services. In light of the attorney's expertise, the general counsel took the call. The two lawyers had a meeting and they hit it off. About a year later, the general counsel gave this lawyer a substantial piece of litigation.

Direct Solicitation Through an Offer of Value

The key to successful cold-calling is the "offer of value." Instead of simply calling and saying, "I want to meet with you to discuss how we can help your business," your call should offer a specific narrow value.

For example, I know an attorney who, as an associate at a large firm used cold-calling and built a relatively large book of business. He did it with a very narrow proposition aimed at a very specific list of prospective clients. He discovered his narrow business proposition one day while researching in the Code of Federal Regulations. He came across a program that provided a substantial benefit to municipalities under certain circumstances. He did some research and found that many municipalities were eligible for the benefit but had never applied for it.

---

to win business. But I would probably recommend that this associate's business development time would be better spent calling on acquaintances at prospective clients before resorting to cold-calling.

From there he developed a value proposition. He would contact municipalities and simply ask whether they were aware of this federal benefit and whether they had applied for it yet.

His next step was simply to generate a list of municipalities and begin contacting them. None of the municipalities' lawyers who were contacted felt that they were the subject of a "cold call." Instead, they were simply under the impression that they were being contacted by an enterprising lawyer who had a piece of valuable information to offer.

As it turned out, many municipalities had no idea that they were eligible for the benefit and retained the lawyer to help them. No single piece of business was very large. But with forty to fifty clients, it all added up to a nice book of business.

This is the kind of narrow business proposition that can be a wonderful "door opener" for a little business that could eventually lead to more business.

And the law is a wonderful source of such types of tiny value propositions. Every area of practice is constantly evolving. Any good tax lawyer knows of many small tax regulations that could benefit numerous businesses. Environmental lawyers know of many ways to save their clients money. Immigration lawyers know of many small ways to help businesses with their immigrant labor force. Any small idea taken from the law that can save a business money represents an opportunity to cold-call a series of prospect companies and start a relationship.

Generally, these campaigns have three steps:

STEP 1: Identify the value proposition.

STEP 2: Identify and clear conflicts with fifty businesses that could benefit from the value proposition. Be sure to identify more than just a handful of businesses. Remember, cold-calling works because you can call many prospects in a short period of time. To call a lot of prospects, you must have a lot lined up. So before you start, build your list complete with telephone numbers.

STEP 3: Develop your call script. It should sound like this:

> ▶ "Hi. This is Joey Asher. I'm a tax partner with the law firm Smith and Williams."

▸ "I'm calling you today in relation to a new provision of the tax code passed last month that allows some of our clients to lower their effective tax rate by a full percentage point. I'd love to meet with you for about thirty minutes to discuss whether the provision applies to you."

▸ "Can we meet next week?"

PROSPECTING BY MAIL: MAKING THE COLD CALL EASIER

The best fishermen make a lot of casts. The same is true for the best business developers. Here's a classic tactic that works. Pick fifty businesses that would be good clients. Clear them all for conflicts and determine who in each firm is the likely decision-maker. Then write a letter to each with an offer.

What kind of offer?

▸ A personal update on the tax laws
▸ A free explanation of a tool to help companies comply with the Sarbanes-Oxley law
▸ An invitation to an in-house seminar
▸ An invitation to a CLE presentation
▸ An intimate dinner/networking event with an expert on corporate governance

Send the letters on a Monday and do follow-up calls the following Thursday.

But what do you say in the letters? Here are a few sample letters that work:

Dear Jack:

As you may know, Congress just passed a major revision of the corporate tax laws. These laws have major implications for businesses such as Southern Metal Finishing. For example, under certain circumstances businesses can cut their effective tax rate by 10%.

Our firm has developed a fifteen-minute presentation that explains how businesses like yours can maximize the benefit from the new law.
I'll call you in a few days to determine your interest.

Or how about:

Dear Jack:

As you know, Congress has passed a set of new workplace safety regulations that are highly complex and can require expensive compliance. Our firm has developed some interesting strategies for dealing with these regulations in an inexpensive manner.
We'll be explaining these strategies in a free seminar offered at our firm next month. We'd like to invite you to this seminar.
I'll call you in a few days to determine your interest.

What do you say in the follow-up call?

Step 1: "Hi. This is Joey Asher, with Smith and Williams. I'm following up on correspondence that I sent you earlier this week."

Step 2: "I sent you a letter inviting you to a dinner at the Ritz-Carlton on [date]. This is going to be an intimate dinner with Charles Elson, one of the top experts in the area of corporate governance."

Step 3: "Would you be interested in attending?" If the answer is "no," be ready with a "back-up offer" such as, "I understand. We publish monthly newsletters on business development topics. Would you be interested in receiving some of them?" Even the most reluctant prospects will probably accept a back-up offer.

Does this technique seem too "pushy" for a big-time lawyer? Maybe. But a little *chutzpah* is sometimes what it takes to win business.

Steve Whitehead, General Counsel at Randstad North America, recalled mailing prospecting letters cold to forty large businesses when he was still a partner at a major southeastern law firm. He knew this was a pretty unorthodox thing to do at a large law firm. But as Steve put it, "What the heck. It wasn't like I had them as clients. So I had nothing to lose."

And guess what? Steve received a call in response to the mailing. The call was from an in-house lawyer at a Fortune 100 business. Steve's firm didn't get any legal work immediately. The courtship took time, with Steve inviting the in-house lawyer to speak at a law firm seminar. But eventually that cold contact led to a substantial amount of legal work. "We cast out a line and landed Moby Dick," recalled Whitehead.

TRY COLD-CALLING: IT WORKS

Very few lawyers whom I've met are willing to try cold-calling. It smacks of the most grotesque sales activity. Some lawyers view cold-calling as no different than hawking exercise equipment on late-night television. But I see nothing wrong with cold-calling so long as it is done creatively.

And even though some lawyers view cold-calling as anathema, I've met many lawyers who cold call in certain circumstances and have experienced success.

So scoff if you want. But cold-calling has been in the business arena for a long time because *it works*. And some of your colleagues are finding that it works in the legal profession as well.

CHAPTER **6**

The Old Standbys:
Articles, Speeches, and Bar
and Trade Associations

NONPRODUCTIVE BUSINESS DEVELOPMENT ACTIVITIES

I'm amazed at the activities that many lawyers refer to as "business development," such as writing articles, giving speeches, and engaging in bar activities. I'm not opposed to these activities *per se*. They can be wonderful ways of contributing to the legal community. But because of the way these activities are undertaken by most lawyers, they do not constitute business development.

Why is this true? Because these activities rarely lead to business! Surely, "business development activity" ought to result in getting hired by actual clients who will pay actual dollars for actual legal work. Otherwise, the concept is a misnomer.

When I was practicing law I knew a lawyer who would submit a scholarly article to a law publication every year. He would bill the time he spent writing each article as "business development." The articles looked great on his résumé that is posted on his firm's web site. But this attorney would be hard-pressed to identify any work that has resulted from those articles.

Similarly, I know an intellectual property lawyer who speaks at two or three IP conferences a year but has no new clients from these conferences. He counts these speeches toward his firm's required "business development" hours. When he recently returned from speaking, I asked if he had any leads. "No," he said. "The conference was mostly for other IP lawyers."

And we all know people who are active in bar activities but get no business from their work.

However, a little follow-up and the proper direction can turn these traditional activities into productive business development tools.

WRITING ARTICLES TO GET BUSINESS

Many lawyers write articles in the name of "business development." And I often hear lawyers complain that, "I wrote that article and didn't get anything out of it." That's because article writing is usually about "credentialing," not developing business.

But articles, once you've written them, are fine for leveraging your way into a business relationship. Here's how.

STEP 1: Write an article that you know is a hot topic for your key prospects and have it published.

STEP 2: Reproduce the article nicely and send it to your best prospects along with a personal note detailing how the law applies to each prospect's specific company.

STEP 3: Follow up with telephone calls offering to discuss, at no charge, how these issues apply to each prospect's business.

And if you're going to write articles, at least try to publish them in periodicals that your prospects might actually read. I know a lawyer who focuses her practice on nursing homes. She publishes articles in trade publications aimed at the nursing home industry, and then sends the articles to her clients and prospects.

This lawyer's focused approach has generated far more business than if she were to write purely legal analyses for bar journals that are read solely by other lawyers.

LEVERAGING SPEECHES

Speeches can be a wonderful way to connect with prospects. But you can't just give a speech and leave. You must also leverage the chance to connect with prospects.

One of the biggest missed opportunities for building relationships takes place before and after the speeches that lawyers give to bar associations, at industry conferences, and for CLE presentations. In any audience of fifty to 100 people, there are likely five to ten good prospects. If you don't find some excuse to call them up and make contact just before or after you give your speech, you will be wasting an opportunity.

I recently worked with a patent lawyer who was giving a speech to an industry conference. He created and delivered an effective speech, and the attendees gave him the highest marks on the evaluation forms.

"So did you get any good contacts out of it?" I asked.

He looked at me with a slightly puzzled expression. "I met a few lawyers who used to be with our firm," he said. But he had failed to contact any of the real prospects in the audience.

The real shame of the lawyer's omissions is the sizeable potential of this missed opportunity.

What should he have done? The following two things:

(1) Obtain from the conference organizer a full list of all the participants and contact information, and then get in touch with some of them. Indeed, many business developers refuse to speak at a conference unless, prior to the conference, the organizer provides a list of all attendees complete with e-mail addresses and telephone numbers.

(2) Contact the best prospects either before or after the conference.

> ▶ If you're calling beforehand, you can say, "I see that you're attending my presentation next month. I'd love to speak to you when we get there. Is there anything that you're particularly interested in that you'd like me to address?"
> ▶ If you're calling afterwards, you can say, "I see that you attended my presentation. I'd love to hear your view of the issues I discussed. I'd also like to learn about your business. Are you interested in a meeting next week?"

Many people give presentations and wonder why they don't get much business as a result. But those lawyers don't get new business because they do not realize that people won't hire you unless and until they believe you can solve their business problems. When you give a speech, you are addressing a roomful of people who are already interested in what you have to say. If you do a good job, they will probably be that much more interested in following up by speaking with you. So pick up the telephone and try to connect with the people who could bring you business. What have you got to lose?

BAR ACTIVITIES FOR REFERRALS

Too many people consider bar work to be business development when it's nothing of the sort. The problem with bar activities from a business development standpoint is that most of the time you're schmoozing with your competition, not your prospects.

If you get business through referrals, then bar activities work great. Just make sure that you connect with people who can send you business.

If you have a niche practice in trusts and estates, connect with litigators who can send you their clients who need wills. Woo referral sources just as you would any other prospects, meeting with them and letting them know how you can help their clients and refer *them* business.

CAPITALIZING ON TRADE ORGANIZATION LEADERSHIP

For many lawyers, trade organization work is far more effective for developing business than getting involved in bar activities. And if you're going to join a trade group, remember the following admonition: "Never join an organization that you don't want to run."

Young lawyers hear advice like that from top rainmakers in many law firms. And for the most part, this is sound advice. But if you want to make community involvement a cornerstone of your business development work, pick an organization that will put you in contact with business prospects. Just any organization will not do. (That's not to say that you shouldn't get involved in the American Cancer Society or the United Jewish Appeal. Just don't expect such work to generate numerous business opportunities.)

For example, the prospects for Scott Petty, a top patent lawyer at King & Spalding, are high-tech business people. So it was wise for Petty to take a leadership role in the Entrepreneurial Forum for the Technology Association of Georgia.

Every month, the Entrepreneurial Forum features speakers on topics of interest to technology entrepreneurs. I attended one of the programs where the speaker was the founder of several very successful high-tech companies. She attracted approximately 200 high-tech business people to a 7:30 A.M. breakfast meeting at the King & Spalding offices.

As a result of this program and others, Scott has become the leader in an organization that features must-attend events by many of Scott's most important prospects.

Another lawyer who uses trade organizations effectively is Michael Golden, a corporate lawyer with Arnall Golden & Gregory. His prospects are business owners. Golden has therefore opted to become deeply involved in the Young Entrepreneurs Organization. At every meeting he can connect with the top young business leaders in his community.

Regardless of the type of law you practice, there is an industry association in which you can get involved to build relationships with your prospects. And if you become a leader in such an organization, you will have opportunities to build numerous strong business relationships.

THE INTIMATE DINNER EVENT WITH A BUSINESS EXPERT

A variation on the "trade organization" tactic is to organize a small function of your own that is geared toward a specific group of people. The beauty of this tactic is that prospects get great value and you get a strong start on a business relationship. Don't be surprised if prospects actually call you asking to attend your event.

Ideally, you should plan an intimate event with no more than about ten people at a very nice restaurant or club. Be sure to invite a guest who can help your guests better understand their own businesses. The expert should not be a lawyer but, rather, should be an expert on a topic of interest to your prospects. Your goal is to add value to the prospect's business.

Whom do you invite as the "special guest"?

▸ If you're an environmental lawyer, invite a key EPA administrator or an expert in technology for complying with the Clean Air Act.
▸ If you're an electric utility lawyer, invite an economist to discuss the implications of electric power deregulation.
▸ If you're a tax lawyer, invite a tax commissioner. If you can't get a current commissioner, get a former commissioner.
▸ If you're a banking lawyer, invite a bank consultant.
▸ If you're a corporate lawyer, invite an expert in corporate compensation or corporate governance.

Once you've lined up the guest, choose fifteen prospects to invite to the event. The prospects can be potential new clients for your firm or existing clients who need to be "cross-sold" on your area of expertise.

Then call them up and invite them to the event. What do you say?

STEP 1: "Hi. This is Joey Asher. I'm a partner at Smith and Williams."

STEP 2: "We're having a small dinner/networking event next month. Attending the dinner will be Janet Miller, former head of corporate taxation for the state of New York. She now has her own consulting firm. This is going to be a great chance for you to get insight into the inner workings of the state tax department."

STEP 3: "The event is to be held at 7:30 P.M. on March 21st at the Ritz Carlton dining room. Would you like to attend?"

This is a surprisingly easy way to build relationships because the dinner has considerable value to the attendees. Your clients and prospects will want to participate for several reasons:

> ▸ They will receive a free dinner at a nice place. Pick a hot new restaurant and reserve a private room. If you can't get a private room, schedule your event at a private club with a quiet room where you can be sure that participants will be able to hear the discussion.
> ▸ They will have a chance to learn more about their industry. Spend some time thinking about who you'd like to invite to the dinner. Pick people who are on the cutting edge of an industry trend.
> ▸ The event will be exclusive. Because you're only inviting a small number of people, the dinner will have the feel of an "private event." That exclusivity adds to the perceived value.

So now that you have planned the event, what do you do next? The key to a good event is to give everyone a chance to participate and trade ideas. The presentation should not be merely a speech by the guest of honor. Following is an agenda that works:

> ▸ *Networking:* Let people introduce themselves and chat for a while.
> ▸ *Introductions:* Before introducing the guest of honor, let the other participants introduce themselves, including their backgrounds.
> ▸ *Guest of honor introduction:* Briefly introduce the guest of honor.
> ▸ *Guest of honor brief comments:* It's important that you tell the guest of honor to limit the length of his presentation to

a maximum of five minutes. In addition, make sure the keynote "speech" is informal. Finally, there must be no PowerPoint presentations under any circumstances.

▶ *Q&A for prospects and guest of honor:* After the initial remarks by the guest of honor, get the questions started by asking him or her a question. Be sure to prepare questions for the participants as well. Ask them their views on the key issues facing their industry. Make sure that you're actively soliciting input from all participants, e.g., "Sally, what does your company do in this area?"

The greatest advantage about this kind of event is that you can learn about the key issues facing the participants' businesses. For example, if you're an environmental lawyer and you arrange for a clean air technologist to speak, you should listen carefully to the prospects' comments and questions. You might well hear the prospects discuss a legal problem about which you can help.

Once the meeting is over, you should have developed a strong relationship with all of the prospects who attended. So don't stop! You need to call them all and arrange meetings to discuss their business. This will be another easy telephone call. Who wouldn't meet with you after you've fed them a nice meal and introduced them to an industry expert?

CONCLUSION: TURNING OLD STANDARDS INTO BUSINESS DEVELOPMENT

Let's put this issue in the language of tort law. If, as a direct result of your activity, "new business" is "reasonably foreseeable," then that activity can be characterized as business development. Unfortunately, writing articles, attending bar functions, and giving CLE speeches—at least as undertaken by most lawyers—just doesn't usually pass that test.

However, with some follow-up and direction, these activities can become significant business generators.

CONNECTING VALUE:
HELPING BUSINESSES
SUCCEED

II

Here is some ridiculous business development advice that you hear all the time: "To win business you need connections. So go join an organization."

Sure, connections help you develop business. But I find that many lawyers have plenty of connections and are very community-oriented people. Unfortunately, connections don't become business unless you use those connections well. And that is where most lawyers fail.

One example is an attorney whom I'll call Carrie. Carrie is very well "connected." She is extremely active in her child's prestigious private school. She campaigns actively for her favorite political candidates. She is on the board of several charities. Carrie knows everyone in town. And everyone knows Carrie.

But as a partner for a large commercial firm, Carrie generates little business. And her story is common. Lots of lawyers have lots of connections but generate little or no business.

Why don't these connections generate business? Because business people don't hire lawyers out of friendship alone. As was said previously, business people hire lawyers for only *one reason:*

> **Business people hire lawyers whom they believe will help their businesses succeed.**

So you can be best friends with every CEO in the Fortune 500 and you still won't generate any business if you can't show how you can provide value. But, if you can show how you can help a business succeed, that is, demonstrate "value," then you *will* get business. Maybe not immediately. But if you show enough businesses that you can provide value, your telephone will begin to ring with clients waiting to hire you. Guaranteed.

How to Convert Contacts into Business

Let's assume that you're doing a great job of prospecting. You're building connections through networking or speaking at conferences. Now you must convert those contacts into business by making those contacts see you as a person who can help their businesses succeed.

Converting contacts into business takes the following three steps:

Step 1: *Get a meeting with a decision-maker.*

Business owners and others who hire lawyers will not spontaneously start thinking of you as a value provider. Business owners, as a rule, do not assume that you even are interested in their business. In fact, business owners spend virtually no time at all thinking about you.

With that in mind, you're going to have to find a way to make business owners know that you want their business and that you can add value to their firms. There is only one way to do that consistently. You have to call your connections on the telephone.

Once you get your contacts on the telephone, you must ask them to meet with you to discuss how you can add value to their businesses. This telephone call may be the most intimidating aspect of getting business. But once you learn how to do it, you've completed the first step toward growing your practice.

Step 2: *During the meeting, learn what the decision-maker believes he needs to succeed.*

Note that I did not entitle this section, "Tell the decision-maker what a great lawyer you are." Note also that I did not call this section, "Tell the decision-maker how many prestigious clients you have." Neither did I call it, "Tell the decision-maker that you went to Yale or

Harvard or NYU and clerked for Justice David Souter" nor "Tell the decision-maker how you just won a $10 million judgment for another client."

The key to getting a person to hire you as his or her lawyer is to focus on *the client's needs.* That means listening to *business goals,* truly seeking to understand what the client *values* in a lawyer, and trying to understand *how you can help the business succeed.* That's not to say that your qualifications are never relevant. But no one cares about your qualifications until you convince your prospect that you understand his or her needs and can provide a solution. This is the biggest mistake lawyers make in dealing with decision-makers. They talk about themselves before listening to the prospect.

STEP 3: *Package your legal service as a solution to the prospect's business needs.*

Once you've listened to the prospect and understand what he or she thinks is needed, tell the prospect how you can provide a solution. You must demonstrate that you've been listening to his or her needs by explaining what you've been told and discussing how you think you can contribute to the business's success.

Those three steps are what separate the true business developers from the lawyers with lots of connections but no business. The only way to get business is by making decision-makers see you as a value provider. And the only way that happens is if you *make* it happen.

TURNING CONNECTIONS INTO BUSINESS

Frankly, I'm not too worried about your connections. If you're like most lawyers, you're probably pretty well-connected. You probably serve on the school board, or raise money for your school, or coach a soccer team.

My concern is how you're going to make the business owner you've met through your board work or soccer coaching begin to see you as a resource. Because that's the only way you're going to win that business. No one is going to hire you just because, as I've heard some attorneys say, "They know I'm a lawyer."

They're going to hire you if they perceive you as someone who can add value to the business. To make prospects see you that way, take action that will *make* them see you that way.

CHAPTER 7

What Do Decision-Makers Want?

CONSIDER THE FISH

DIFFERENT VALUE EQUATIONS

EVEN GREAT LEGAL WORK DOESN'T ALWAYS GET YOU BUSINESS

THE BUSINESS DEVELOPMENT CYCLE

CONSIDER THE FISH

I was watching a fishing show on television when the host suggested a great sales tip that any business lawyer would do well to adopt. "To catch a fish," this renowned fisherman said, "you have to consider the fish."

"Consider the fish!" Now that's what I call great business development advice.

In other words, if you want to win business, you have to "consider the client." That is, to win a business client, you need to consider what that business values in a lawyer.

As a result, I speak regularly with in-house lawyers and general counsels to learn what they value in an outside counsel. And every time I question them, these in-house lawyers say virtually the same thing: they want outside counsel who *understands how to add value to the business*.

This emphasis on adding value is far more important to general counsels than outstanding legal expertise, which many GCs view as important but far easier to find.

"You need to understand my perspective of value," says Bruce Richards, an attorney and former GC at Certegy and Equifax. "You want to think about how you can meet my needs as far as the desired value equation."

What, then, is a "value equation"? A value equation is simply what the customer cares about most in a lawyer. And in any business development process, your goal as the individual who is seeking the business is to find this out.

DIFFERENT VALUE EQUATIONS

The "value equation" that I hear most often is, "They need to understand my business." In other words, if you're going to give advice on a client's ERISA plan, the client wants a lawyer who can deliver more than just the "right answer." The client wants to know how the answer will impact the rest of his or her business.

"In general I place a very high premium on the attorney's ability to learn about my business," says Richards.

"For example, let's say that we're developing a marketing strategy for a new, highly regulated financial service. My outside lawyer, who is an expert in the regulations, may need to focus with me on tweaking the service design in ways that will pass muster with the regulators without compromising the strategy and the service's appeal to the customer," says Richards. "It's very useful for outside counsel to have a business sense. Not just to come in and say, 'Here's what the law says.'"

But some GCs focus on values other than understanding the business. A value model of some clients relies on getting the work done quickly at low rates. Other businesses want their outside counsel to be able to work well with the company managers, placing a high premium on being able to communicate with laymen.

How do you find out what a particular in-house lawyer values?

Well. . . . You ask her what she values. Then you listen. If you want the business, you find a way to give her what she wants.

EVEN GREAT LEGAL WORK DOESN'T ALWAYS GET YOU BUSINESS

Understanding the customer's business is not what lawyers tend to think of first when they are asked what clients value most. I recently did a workshop with a group of litigation partners at a very prestigious firm in New York City. At one point in the program I asked them to list what *they perceived* as the primary reasons why a company selects a particular lawyer or firm. No one said anything like, "They want someone who understands the business."

Instead, they said that GCs value "Expertise." "They want great lawyers." "They want someone with a lot of experience." And so on.

But let's be clear about something: *Great legal work is not what most in-house counsel value most in their lawyers.* Great legal work is taken for granted. In-house counsel won't even consider hiring you if you're not a great lawyer. "For me, a reputation for high-quality work is just a starting point," says Richards.

That is, people who hire lawyers value great legal work in the same way that people who buy cars value an engine that runs well. Sure, the engine is important. You certainly wouldn't buy a car without a good engine. But a reliable engine isn't usually central to the purchase. It's taken for granted.

For Mike McGuire, the head of the real estate law department for The Home Depot, the value equation comes down to willingness to do business "The Home Depot Way." "We don't just need good lawyers," McGuire says. "We need good lawyers who are willing and able to work within our systems and enter into a long-term partner relationship."

And that's not as simple as it may seem. To be a real estate lawyer for The Home Depot, you have to comply with its billing methods, stay within accepted per-deal budgets, and turn in timely and complete closing binders. "We expect perfection from our firms and, unfortunately, perfection is an elusive goal," McGuire says.

Because of the specific standards, McGuire told me that only three or four firms per market are usually chosen to do The Home Depot's real estate work. Moreover, there are some major firms with terrific lawyers that don't always qualify. McGuire mentioned one well-known firm with a lawyer who has been courting Home Depot aggressively. "I like the lawyer and his firm a lot," McGuire said. In fact, he indicated that the firm clearly has the technical expertise to do the average Home Depot real estate deal. And the lawyer is highly qualified. "He's a fabulous lawyer," McGuire said. But that lawyer's firm is not willing to do the standard Home Depot real estate work within the billing rates that Home Depot expects.

"We don't care about how fancy your office is," he says. "That doesn't mean anything to us. We just want top-notch service at the best price."

THE BUSINESS DEVELOPMENT CYCLE

What does all of this mean for a lawyer who is seeking the business of these in-house lawyers? That winning business is not about impressing prospects with your résumé. Instead, business development is about trying to discover the prospect's values or needs and then showing how you're both well-qualified and positioned to provide that value and fulfill those needs.

In fact, that's the business development cycle in a nutshell:

STEP 1: Meet with a decision-maker.

STEP 2: Discover what he or she needs and how she expresses that need.

STEP 3: Show the decision-maker how you can fulfill that need.

This is not to say that your impeccable résumé of winning deals isn't relevant. Sure it's relevant. But only to the extent that those deals reassure the decision-maker that you can satisfy his or her needs.

So if you want to catch a fish, you have to consider the fish. And if you want to catch a client, you have to consider the client. That means listening to the client and trying to understand what he or she values. Unless you understand those needs, your great résumé is worthless.

CHAPTER **8**

Turning Contacts into Clients: The Telephone Call

FACING UP TO THE UNAVOIDABLE

"BUT I DON'T WANT TO SOUND LIKE A SALESMAN"

OVERCOMING CALL RELUCTANCE

SUCCESSFUL PROSPECTING CALLS START WITH A PLAN

THE CALENDAR ASSAULT THEORY

DANGER SIGNAL: "TELL ME WHAT YOU THINK OF THIS PROBLEM"

"I'M GOING TO BE IN SAN FRANCISCO"

REHEARSING WITH A SCRIPT

RITUALS FOR OVERCOMING CALL RELUCTANCE

THE IMPORTANCE OF MAKING LOTS OF CALLS

FACING UP TO THE UNAVOIDABLE

A telephone call to a prospect is an *unavoidable act of sales*. It's unavoidable for you because business development simply won't happen consistently without it.

To understand this concept, let's be clear about what prospects *don't* do. They don't sit in their office and create "to do" lists that include, "Be sure to contact that lawyer I met the other day to see how he can help me make more money." Prospects simply aren't thinking about you.

Once you've met the prospects, it is best that you assume they will never think of you again. Ever. And if you don't call them up and ask for a meeting, they will simply continue about their business without giving you a second thought.

It's not that they don't like you. But they have other things to do that seem more important. So you can put off making that call as long as you want. But the telephone call is unavoidable if you want to development business.

The wonderful thing about telephone calls is that they're unavoidable from the prospect's perspective as well. A direct communication from a known contact is something that most people will not avoid. If you call them, *and they know you* (I'm not talking about cold calls here), most people will accept your call or call you back. If they don't return your call, they will eventually take it once you catch up with them on a subsequent attempt when they're in the office.

"But I Don't Want to Sound Like a Salesman"

The problem with telephone calls to prospects is that, for lawyers, this is the most "sales-y" part of the process. I hear, "I don't want to be a salesman" from lawyers all the time. And as a lawyer turned salesman, I don't take offense at this obviously sales-phobic statement. Sometimes I wonder if there is any fate worse for a lawyer than to be perceived as a salesman.

But whenever I hear someone say, "I don't want to sound like a salesman," I immediately think that this is a person who doesn't understand selling when it's done right. Sales is not about asking for favors. It's not about "slicking" a prospect into doing something he wouldn't otherwise do. It's not about getting a prospect a "great deal on a used car."

Great salespeople think in terms of equipping their prospects with resources for success. And if you approach the process with that attitude, you shouldn't be worried about appearing to be a "salesperson." You'll be doing things that add value to the prospects' businesses.

And your prospects don't view lawyers who call them seeking to build a relationship as "slick salespeople." Most in-house lawyers with whom I've spoken welcome contact from people whom they know want to help them. Most in-house lawyers consider close contact with the general legal community to be a major aspect of their job.

"As a general counsel, I have always sought a lot of relationships within the legal community," said Bruce Richards, former General Counsel at Equifax and Certegy. "Among other benefits, tapping into your network is a great way for a corporate counsel to obtain quick answers to a lot of legal questions and get free advice from others who've faced similar issues."

And every general counsel that I've ever spoken to has told me the same thing. If they know you, usually they'll meet with you. Many of them consider building a reservoir of resources in the legal community to be an important part of their job.

The fact that so few lawyers actually make such phone calls provides a great opportunity for those who are willing to do so. For example, I know one attorney who was reluctant to call the General Counsel of a major pharmaceutical company even after being urged to do so by the company's accountant. "They are expecting you to call them," the accounting firm's representative told the lawyer. Finally the lawyer called, after much coaching from the accountant. The General Counsel took the call, set up a meeting, and gave the lawyer some business.

OVERCOMING CALL RELUCTANCE

Of course, for many lawyers, an intellectual understanding that prospects accept calls from lawyers who sell their services is not enough to get that call made. Many lawyers are still hesitant to pick up the telephone.

If you're not worried that you'll sound like a salesman, perhaps you're worried about something else. Maybe you're worried that you'll sound needy, or stupid, or unskilled, or amateurish.

Or perhaps you're worried that you'll be "bothering" the prospect. Or maybe you're worried that the prospect already has another lawyer whom he loves so much that he can't ever consider hiring other counsel under any foreseeable set of circumstances. Or perhaps you're just a little scared.

Salespeople have a name for this fear: *"call reluctance."*

When it comes to call reluctance, I feel your pain. Truly I do. I've stared at my telephone for hours, frightened to pick it up. I've come to work on days when that telephone handset felt like it must have been made of solid lead. I know that when you're just getting started in business development, it's hard to make business development calls, even when you're calling people you know (just try making cold calls for a few days if you really want to really feel dread when you look at a telephone).

But call reluctance can be overcome. First, ask yourself the following question every time you hesitate to pick up the telephone to make a business development call:

"Do I have the business now?"

For me, that simple question is kryptonite for "call reluctance." If the answer is "no," then all reasons for not picking up the telephone become nonexistent. Why? Because if you experience rejection during a call, then you're *already* experiencing the worst-case scenario: *not getting the business.*

I don't generally throw around typical motivational phrases. They usually seem hokey to me. But I've yet to find anyone who has a better approach to this issue than hockey legend Wayne Gretzky, who said, "You miss 100% of the shots you never take."

So, the next time the telephone receiver looks a little heavy, think of the Great Gretzky and take a shot.

SUCCESSFUL PROSPECTING CALLS START WITH A PLAN

If your prospecting call is handled right, your chances of obtaining a meeting are pretty good. After all, you're calling someone you already know. So if you sound confident and give the prospect a sense of the value you might provide, your prospect is probably going to agree to meet with you.

Following, therefore, is a simple formula that you can use to make a telephone call:

STEP 1: *Greeting.* Introduce yourself and remind the prospect how you know each other. "Hi Fred. This is Joey Asher with Smith and Howard. You and I met last week at the Society for Human Resource Management meeting. We sat next to each other during the keynote address."

STEP 2: *Transition to business/hook.* Move quickly to the point of the call. "Let me tell you the reason for my call. I'm calling to discuss business. When we were chatting at the conference you mentioned the chemicals disposal issues that your firm is facing. As an environmental lawyer, I might be able to be a resource."

STEP 3: *Ask for the meeting.* "I'd love to learn more about the issues that you're facing. Can we meet for about thirty minutes next week in your office? Are you free next Wednesday."

The Greeting: Speak Slowly and Limit the Chit Chat

Imagine the prospect sitting at his desk in the two minutes before his telephone rings with you on the line. What has he been doing? He's been working. Reviewing budgets, fly-specking contracts, balancing his personal checkbook. Whatever he's been doing, he has certainly not been waiting for your telephone call. Remember, he hasn't been thinking of you at all.

So when he picks up the telephone, speak slowly, pronounce your name carefully, and pause, giving the prospect a moment.

"Hi Fred, this is Joey Asher of Smith and Howard." Pause briefly to let the information sink in. The prospect is most likely wracking his brain, trying to remember you.

After the brief pause, assuming that the prospect doesn't immediately start a familiar conversation, remind him how he knows you. "We met last week at the SHRM conference in Orlando. We sat next to each other at the keynote address."

Pause again. Remember, the prospect is likely trying desperately to remember who you are. Pretty soon everything is going to click into place and he'll say something like, "Oh, hi Joey. How are you? Did you enjoy the conference?"

And from there you should take the cue from the prospect to engage in brief chit chat. But don't linger too long on the chit chat. If the prospect wanted to have a social conversation, he'd call his fraternity brother. You want to move quickly to the second step.

Transition to Business

When you're calling "warm" prospects (people you know socially or through a business or civic network), one of the most challenging things is to take the relationship to the "next level." Indeed, many lawyers have plenty of contacts but never get business because they don't know how to transition the relationship from social to business.

The key to transitioning to the "next level" is a short, two-sentence phrase:

> *"Let me tell you the reason for my call. I want to discuss business."*

This little statement is what you say once you've finished with the "chit chat" portion of your call. So the conversation might sound something like the following: "Well, I also had a nice time at the dinner party the other night. But let me tell you the reason for my call. I want to discuss business."

This little sales pirouette is one of my favorite phrases in the sales repertoire. The two short sentences are simple, unassuming, and non-threatening. Yet what they convey is incredibly powerful. These two little sentences say, "I'm interested in taking control of this relationship and directing it toward finding a way that we can have a business relationship."

Those two phrases also convey confidence and command respect. I have made countless business development calls in my life. And virtually every time I have said those two little sentences, I have received the same response. Typically, that response is:

"Okay."

Sometimes, the response is, "All right." Occasionally, it is simply, "Sure."

But, most important, I am never told, "No ... interested in discussing business with you. You scumb... never heard of anyone else getting such a response.

You might think I'm making a big deal over a small thi... ...er all, this is not what salespeople call a "close." These a... not statements that "ask for the order." And you're not going to get an engagement from these statements. At least not yet.

But the statement "I want to discuss business" marks a critical turning point in any relationship. Suddenly, what was once a casual relationship has entered the realm of business. Suddenly, you have permission to discuss ideas for doing things together that will benefit you both financially.

And that's important if we remember the most fundamental aspect of business development: *Business people hire lawyers whom they believe will help their businesses succeed.* Prior to hearing the "magic phrase," the prospect probably never considered you as someone who could add value to his business.

Now, by your uttering the magic phrase, that has suddenly and dramatically changed. By responding "okay," the prospect has agreed to consider you as a business partner. Maybe he's not considering you seriously yet. But you're referenced in a materially different part of his brain now. You've been re-categorized from "friend" to "friend and potential business partner." And that's huge. That's where business development really begins.

The Hook: Showing Some Value

After you transition the conversation to business, you can then attempt to show value to your prospect. And that is what you do with your *"hook."* The "hook" is a simple statement that "hooks" your prospect with a suggestion of the kind of value you can provide to the prospect's company. Typical hooks are as follows:

Corporate lawyer: "I noticed that your firm is in the process of expanding through acquisition. I'm a corporate lawyer who has helped many companies like yours, and I'd like to learn more about your business and perhaps get a sense of how we might add value."

Employment lawyer: "You mentioned that your firm has a number of employees. I'm an attorney with considerable experience helping companies deal with employee issues. I'd like to learn more about your business and perhaps get a sense of how we might be a resource."

Environmental lawyer: "You mentioned that your firm is involved in manufacturing. I'm an attorney who has helped many companies find interesting solutions to environmental challenges. I'd love to learn more about your business and get a sense of how we might be a resource."

Securities lawyer: "I know that your firm is involved in a number of securities matters. I'm an attorney who has helped many companies find interesting solutions to securities issues. I'd love to learn more about your business and get a sense of how we might add value."

Real estate lawyer: "I know that your business is involved in numerous land acquisitions across the country. I'm an attorney who has a good deal of experience helping companies buy and sell property. I'd love to learn more about your business and get a sense of how we might add value."

Corporate litigator: "Like any businessman, I know that you're involved in disputes. I'm an attorney who has much experience helping businesses prevent disputes. I'd love to learn more about your business and get a sense of how we might add value."

Litigator focusing on high-tech: "I know your firm makes enterprise software. I have a lot of experience working with software firms. I'd love to learn more about your business to see whether I could be a resource for you." (This example can be used for anyone with an industry focus.)

Intellectual property lawyer: "I know that your business handles many intellectual property matters. I'm an attorney who has considerable experience helping companies maximize the value of their intellectual property. I'd love to learn more about your business and get a sense of how we might add value."

Tax lawyer: "I know that your business spends a great deal of time trying to keep the effective tax rate as low as possible. I'm an attorney with a good deal of experience helping companies lower their taxes as much as possible. I'd love to learn more about your business and get a sense of how we might add value."

Corporate finance lawyer: "I know that your business is involved in many complex financial transactions. I'm an attorney who has much experience helping companies finance complex projects. I'd love to learn more about your business and get a sense of how we might add value."

Healthcare lawyer: "I know that your business handles many complex healthcare issues. I'm a healthcare lawyer who has been helping healthcare organizations for many years. I'd love to learn more about your business and get a sense of how we might be a resource."

As you can see, when you prepare your hook, the goal is not to suggest specific legal work that you could provide. Rather, you simply want to suggest generally how you might provide value to the prospect's company. Then you want to show an interest in learning more about the prospect's business.

This approach is consistent with what people who hire lawyers tell us about *how* they hire lawyers. They're interested in someone who will take the time to become a true business counselor, rather than someone who is simply a solver of specific legal problems.

Once you've suggested the value that you can provide, it's time to move to the final step.

Ask for the Meeting

Asking for a meeting ain't brain surgery. But it's a critical part of the process. At every stage of a sale, you must tell the prospect what you want. In this case, you want a meeting. So you need to ask. The best way to ask is to have a specific date and time in mind. It's also a good idea to give the prospect a specific sense of how long the meeting will take.

> *"I'd like to stop by your office for about thirty minutes to discuss your business. Are you available next Thursday morning?"*

Telling the amount of time you need helps you get the meeting. The prospect thinks, "Well it's only thirty minutes, why not?" Chances are that he will give you an hour.

Suggesting a specific time also helps you get the meeting. It makes the decision easier for the prospect. By suggesting a time, you've immediately gotten the prospect to start looking at her calendar. You've bypassed the mental process of finding a time to meeting ("Let's see, when do I have time available?"). Instead, the prospect just looks at the calendar and determines whether that specific time is available.

THE CALENDAR ASSAULT THEORY

Remember that the sole purpose of your telephone calls is to get a meeting with prospects. I like to consider these calls a "single-minded assault on their calendars." Once you get the meeting, GET OFF THE TELEPHONE. Say, "I'm looking forward to seeing you next week. Have a great weekend! Goodbye."

No matter how tempting it might seem, do not under any circumstances say, "So tell me a little more about the SEC investigation that I've been reading about." At this stage of the sale, nothing good and plenty of bad can come from such questions.

Consider what the possible answers are:

"Well, a case has already been brought by the SEC and we've retained counsel. Come to think of it, right now I'm pretty overwhelmed with that case, so can you call me in a couple of months when that matter is finished?" *Your extra question cost you a meeting.*

"Actually, the SEC was wrong and has withdrawn the complaint." *Your extra question made you look uninformed and out of the loop.* Maybe the prospect will not cancel the meeting. But you're going to have a tougher time building a strong relationship.

"Actually, I'm very interested in your view on that. Tell me...." *Your extra question has you stuck on the telephone giving half-baked legal advice.* And if the prospect doesn't like what he hears, he'll never hire you.

You're never going to get the business unless you build the relationship. The way to do that is gradually learning about the business first and then starting to solve legal problems. So when you're on the telephone, just get the meeting arranged and get off the line.

DANGER SIGNAL: "TELL ME WHAT YOU THINK OF THIS PROBLEM"

Just as you should never ask an extra question once you've gotten a meeting on the telephone, you should avoid letting the prospect get you roped into an impromptu discussion of a legal issue. For example, it's very common for a prospect to say, "You're an employment lawyer? Let me ask you about this employee I have."

Avoid answering those questions. Instead, here's what you say:

(1) *If you've already gotten the meeting:*

"You know, we deal with a lot of issues like that, but what we do depends a lot on your business and your goals. And that's what we're going to talk about when we meet next week."

Or,

(2) *If you haven't gotten the meeting yet:*

"You know, we deal with a lot of issues like that. But how we handle them depends a lot on your business and your goals. I'd love to learn more about those things. Can we meet next week?"

Once again, the goal of these telephone calls is not to solve legal problems. The goal is to get the prospect to agree to meet with you. All you're doing is making an assault on his calendar. Avoid doing anything else during this telephone call, especially displaying your expertise as a lawyer. That expertise will be on ample display later in the process.

I'M GOING TO BE IN SAN FRANCISCO

One neat trick to help you get the meeting is to tell someone that you're going to be in town and would like to meet. Here's what you do. Next time you're going on a trip to, say, "Philadelphia," about two weeks before the trip, contact a prospect in Philly. Here's what you say:

STEP 1: *Greeting.* "Hi, this is Joey Asher of Smith and Howard. You and I met last month at the energy marketing conference."

Step 2: *Transition to business/hook.* "The reason for my call is to follow up on our discussion. You mentioned challenges that your company is facing regarding compliance with the new FERC marketing regulations. I'm an electric utility lawyer with a great deal of experience dealing with FERC. *I'm going to be in Philly in two weeks.* While I'm in town I would love the chance to stop by your office for about thirty minutes to learn about your business and discuss how I might help you add a little value."

Step 3: *Ask for the meeting.* "Are you available on March 22nd in the morning?"

For some reason, telling people that you're going to be in town and would like to squeeze in a meeting with them makes people more likely to give you a meeting. Perhaps the prospect thinks, "Well, if you're going to be in town, I guess I'd better take advantage of this opportunity."

I know salespeople who set up entire sales trips by telling their prospects that they "plan to be in town" and would love to set up a chance to meet. Often these salespeople don't buy the tickets until they confirm the meetings.

REHEARSING WITH A SCRIPT

If you're not used to making these kinds of calls, then you should use a script. And you should also rehearse. I know one lawyer who writes out exactly what he plans to say every time he makes a prospecting call. Then he practices what he wants to say out loud.

"I don't want to sound scripted," he says. "But I also want to sound cogent."

Having a script won't make you sound stiff. It'll just give you a crutch if you need it.

And rehearsing helps assure that what you say sounds good. This is important. You must sound good, although not too formal. Too often people construct cleverly written scripts that sound stilted.

Try practicing your script once into your answering machine. And listen to how you sound. If it sounds simple, cogent, and clear, you're ready.

Rituals for Overcoming Call Reluctance

If you're a tennis fan, then you might remember tennis star John McEnroe's famous ritual before every serve. He would bounce the ball a couple of times, look over his right shoulder at his target, and then would stretch forward with his racket before making his toss and unleashing a great shot.

Part of what made that shot great was McEnroe's ritual. Similarly, if you undertake some ritual before making a prospecting call, this can help you deal with the call reluctance that plagues many new business developers.

I suggest a three-step ritual:

Step 1: Write out your script on a sheet of paper.

Step 2: Practice saying the script out loud several times until you're certain that you can say it confidently.

Step 3: Pick up the telephone and dial.

Steps 1 and 2 of the ritual are really all the preparation you need. Once you've completed these steps, there is no excuse for not moving forward, picking up that telephone, and dialing. You may not become a world champion like McEnroe. But you'll serve up your share of aces.

The Importance of Making Lots of Calls

When I was trying to lose weight, I bought a book by a Harvard diet researcher who reviewed the advantages and disadvantages of competing diets. The book pointed out that there was only one diet activity that correlated with substantial weight loss close to 100% percent of the time. That activity was keeping detailed track of all the calories you ate every day.

Simply keeping track of your calories, research showed, resulted in weight loss in 95% of people who did this religiously. So that's what I did. I wrote down everything I ate and the associated calories in a little notebook. It wasn't easy. But I did it and I lost weight. That notebook was my silver bullet for diet success.

Similarly, I often hear lawyers ask for a silver bullet for business development success. In my opinion, there is only one activity that, if done consistently, will develop business for you. That activity is making telephone calls to decision-makers and setting up meetings to discuss their businesses.

Now let's be clear about something. I'm not assuming that you will subsequently conduct the meeting like a seasoned business developer, confidently employing all the consultative tactics that I'll describe later in this book. I'm not even talking about using the calling scripts that I've outlined above in this chapter. *I'm merely talking about making the calls, and showing up at the appointments.*

Every lawyer whom I have ever met who has regularly engaged in that practice—and there are many—has become a successful business developer.

Over and over in my coaching, I see it start to work almost instantly. Recently I was working with a litigator who wanted trademark infringement business from a company that had started doing business in South America. "Go meet with them and discuss what they're doing," I said.

This lawyer made the call, went to the meeting with a colleague, and they came back with some trademark work.

A patent lawyer wanted work from doctors who had invented some medical equipment. He also had a list of physicians who were former clients from whom he had not heard recently. I said to him, "Try giving them a call and saying, 'How's it going?'" In the first day of calling, one of the doctors said, "You know, I was meaning to call you!" The lawyer got some business.

A corporate litigator said he had a friend who owned a small manufacturing business. I suggested to him, "Why don't you just call and say you want to take him to lunch to discuss his business." Six months later he had a small matter from his friend.

Why is making calls the best correlation to business development success? Because the only way that you can reliably make business come to you is to put yourself in the room with the people who can hire you and show how you can add value. That can't happen without a call to that decision-maker.

Calling Beats Writing Articles

Calling decision-makers is far superior to the most common business development activities. Speaking at trade shows and at lawyer conferences is wonderful. I recommend it for getting your name out into the marketplace. And sometimes a decision-maker or referral source will hear you and recommend you. But what you say in a speech rarely addresses the specific concerns of a business. As a result, the business you receive is irregular.

Writing articles is even less advantageous. If you make a speech, people at least can appraise you in person. But when you publish an article, the reader often assumes that the piece may not even have been written by you.

Networking is fine too. But networkers don't get business based *solely* on knowing many people. Just because you meet a business owner through your work with the Boy Scouts doesn't mean that business owner thinks you can help her business succeed.

Each decision-maker may have dozens of friends who are lawyers. To get the prospect's business, you must convince the prospect that you—and not some other lawyer—can help her make money. And to do that, you're going to have to call her up on the telephone, ask for a meeting to discuss her business, and then show up at the meeting and have the discussion.

I know This Isn't Easy

What I'm proposing is not easy. Many people would die before they would pick up the telephone and call a decision-maker.

But I'm not proposing that you get a list of 500 decision-makers, start calling them during dinner, and ask if they're interested in switching long-distance telephone carriers. I'm not proposing offensive cold-calling.

I'm proposing that you call the people you *already know* who are in a position to hire you or at least introduce you to decision-makers within their business. I'm proposing that you start to capitalize on all that exhausting networking that you're doing with the local Chamber of Commerce. I'm asking that you simply follow up with that in-house lawyer who happened to sit next to you on the airplane and said, "I'd love to hear from you." I'm asking that you follow up with the business people who heard you speak at a recent trade conference and gave you a warm round of applause in appreciation for your remarks.

Of course, I know that even making these "warm calls" is not easy, especially for those who have never done it. But that doesn't change the fact that making the calls is the single biggest predictor of business development success.

Make the calls. Show up. Get business.

Guaranteed.

CHAPTER **9**

Selling Requires Listening

BASIC LISTENING

CONSULTATIVE SELLING: DR. PIERCE, SNAKE OIL SALESMAN

LISTENING BEFORE BUSINESS DEVELOPMENT CALLS

THE BIGGEST MISTAKE: FAILURE TO LISTEN FIRST

A LISTENING SUCCESS STORY

ABOVE ALL, YOU CAN'T LISTEN TOO MUCH

BASIC LISTENING

You can read a thousand sales books to learn how to conduct a business development call. And they will all propose a "method" for conducting a call successfully. Books will describe methods for asking questions. They'll give you various instructions to follow if you want to win the business.

And this book is going to outline a method as well. But more important than any method is the basic idea that all of these methods have in common: *listen for needs and propose solutions*.

"Consultative selling" is basically a three-step process.

STEP 1: Determine where the business is now.

STEP 2: Find out where the prospect wants the business to be and if there are any barriers holding the business back.

Step 3: Suggest ways that you can help the business achieve its goals.

Consultative Selling: Dr. Pierce, Snake Oil Salesman

It might be helpful to take a lesson in consultative selling from Doctor Ray Vaughan Pierce. Because if Dr. Pierce wasn't much of a doctor, he was one heck of a salesman.

Dr. Pierce was a "healer" who practiced "medicine" in the late 1800s and early 1900s in rural America. He traveled around the country selling a product called "Dr. Pierce's Golden Medical Discovery." Like many medical products of the time, this herbal elixir allegedly could cure virtually any common ailment from headaches to diarrhea to a runny nose.

What is particularly interesting is how Dr. Pierce sold this product. He wasn't the usual carnival huckster, selling his snake oil from a suitcase. Rather, Dr. Pierce would travel the country setting up shop in local offices where he would make appointments with patients.

What is especially fascinating is how Dr. Pierce conducted the appointments. That is, he used a classic "consultative" sales approach.

Dr. Pierce might start the appointment with the traditional, "Where does it hurt?"

"I have a toothache," the patient might say.

"Really? I'm sorry to hear that. I know how painful that can be. Tell me, how is that affecting you?"

"Well it hurts like hell. And it's causing me to have a headache all the time. Doc, you really have to help me here."

"I can imagine that's horrible. How is this affecting your sleep?"

"Sleep? Who sleeps? I haven't had a good night's sleep in a couple of weeks. I have to drink myself to sleep. And as a result, I'm exhausted at my job. It's horrible."

And so the conversation would continue with Dr. Pierce dutifully writing down all the information. Then he'd make a show of thinking about the problem and finally he'd look at the patient with his verdict.

"I have something that will help that toothache and will help you get some sleep. It's called 'Dr. Pierce's Golden Medical Discovery.'"

And of course he'd make the sale.

LISTENING BEFORE BUSINESS DEVELOPMENT CALLS

The reader should not interpret this story as encouragement to be a "snake oil salesman." I'm certainly sensitive to the concerns of most lawyers about appearing to be too "sales-y" in their business development meetings.

But look at what a masterful job Dr. Pierce did in selling the client. He knew from the beginning what the cure was going to be. And he also knew that to make the sale, he had to be patient.

Rather than jump right in with the solution, Pierce listened to his client describe the problem. He did what great business developers always do: *he listened first.* He wanted to give his prospect the feeling that he truly understood the problem. And he knew that the only way to accomplish that was to let the prospect talk and tell "where it hurts."

Consider what would have happened if he had pulled out his bottle of the "golden medical discovery" as soon as the patient had said "I have a toothache." The prospect would probably not have been as quick to reach for his wallet. He certainly wouldn't have been as confident that the good doctor understood his medical problem. He would have thought, "How he can be so sure? He hasn't even heard about how bad this is."

Lawyers should take a lesson in business development from Dr. Pierce. He practiced the number one rule of a sales call: listen first and let the prospect describe the issues he faces from his perspective. Let the prospect tell you about his world. And keep listening.

THE BIGGEST MISTAKE: FAILURE TO LISTEN FIRST

Repeatedly I see lawyers who jump into a conversation with a solution to a legal problem far too soon. And this is understandable. We lawyers often know five minutes into the conversation exactly what needs to be done to solve the prospect's legal problem.

For example, I was working with a litigator at a large New York firm and we were role-playing a business development call. Playing the role of the prospect, I knew that this lawyer was a wonderful employment litigator. So a few minutes into the role-play I let slip the following tidbit: "We're having a problem with some of our employees in the area of sexual harassment."

Now the right thing to do in this sales call (what Dr. Pierce would have done) would have been to say something simple such as, "Oh really? Tell me about the problem." And then to listen. This is the right response even though there is virtually nothing that the prospect can tell the lawyer that the lawyer needs to know to determine whether he is qualified to handle the case. Of course he can handle the case. He's a great employment litigator. He's done it all. And he wins virtually all of his cases.

And with that in mind, what did this great lawyer do? He said, "Do you have anyone yet to represent you in this matter?"

Whoa! Be cool, Ringo!

The business isn't going to disappear in the next five minutes. You don't need to pounce just yet.

Rather than attack, sit back and ask a few questions. Listen. Let the prospect know that you're the kind of lawyer who listens to clients and tries to understand business goals. Try to learn more about the case. The additional information will help you understand this prospect better.

Sure, the ultimate solution is going to be "Dr. Pierce's Golden Medical Discovery." But before unleashing your solution, let the patient describe "where it hurts." It makes the patient feel better. And if you want the business, that's a good thing.

Even if what he tells you doesn't change the legal solution, your listening will make him confident that you understand his businesses problems. Your listening will make the prospect believe that you understand how to add value to his business.

A LISTENING SUCCESS STORY

One lawyer who knows the value of listening is Bob Pile, a partner at Sutherland Asbill & Brennan. Before attending law school, Bob sold computer equipment for Digital Equipment Corporation. By selling computers, Bob learned that the way to sell is to listen first.

His success stories are many. But he told of one occasion where he and one of his partners made a special trip out west to a large business client that had given Sutherland much legal work.

They went to the client and said, "You're an important client to us. We want to know how we can help you." Added Pile, "It was a classic sales call. It was the kind of call on which a regional sales director in the computer business would go."

They didn't use PowerPoint. They didn't bring a bunch of firm brochures. "We just talked about their business," Pile said.

After listening carefully, they followed up with a letter to the client detailing several areas where Sutherland could be helpful. The business hired them for a large project.

So, if you want to develop business, just listen to the client. Let it tell you what it needs. Then find a way to comply.

ABOVE ALL, YOU CAN'T LISTEN TOO MUCH

The biggest mistake made by people who are new to sales (and this includes lawyers as well as everyone else in sales) is that they don't listen enough. Most people are so eager to make a sale that they start talking about their solution too soon.

This is not good. You have to listen and let the prospect tell you his story. Let him tell you where it hurts. Let him tell you how it's affecting the business.

You think that you already know all that stuff. But if you want the business, the prospect has to *know* that you know all that stuff. And the only way that the prospect can know that is if he tells you.

So don't jump up and open your mouth as soon as you see something that you can sell.

Be cool, Ringo.

CHAPTER **10**

The Sales Call: Mining The Gap

INTRODUCTION

In the London subway, sometimes the train will stop and the riders will have to carefully step over a gap between the platform and the subway cars in order to leave the cars. If you aren't careful, of course, you could fall down under the platform. Therefore, in order to remind passengers of the gap, a recording of a lovely female British voice is broadcast every time the subway doors open for new passengers. The voice says, "Mind the gap!"

I think of that voice every time I plan a business development meeting. But instead of saying "Mind the gap," I want the British voice to say *"Mine the gap."*

Clearly, that is what you're doing every time you're conducting a business development call. You're mining the gap between what the prospect has in his business and what he wants. That is, you're trying to find ways that your firm can help the prospect achieve his goals.

Finding that gap is the most important job of a lawyer in a business development meeting. You find that gap by what salespeople call the "consultative process." "Consultative selling" is really just a fancy term for listening to the owners in order to understand a business and its needs, and then proposing solutions to meet those needs.

As I suggested in the previous chapters, *"consultative selling"* is basically a three-step process:

STEP 1: Determine where the business is now.

STEP 2: Find out where the prospect wants the business to be and if there are any barriers holding the business back.

STEP 3: Suggest ways that you can help the business achieve its goals.

That's consultative sales in a nutshell. You can read dozens of books on "consultative sales," "spin sales," "partnering," "creative selling," "win-win sales," etc. But the essence of all the books is: (1) listen in order to understand the prospect's aspirations and (2) then suggest how you can help the prospect achieve those goals.

THE MODEL MEETING: AN OVERVIEW

To conduct an effective consultative sales meeting, it's helpful to follow a model. We have therefore provided an overview of an effective four-step model: (1) opening, (2) situation, (3) solution, and (4) the next step.

Opening: Getting the Meeting Started

(1) *Opening the meeting/small talk:* This is the beginning of the meeting where you shake hands and chat about the weather, sports, something you see on the prospect's wall. ("My! What a wonderful collection of model ships you have.")

(2) *Meeting objective:* This is a brief introduction that sets the stage for the meeting. The goal here is simply to let the prospect know that your intention is not to talk about yourself but, rather, to talk about the prospect's business. "What I'd like to do is discuss your business and get a sense of how we might be a resource. Is that okay?"

Situation: A Conversation about the Prospect's Business

(1) *Summary statement/question:* This is the kick-off to the probing section of the meeting. First, throw out a topic of discussion related to the prospect's business. "I know that a lot of manufacturing businesses are dealing with labor shortages. How is your business managing?" Don't start with a question that implies you know nothing about the business such as, "So tell me. What are your goals?"

(2) *Probe with questions:* You should not give the prospect the "third degree." Rather, you should simply show interest in the business and have a discussion about the issues as they pertain to what that business is trying to achieve. Avoid topics that suggest you've identified a legal solution. For example, don't blurt out, "Have you gotten legal counsel yet to deal with the pending anti-trust claim?" This step should comprise the bulk of your meeting.

Solution: Representing Yourself as a Resource

Solutions and suggestions: Here is where you simply identify areas where you as an attorney might be a resource. For example, you might say, "Well, I see two areas where we might be a resource. It sounds like you have some issues with the proper disposal of some chemicals. We might be able to help you with that in a way that would save you money. Also, it sounds like you have some challenges with employees who are making discrimination claims. We can help you there as well."

The Next Step

(1) *Follow-up:* This step gives you a chance for some follow-up. For example, you might propose to give the prospect something for free. Or, if you've uncovered some minor matter that you could research, offer to research it at no charge. Or, if there is an educational program that the prospect may need, offer to come and speak about the topic to the prospect's employees.

(2) *Asking for the business:* In many businesses, it's appropriate at the end of a meeting to ask for an order. In the selling of legal services, such directness is probably not appropriate. Instead, just say something like, "I know that hiring a lawyer is a big decision. But I'd love the opportunity to do a small matter for you in the future."

THE MODEL MEETING: UNDERSTANDING THE CONCEPTS

The key to running a business development meeting well isn't slavishly following a model. Instead, the key is to understand the underlying concepts so that you can achieve your ultimate goal of building the relationship and making the prospect consider you to be a resource for building his or her business. With that in mind, let's discuss steps for running an effective meeting and explaining the concepts behind them.

Setting the Stage for a Prospect-Focused Meeting

At the beginning of a business development meeting, the prospect generally doesn't know what to expect. He doesn't know whether you intend to pull out your firm brochure or launch into a dissertation on tax law. As a result, it's always helpful to take control at the outset and assure the prospect that the meeting will be about him/them/their company and adding value to the business.

You can be creative about accomplishing this goal. However, I recommend beginning with a brief, two-sentence statement that clearly declares what you intend to do during the meeting. Keep it simple. For example:

> "Thanks for meeting with me today. I really just wanted to learn about some of the challenges you see in your business and find out whether or not we might be a resource for you. So if it's okay, I'd like to start by asking you just a few things about your business."

Think about what these statements do. They:

- ▸ Transition easily to business from the "chit-chat" portion of the meeting.
- ▸ Give the prospect the comfort of knowing that you have a plan for the meeting. The prospect thinks, "Thank goodness I don't have to figure out what to do here."
- ▸ Focus on the prospect's favorite subject, the prospect himself.

Conversing with the Prospect about His Business

Starting the Conversation with a Little Red Meat

All that really matters during the second part of the meeting is that you get a conversation going about the prospect's business. Remember that you'd love to find out what challenges the prospect is facing in achieving his goals and how you as a lawyer might help him overcome those challenges.

Unfortunately, you can't really start the conversation by saying, "So, Bob, tell me what challenges you're facing in running this business." You would sound like you know absolutely nothing about Bob's business or the industry. It is important that you start the conversation by giving the prospect a sense that you've done a little homework.

We therefore suggest starting the conversation by throwing out a relevant conversation topic a/k/a "red meat." For example, if you have read on the Internet that the prospect is on a buying spree, acquiring smaller companies to speed growth, you might start with the following:

> "The trade magazines have a lot of information about your acquisition strategy. How many businesses are you trying to buy right now?"

Or you might try something like:

> "I've read about your buying spree, and I assume that integrating all those businesses into your company is a real challenge. Is that true?"

Or you might even try:

> "I see that you're buying a lot of companies. Is that because your competition is doing the same?"

It really doesn't matter exactly what question you ask. The key is to say something semi-intelligent to get the conversation started. Even if your assumptions in the question are wrong, the prospect will realize that at least you're thinking about his business. That thought provides some "red meat" to bait or lure your prospect into a conversation.

Some Conversation Goals

Of course, you don't want to have a random conversation about the prospect's business either. You want to accomplish some goals in the meeting. Important goals include the following:

Identify Barriers to the Prospect's Business Goals

Once you've gotten the prospect speaking generally about his business, you can usually steer the conversation easily to the company's goals, barriers, and strategies. Some good questions include:

- ▶ "What are you trying to accomplish with the acquisitions?"
- ▶ "What types of companies are you trying to buy?"
- ▶ "What is your strategy for growing sales?"
- ▶ "How are you trying to cut costs?"
- ▶ "What is the biggest cost that you face in your business?"
- ▶ "What is the single biggest problem that you face with your employees?"
- ▶ "What is the toughest job you have to fill and why?"
- ▶ "What is the biggest employee management challenge that you face?"

Ultimately, you must use your judgment and your knowledge of business generally to determine how to focus on the prospect's needs. Just listen for the challenges that the prospect faces. Those challenges are your key to providing value. Note also that the best questions call for broad, expansive answers rather than a "yes" or a "no." This is not cross-examination where you are expecting short "yes" or "no" responses. Contrary to much legal training, it's okay to ask questions to which you don't know the answers. Ask open-ended questions that expand your knowledge of the prospect's business.

Identify Legal Needs

When the prospect mentions a practice area where you or your firm can do legal work, be careful not to pounce. Instead, ask a few questions: "So you say that there is a potential sexual harassment claim by some of your women employees? What do you know about it so far?"

In addition, there's nothing wrong with trying to identify who does the legal work for the firm. For example, if the prospect mentions that there are a lot of chemicals involved in the business, ask which law firm handles its environmental legal work. If the prospect mentions that they have many employees, ask who does their labor work. Even if the prospect already uses a firm (and it usually does), chances are that the firm will be conflicted out of the work at some point, or may even fall out of favor. Then you might be sitting pretty.

Identify What You Can Do Now for Free

You read it right. For free. One of the best ways to start to build a relationship with a prospect and learn his business is to suggest small things that you might do for free as a way to build the relationship. Many general counsels have told me that they really appreciate it when lawyers offer free advice or research, even if it's minor.

"How about the law firm proposing to do an audit of our labor and employment practice?" one general counsel told me. "It will give you a chance to demonstrate your expertise and let you learn a little about our business."

Almost every general counsel with whom I spoke welcomed offers of presentations on the latest legal issues.

You could also invent a simple tool to help the prospect comply with a particularly complex set of regulations. For example, the next time a complex set of federal environmental regulations is enacted, why not create a simple spreadsheet that an in-house counsel can use to stay in compliance? You could offer to come to the prospect's firm and spend an hour showing the relevant compliance management how to use the tool to stay in compliance with the regulations.

Or why not simply offer to do a quick bit of analysis of a legal problem for free? "If you'd like, I'd be happy to check a few cases on the problem you're having with the SEC. I'll do it at no charge and send you an e-mail with my findings."

Showing Yourself as a Resource: You Can't Sell 'Em if You Don't Tell 'Em

It's very important that you let the prospect know exactly how you can be a resource, now or in the future.

If you're an environmental lawyer, you need to let the prospect know exactly how you can help his business. For example, you might say:

> "I've heard you mention several challenges you're facing regarding disposal and clean-up of chemicals. We can help you stay in compliance with federal regulations. And to the extent you ever find yourself in a situation where the EPA challenges something you're doing, we can help you."

If you're a tax lawyer you might say:

"I've heard you mention that you're buying several companies. There are probably some things that you can do to ensure that the acquisition keeps your effective tax rate as low as possible. Also, in the future, you might find yourself having to deal with challenges from the IRS. We can help you in those situations."

Or, if you're a labor lawyer:

"I see that you're trying to make sure that your factories are in compliance with the new OSHA regulations. We can do an audit to see how you're doing there. And if you ever find yourself faced with an employee who is not happy with you and is threatening a suit, we can help you."

Closing/Next Steps/Asking for the Order

At the end of the meeting you should do two things: (1) ask for the business and (2) suggest a follow-up plan. In the sales world, this is known as "closing."

In fact, many lawyers ask me for "closing techniques." "I need to know how to close the deal," one managing partner told me.

It's a funny question to hear from lawyers because closing techniques are overrated and don't even work in industries where participants are more accustomed to sharp sales tactics.

I met a real estate salesman who said that he used the following closing technique: When he was finished discussing a sale with a prospect, he would produce from his briefcase a contract with the prospect's name typed below the signature line. He then would place the contract in front of the prospect and roll a pen across the table.

"The beauty of this technique," this salesman explained to me with apparent seriousness, "is that the prospect has to grab the pen to keep it from rolling into his lap. Once the pen is in his hand, he's likely to sign."

When this salesman told me about his technique, I found it hard to keep from laughing. I doubt such a sales technique, if it ever worked, works today. Certainly, slick closing techniques are useless in the legal services context.

The fact is that there are no magic words to "close a sale." Buyers of legal services are too sophisticated. And you can't force a prospect to buy from you. What you *can* do is make sure that the prospect understands how you can add value to his business.

With that in mind, the best "close" is simply to let the prospect know that you'd like to be considered a resource in the future. The following language works:

> "I know we've talked about a lot of issues. I hope that you can see that I'm available to help you in several areas including _____ and _____. Hiring a lawyer is a big decision. But I hope that you'll consider me and my firm. We'd love the chance to do your work."

This statement is about as close to "asking for the order" as you should come. But you definitely should ask. Letting the prospect know that you want the business is important. People are flattered to know that a lawyer considers their business valuable.

Suggesting a Next Step

Your next move should be to make sure you stay engaged with the prospect in some way. Therefore, suggesting a plausible next step is important. The logical next step depends on the prospect and what he has told you during the meeting. Three particular next steps are most logical:

(1) *The next step toward representation:* In the extremely rare case where it looks like the prospect really needs you for some legal work, then you must suggest the next step toward formalizing the representation. That next step may be simply sending over an engagement letter. But it may also be an interim step such as a meeting with another member of the management team or with an in-house lawyer.

(2) *The next step toward free service:* Usually the prospect won't ask you to represent him during the initial meeting. In that case, a great next step is simply to offer a free service. You can offer to return to do a seminar. You can offer to "look into" a

legal issue that the prospect has wondered about during the meeting. You can offer to do an audit of one of the business's activities and detail potential legal exposure.

(3) *Follow-up:* At the very least, ask the prospect for permission to stay in touch and keep him abreast of key legal issues. When the prospect says "yes," you'll have permission to call him with future ideas. So when a labor relations seminar comes up, you can call him and invite him to join you. Or when you have an idea to save taxes for his business, you can call him up and offer to come out to his office and show him the idea.

WHEN THE DECISION-MAKER IGNORES THE COMPANY'S BIG PICTURE

When your clients are very large businesses, you'll be calling on people who aren't necessarily focused on the big picture of the entire enterprise. The in-house counsel who oversees real estate deals for a large retailer doesn't necessarily want to have a discussion with you about the key factors that affect growth. And the associate general counsel for insurance for a drug manufacturer isn't necessarily interested in the pipeline for new drugs.

But that doesn't mean you don't focus on the big issues that are facing that particular decision-maker. For example, if you're speaking with an in-house counsel in charge of real estate, you can focus on his likely issues. Chances are they're something like the following:

- ▶ What are his current goals for managing his department?
- ▶ What are the challenges he faces in managing the real estate acquisition process?
- ▶ How does he measure success regarding a particular acquisition?
- ▶ What is the biggest barrier to success in closing deals?

It doesn't matter who you're speaking to. You still need to learn that person's goals and determine the barriers to those goals. You'll succeed in making sales when you help your prospect begin to get past those barriers.

GETTING BUSINESS EVEN WHEN YOU CHARGE HIGH FEES

Often a company will refuse to hire a great firm because of high fees. And if you're one of those firms, that can be frustrating, especially if you insist that you won't cut your fees no matter what.

But don't give up. The reason for your high fees is (or should be) that you're a desirable lawyer when the company is in trouble. In that case, make sure you're clearly positioned in the prospect's mind as a "bet the company" lawyer.

I know a corporate lawyer for a large firm that has a reputation for charging extremely high fees. The general counsel told him that he would love to hire him, but that he was too expensive. The corporate lawyer understood but said, "Call me when you're in big trouble and we can help."

Then this lawyer stayed in touch, calling every six months and leaving the general counsel a voice mail saying, "Hi. This is _____. Just wanted to check in and find out when you're going to be ready to hire a real lawyer."

That may sound too aggressive. But it can be said with finesse. And this lawyer said it with a smile in his voice so that the general counsel took it in a positive way. Indeed, about a year later, the general counsel found himself with a serious problem and placed a call to the expensive lawyer. "I need you. Can you come over here next week?"

This expensive lawyer won the business because he positioned himself in the general counsel's mind as the "bet the company" lawyer. When the stakes became very large, the lawyer got the call.

Indeed, many general counsels will consider you to be the lawyer to consult in a specific situation and not call you until that situation occurs.

THE BEST SALESPEOPLE ARE PROBLEM-SOLVERS

Lawyers tend not to be very good salespeople. But you wouldn't know it to read the brochures of some of the top law firms. Indeed, those brochures contain some wonderful sales advice and the lawyers would do well to follow that advice.

One major firm has a brochure that quotes a long-deceased partner as follows:

"Whenever combined effort is required, there must be some form of teamwork. There are two kinds. One kind is based upon the easy realization that teamwork is mutually advantageous. *The other kind is where one helps another for the joy of helping and the zest of adding to the success of the organization."*

I don't think I've ever read better advice for conducting a sales call. The best salespeople go to a meeting and put aside their own sales needs. Instead, they focus solely on the needs of the prospect and "the joy of helping and the zest of adding to the success of the organization." If the prospect finds a way of "adding to the success of the organization" that also happens to include legal work, so much the better.

But for the best salespeople, the prospect's needs come first, whatever those needs happen to be.

For example, I know one good business developer who called on a prospect and was unable to identify any serious legal needs. However, the prospect mentioned how he was completely flummoxed by squirrels in his basement.

Was this business developer discouraged? Not at all. Instead, the developer put his prospect in touch with a good exterminator. Several months later, the developer received a call from the prospect offering some billable work. The prospect saw him as a problem-solver.

That's what business development is all about.

This Ain't About You; It's About the Prospect

There's a joke that could be told about the mistake that most novice business developers make during business calls. The joke concerns a self-centered person at a cocktail party.

"Enough about me," he says. "Let's talk about you! Tell me, what do you think of me?"

If there's nothing else that you remember from this chapter, remember that when you're trying to develop business, *don't focus on yourself.* Focus on your prospect's needs. Then offer ideas on how you can help meet that prospect's needs.

The biggest mistake that lawyers (and all salespeople, for that matter) make is thinking that they are the most important people in the room. For example, a lawyer I know described a meeting with an in-house lawyer at a large company. She thought the meeting had gone very well.

I knew the in-house lawyer and asked him how the meeting went. "She talked too much about herself," he told me. "She didn't seem very curious about our business."

When I first began selling, I called on a friend who was a very good software salesman and asked him to a baseball game. I had this rather naïve view that he could teach me to sell over a beer and a hot dog. And so we took our seats and chatted a while before getting down to business.

"So tell me, Dan," I said, "how do you sell?"

"Just shut up and listen," he said. "Most salesmen talk too much. Listen to your customer. They'll tell you how to sell them."

I've read dozens of sales books and still haven't come across better advice. The best business developers understand that you just have to listen carefully to your client and he will tell you how to sell him.

CHAPTER **11**

Winning
Beauty Contests

WHAT DO PROSPECTS WANT TO HEAR?

CLIENT FOCUS IN ACTION

HOW TO ORGANIZE A BEAUTY CONTEST PRESENTATION

A COMMENT ON STYLE: WHY IS IT CALLED A "BEAUTY CONTEST"?

SOME FINAL THOUGHTS ON BEAUTY CONTESTS

WHAT DO PROSPECTS WANT TO HEAR?

Imagine that you're sitting in a waiting room, preparing to pitch for business with a Fortune 500 company. You're part of the fourth team of lawyers to make a pitch. Your team will be making the last presentation of the day, and when you and your partners walk into the conference room, you see that the three in-house lawyers who will make the decision are tired.

There are empty soda cans and coffee cups everywhere. The decision-makers are desperately consulting their BlackBerrys in an effort to catch up on all the work they've missed that day. They turn to you and say, "Okay. We've got about forty-five minutes. Let's hear what you've got."

So what do you do?

If you're like a lot of firms, you all smile, thank the "judges" for inviting you, and begin by launching into a PowerPoint presentation which often begins something like this.

"Let me start by giving you a little history of the law firm of Miller and Winston. We actually are the longest continually active law firm in Indiana, with our founding partner, Jeremiah Winston, having come over to America on the Mayflower. Of course you know that Jeremiah's son Jimmy served as Postmaster General under President John Adams [or some such nonsense]."

And here is what the in-house counsel hears:

"Blah blah blah blah blah blah blah blah blah blah blah blah blah blah blah blah blah blah blah blah blah blah blah blah blah blah blah blah blah blah blah blah blah blah."

That is, nothing you've said moves the client closer to solving its problems. Nothing you've said moves the client closer to winning the lawsuit. Nothing you've said gets the firm closer to negotiating the agreement. Nothing you've said helps this company. Period.

So let's just get this out of the way right now because so many law firms love to flash their credentials in beauty contests.

No one cares that you work for a prestigious law firm. All the firms invited to present at beauty contests are prestigious.

And no one cares that one of your partners was a U.S. Senator, or Governor, or former Postmaster General. Unless the former U.S. Attorney General is going to be handling the case personally, it's meaningless. Moreover, the former Ambassador to Taipei was a partner in the last law firm that made a presentation.

Finally, no one cares that your managing partner once clerked for Justice Sandra Day O'Connor. Unless Justice O'Connor could decide this case, it's irrelevant and a waste of oxygen to bring it up.

Maybe that information will impress your summer clerks. But as I speak with in-house counsel, I hear the same thing over and over: they're not impressed. So leave it out.

What *do* they want to hear?

▶ *They want to hear your plan for helping them.* They want to hear your strategy for managing the labor agreement negotiation. They want to hear how you're going to help lower their effective tax rate. They want to hear how you're going to keep the class action case from going to trial.

▶ *They do want to hear about your qualifications, but only as they relate to the issue at hand.* The fact that you won a $100 million judgment in a highly publicized antitrust action is of no interest if you're trying to win employment discrimination work. However, if you've worked on similar litigation in the past (especially the recent past), bring that up.

▶ *They want to know that you understand how the matter at hand fits into their business's big picture.* Sure, they want to win the lawsuit. But they'd also love to hear how you're going to help prevent similar lawsuits in the future.

▶ *They want to know that you have a strong sense of how much the matter will cost.* If you say that the litigation will cost $300,000, they'd like to know that you're not just pulling this number out of thin air. They want to be convinced that they're not going to have to pay more than that.

▶ *And finally, they want to hear what you have to say in a way that makes them like you.* That's right. There is a totally superficial aspect to the beauty contest. They're going to have to spend a lot of time with you. They want to like you.

In other words, the lawyers who win beauty contests are the ones who do a very good job of helping the client know as much as possible about what it's going to be like having them as their lawyer.

The ones who lose beauty contests talk about their firm's history.

CLIENT FOCUS IN ACTION

An example of how client focus can win a beauty contest comes from the Vice President for Employment and Labor Law at a Fortune 500 company whom I interviewed recently. This in-house lawyer, whom I'll call Janet, described how she held a beauty contest to find a firm to handle a major piece of litigation.

She invited four firms, including one that was clearly her favorite, a firm that had done good work for her and her company. She also invited one firm solely because of a recommendation from a colleague, although she didn't know the firm very well.

This outsider firm came extremely well-prepared. "They were very thorough from the standpoint of analyzing the case we were interested in," she said. She also said they not only had a plan for handling the case effectively, they had thought through the business implications of the case and proposed a plan for conducting training to ensure that this type of case would not arise again in the future.

As for their experience, they focused on what was relevant experience, not a routine history of the firm. "Lawyers often give a nauseating discussion of how great their firm is," she said. "It's not helpful at all. They're so full of themselves that you don't want to work with them. If you're personally offensive, who will work with you?"

Instead, this outsider firm came in and really won her over. "They exhibited an expertise, experience level, and demeanor that I knew would work well with our company," she said. "I liked them."

However, the firm that Janet knew well and which had done good work for the company in the past was also a contender. From her experience with the familiar firm, she knew that this firm could have done the work and done it well. But the familiar firm took the beauty contest interview for granted. "They put no time and effort into it," she said. "They were complacent. They took it for granted that they would be the winner."

The result was that she chose the outsider firm. That firm showed it had a clear vision for helping the company win the case and safeguard the business against such litigation in the future.

Note that a third firm in the competition did a nice job of laying out a strategy for winning the case. Unfortunately, however, Janet wasn't convinced that the firm could staff the case properly.

In other words, the key to winning these beauty contests isn't demonstrating that you work for a great firm with a great history. Poor firms don't get invited to beauty contests. The key to winning is focusing like a laser on the challenges and concerns being faced by the company that is running the beauty contest.

How to Organize a Beauty Contest Presentation

As lawyers have learned, determining the right approach to resolving a legal problem is usually a highly interactive effort. Lawyers often sit with colleagues or their client and discuss the impact of various resolutions to a problem. The format for a beauty contest should roughly reflect that strategy.

When pitching for business, we therefore recommend an interactive presentation. "The best approach stresses interactivity," one General Counsel told me.

In fact, if you're doing this right, the presentation won't even be recognized as such. Instead, your statements will resemble a choreographed chat about the challenges facing the client's company.

The section of this book dealing with presentations introduces a simple Formula for organizing a presentation.[1]

The Formula emphasizes keeping the message focused on the listener's needs and limiting the message to three or four points at most. The same method should be used in organizing your beauty contest presentation. The primary difference is that you should build discussion into each point.

Following is a simple organizational method to consider when preparing for the beauty contest.

Opening Meet and Greet

Start with introductions, making sure that each person from your firm is introduced with an explanation as to why he or she is there. "John will be the partner overseeing the project. If we go to trial, John will first chair the case. Cindy will be the lawyer involved in the case on a day-to-day basis." If you don't have a role to play in the legal matter or are not the relationship partner, don't attend the beauty contest presentation. Don't ever include your prestigious litigator as a "showpiece." That is phony and doesn't help build the relationship.

---

[1] See Chapter 15 *infra*.

Message Objective

After the introductions, give a single sentence overview of why the prospect firm should hire you. It should be simple, "big picture," and listener-focused. Examples are:

> ▸ "We've thought through this case and think that we can get you a great result while at the same time put in place a plan to prevent this litigation from happening again in the future."
>
> ▸ "We know that you're trying to take this company into the forefront of the transportation business by focusing on your technology. We think we're well-positioned to help you get there."
>
> ▸ "We know that you're focused on getting these real estate transactions closed within a given budget while at the same time dealing with some challenging land-use issues. We think that we've come up with some innovative solutions that will make you happy."

Preview Statement

Next, and before you begin detailing your ideas for their project, you should quickly preview the main areas where you want to focus the discussion. This ensures that the discussion doesn't "bounce all over the place." It is helpful to focus on the three most important issues that the project faces. For example:

(1) *We want to focus on three areas today:*

> ▸ Our strategy for handling this litigation.
> ▸ How we will ensure that the company can minimize the risk of the litigation actually proceeding.
> ▸ Our budget estimate and how we're going to staff the project.

(2) *We want to focus on three areas today:*

> ▸ How we're going to maximize the value of your patent portfolio.
> ▸ Our process for allowing you to catalog all of your intellectual property.

> ▸ How we're going to meet your budget.

(3) *We want to focus on three areas today:*

> ▸ How we're going to approach this upcoming labor contract.
> ▸ How we're going to help you position yourself for a strong on-going relationship with the union.
> ▸ How we're going to meet your budget.

At this point in the "beauty contest" presentation, don't discuss your three points in detail. Simply give the listeners a quick overview as a sense of where the discussion is headed.

Next Steps: Discuss Your Three Points

Analyze the Issues and Form an Opinion

Next, discuss each of your three points. If you're being interviewed for a class action lawsuit and your first point is, "How we're going to handle the case," then you need to articulate your vision for the case. The more well-thought-out your approach, the better chance you have to win.

One client told me that she hesitated to give a detailed analysis because "that would be giving free legal advice."

So what!

What else are you doing with the time? The best way to get hired is to show that you can articulate a clear, thoughtful, comprehensive approach. There's no better way to show that than to detail your plan. If that means giving some free legal advice, so be it. Most lawyers give out free legal advice all the time. At least in these circumstances, you've got a chance to win some business in exchange for the free advice.

In fact, taking some time to really analyze the client's challenge and then presenting your analysis is the best way to win the business. And your failure to do any analysis at all will probably cause you to lose the business.

I know a lawyer who had spent about a year trying to win some labor work. The company had hired a consultant to bring in some lawyers to interview for a large employment litigation case. The consultant provided the lawyer with a "memorandum" detailing some of the issues.

The lawyer "briefly read" the memorandum, but put no real thought into how she would approach the case. Rather, she read the memo merely with an eye toward seeing whether she was qualified to do the work, which she clearly was. When the prospect started asking her how she would approach the case, she had very little to say, and as a result, she didn't get the work.

If you want to win, put in the time to form some opinions about the client's challenges.

Detail Relevant Expertise

At this point you tell the client about relevant expertise. As you discuss your approach to the client's challenges, tell about how you've solved similar problems with other clients.

"This lawsuit is almost the same as the one that we just finished last month; in that case, we did the following and found it worked extremely well. . . ."

"This labor negotiation is very similar to the one we just completed last month. In that case, we were negotiating against the same union and they raised the exact same challenges that they're raising now. . . ."

Ask the Client for Input

As you begin detailing your approach and discussing your expertise, prod the client to react to your ideas and give you feedback. The goal is to get a discussion going about the issues that the client is facing. The quicker you get the discussion under way and the more robust that discussion, the better chance you have of winning over the client.

However, if the presentation consists only of you and your partners talking to a non-responsive prospect, you're in trouble.

How do you get the client to start talking? Ask some questions. If you've done some analysis of the case, you almost certainly will have some factual questions. How many plaintiffs do we expect as part of this class action? Approximately how many patents do you currently have in your portfolio? What is the latest date that the company would like to close on this acquisition?

You'll also likely have some business or policy questions about the issues involved in the case. What is the business strategy behind the acquisition? What do you think is the root cause of the litigation? What is your company's intellectual property strategy?

In other words, ask the client anything that you'd want to know if they already were your client.

And, of course, once you've begun asking questions, listen carefully to what the client says and incorporate that feedback into your analysis.

As indicated previously, the goal is to give the prospect a glimpse of what it would be like having you as its lawyer.

Keeping the Discussion on Track

The biggest risk of having a "choreographed chat" rather than a rigid PowerPoint-driven, formal presentation is losing control. Opening up the presentation for discussion can lead to numerous questions, which almost certainly will lead you and the prospect down some irrelevant blind alleys.

But that risk isn't reason enough to avoid opening up the floor for any discussion. Rather, you must control the risk with strategies that will keep the discussion on track.

The first strategy is one that we've already discussed: initially previewing the points you plan to discuss. By telling the prospect what you plan to cover during the presentation, you give the conversation some implicit "boundaries." Of course, it is unlikely that everyone will observe the boundaries. But at least everyone will be aware when they've left the "field of play" to focus on an issue that wasn't mentioned at the beginning of the presentation.

The other major strategy is simply to "muscle" the conversation back on track. There's nothing wrong with saying, "Would you like to discuss budget now?" Or, "We've also thought through some ideas for limiting the risk that this litigation will recur. Would you like to hear our ideas on that issue?"

It's generally a good idea to ask the prospect for permission to steer the conversation. If the prospect allows you to move on, you can be comfortable that he probably doesn't have other questions about the current topic.

Closing the Deal

People often ask me about how to "close" the presentation in a "beauty contest." As I've noted before, the sales notion of "closing" is overrated. There are no magic words to make a customer select you. If you're going to be hired, the prospect will make that decision in its own time. Pressuring the customer will probably hurt your chances.

But you can certainly end your beauty contest with strength. Following are two practical suggestions:

(1) *Ask the hiring prospects if they have any other questions for you.* Often the customer will be reluctant to ask something that you need to know. For example, if the client has questions about how you plan to staff the project, you certainly want it to ask those questions. Asking for final questions is one way to coax any final questions from the client.

(2) *Tell the clients you want the business.* "I know that you're looking at some great firms. But it is important that you know we want to do this work for you, and therefore, if you pick us, we'll do a great job for you." That is a strong message to leave with the client. It says that you are eager to get started and that you're not afraid to say so. It also suggests that you're a strong advocate. If you don't advocate strongly for yourself, the thinking goes, you likely won't be a strong advocate for the client.

A Comment on Style: Why Is It Called a "Beauty Contest"?

One of the primary reasons any company holds a beauty contest is to see whether the firm simply likes the people involved. You probably won't get invited to participate if your firm isn't highly qualified to do the work. With that in mind, how you appear stylistically matters a lot.

One element that is particularly important in beauty contests is *enthusiasm*. It's very important that you convey to the prospect that you love doing the kind of work that it needs. You want to be perceived as extremely eager to get started and just brimming with ideas for achieving a great result for the client.

Although everyone's style is different, you should smile, make eye contact, and speak with passion. If you seem uninterested in the prospect, that prospect will likely also be uninterested in you.

SOME FINAL THOUGHTS ON BEAUTY CONTESTS

Imagine that you enter a store to buy a very expensive diamond. But when you go in, the jeweler says, "I have the diamond in the box, but I'm not going to show it to you. Rather, I'm going to tell you all about myself and my background and why you should trust me and buy from me."

Chances are that you won't buy the diamond. You want to see the darn thing!

Buying legal services is a lot like buying a diamond sight unseen. The lawyers look nice. The résumés seem impressive. The offices are fancy. But what will the customer actually receive for his money? It's very hard to tell.

That idea should be foremost in your preparation for the beauty contest. You want to do everything you can in the short time that you're given for your presentation to let the client see what sort of legal work you can provide on this particular case. Moreover, you want to give the firm the benefit of any analysis that you've done. You also want to persuade the firm that working with you over the next months or years is going to be a pleasant experience.

You want to do everything you can to let the client get a glimpse of the "diamond in the box."

CHAPTER **12**

Cross-Selling

INTRODUCTION

Everyone agrees that selling new products to existing customers—a/k/a "cross-selling"—is the easiest way to grow revenue. Virtually every business does it.

"You want fries with that?" may be the most successful cross-selling tactic of all time. Have you ever booked an airline ticket through a travel agent and not had him ask you if you also wanted to book a rental car? That's cross-selling.

Whatever the business, any time a customer trusts you enough to buy one thing, he's more likely to trust you enough to buy something else.

And in a business like law, where trust is paramount, cross-selling is certainly the easiest way to grow a practice in a law firm, especially in a large corporate firm with diversified legal expertise.

So why are so few firms good at it? It's because the key to "cross-selling" is the word "selling." And most lawyers don't understand that if you want to cross-sell, first you have to know how to sell. And the keys to selling are identifying decision-makers, understanding needs, and seeking ways to add value.

WHY JOHNNY CAN'T CROSS-SELL

I did a workshop recently with a very prestigious law firm. Ten highly regarded lawyers attended the program. I began by asking the following question: "How much cross-selling goes on here?" Everyone agreed that virtually no one in their law firm cross-sells.

Want to know why cross-selling doesn't work most of the time? Consider the following true story.

A couple of years ago, an international corporate law firm had completed an acquisition of a smaller litigation boutique. After a few months one of the newly acquired female litigation partners was called into a conference room.

"There were three of my new partners in there and they asked me to sit down," she said. "I had no idea why I had been called in."

"We want to know who your clients are," one of the new partners asked. "We want to learn which ones you think we could do corporate work for." From there, the interrogation intensified as the questioning partners took notes on legal pads, probing for opportunities.

The new partner was understandably flustered and did her best to describe her relatively small book of business. After about an hour of being questioned by her new partners, she was sent away. The discussion ended there. She never again heard from her partners about how they might contribute to growing her clients.

"I don't think a single piece of business developed as a result of what happened," this partner told me. "I have to say I had no idea what type of work these partners did. I have to admit that I still don't."

What's wrong with this scene? I hope it's obvious. No one involved concerned himself with the most important fundamentals of sales: (1) identifying decision-makers, (2) understanding client needs, and (3) seeking solutions.

Also, the partners who grilled the new litigation partner failed to realize that cross-selling is actually a two-step sale. First you have to sell your partner, gaining her confidence to entrust you with information about her valued client. Then together you must approach the client.

EXCUSES FOR FAILURE TO CROSS-SELL

Certainly cultural issues within a law firm play a role in whether partners in a firm cross-sell effectively. But I think that the cultural issues are overrated. Indeed, when cross-selling fails to happen, there are a thousand excuses. Most of them are lame. Here are a few of my favorites:

"The corporate lawyers don't trust us litigators because bad stuff happens in litigation." Nonsense. If the corporate lawyers don't give the litigation to their own partners, the litigation business will go across the street, putting all the business at risk to another shop. That excuse just doesn't make sense.

"My partners don't know what I do." Lack of understanding of the partners' expertise certainly is one reason why cross-selling doesn't happen. But whose fault is that? You can't blame your partners for not selling something they don't know is in their inventory. The burden is on you to promote yourself within the firm.

"We just don't know our partners very well." This is also true. But people who know how to cross-sell find a way to build relationships with people who can help their practice.

"Partners don't want to allow their clients to become institutionalized because it makes their books of business less 'portable.'" I've heard this accusation quite a bit. And it makes

some sense to conspiracy theorists. And maybe it's true for a handful of lawyers. But this exception assumes that lawyers who represent substantial clients are always looking to leave their firms. I don't believe that. And I also have a hard time believing that good lawyers (and most lawyers in corporate firms are very good lawyers) would not want other good lawyers helping their clients. Better service just solidifies the client with the firm. And referring work outside the firm puts the client at risk to the outside firm.

"Our compensation system discourages cross-selling." People certainly act consistently with incentives. Sales have always worked that way. And the best law firms are reexamining their compensation systems to encourage cross-selling. But change happens slowly in law firms, and if you're going to wait for the compensation system to change, you may be waiting a long time.

"My partner is an asshole." This is actually a very good excuse for failure to cross-sell. Often relationship partners will fail to cross-sell simply because they are micromanagers who can't bear letting anyone else touch the client.

There is no doubt that cultural issues play a major role in cross-selling. But in my experience, cross-selling fails in most firms because lawyers simply don't understand the business development process. Too often lawyers rely on their partners to find business for them. That just isn't going to happen very often.

To paraphrase Shakespeare, "The fault, dear barrister, lies not in our partners, but in ourselves."

CROSS-SELLING REVEALED

The lawyers who succeed at cross-selling follow the same basic sales process that we've discussed throughout the book. First you identify a prospect and a decision-maker. Then you seek ways to show the decision-maker how you can add value to his business. You usually have to make a telephone call to set up a meeting. And you have to conduct a meeting where you probe for needs.

The great thing about cross-selling is that you already have a lawyer from your firm who has a relationship with the prospect. That means that the meeting should be easier to get and it should be easier to identify needs. But the process is the same.

THE TWO FACES OF CROSS-SELLING: A TEAM APPROACH

Cross-selling is team selling. There are usually two members of this team:

(1) *The value-adding partner.* This is the partner who "wants in" on one of his partners' clients. This value-adding partner has expertise that the firm client is currently not using or is getting elsewhere.

(2) *The relationship partner.* This is the partner who already has the client and would like to grow it by bringing in other lawyers.

Acting together, these partners can cross-sell effectively. Acting alone, they will have a lot of trouble making headway.

Cross-Selling for "Value-Adding" Partners

The key to cross-selling as a value-adding partner is realizing that you actually have two sales to make before you get to do any billing. First, you have to sell the relationship partner on the value of introducing you to his or her client. Second, once you get the introduction, you then have to make the sale to the client.

Selling the Relationship Partner on Making the Introduction

To sell your partner on introducing you to his client, it helps to step into her shoes for a moment. Most partners only have a few clients. Those clients are very important for their livelihood. So imagine a relationship partner's internal dialogue as she thinks about her precious client. It goes something like this:

> *"I love my client. I love my client. I don't want to do anything to jeopardize my relationship with my client. These clients are hard to get. I'm putting my kids through college on this client. Maybe I could bring in others to work on this account. But only*

if I can be absolutely sure that it makes my client love me more. Oh, I love my client. I love my client."

So how do you get an introduction to this precious client? You have to gain the partner's trust. And you have to make sure that she sees the value that you can provide. In order to do that you must meet with the partner, and start to learn about her client. Together you need to discuss how you can add value to the client. Because trust is involved, it may take several meetings.

Scott Petty, an intellectual property partner at King & Spalding, has mastered the notion that cross-selling is really a two-part sale. "I view the lawyers in our firm as my clients," said Petty. "I service *them.* I can grow a nice-sized practice just doing that."

Of course, he doesn't just *think* of his partners as clients. He *treats* them that way too. He creates a business plan at the beginning of each year that targets which dozen or so "prospects" he wants to "pursue." That prospect list is taken from his firm's client list. "I target certain partners who have certain client relationships and who represent attractive opportunities for an intellectual property practice."

But his plan doesn't stop with the targeting. When Scott says he treats his partners like prospects, he doesn't go in and grill them on how they can give him business. He speaks with them with the intention of figuring out how to add value to his partners' practices by adding value to his partners' clients.

Just as some lawyers might call on a general counsel or business owner, Petty makes business development calls on his partners. "We talk about how I can plug into my partner's practice." That means sitting down and discussing the client and the ways his services might add value.

Once the partner understands the value that Scott can add to a client, he and Petty go the client to discuss how King & Spalding can add further value with Petty's services. "My partners open the door, but I have to close the sale."

In other words, once the first sale is made to his partner, Petty recognizes that he still has another sale to make. He has to sell the business manager or in-house counsel on hiring him to deal with the company's intellectual property issues.

Targeting Specific Opportunities Among the Firm's Clients

Following is a three-step approach to getting opportunities as a cross-selling partner:

STEP 1: Obtain your firm's client list and select ten clients for which you suspect you can add value.

STEP 2: Contact each relationship partner and make an appointment to sit down and discuss his or her client. During the meeting, don't focus so much on specific legal needs about which the relationship partner already knows. Instead, try to understand the big issues and challenges that the client is facing. Then think about how you might add value to that client. Together, you and the other partner can devise the best approach to the client. And usually the best approach is a joint meeting with a client decision-maker.

STEP 3: Meet with the decision-maker at the client's place of business. Remember the lessons of Chapter 10. The goal of a business development meeting is to understand the prospect's needs and challenges. Then you can show how you can add value.

Informing Your Partners About What You Do

Depending on the size of your firm, you might not be able to meet with all of your partners individually to discuss their clients. But you can do your best to sensitize the relationship partners to the ways that you can add value.

With this in mind, you need to systematically make sure that your partners know what you do. That doesn't mean giving in-house CLE lectures on environmental law. Instead, you need to discuss how you add value to your clients and where your partners might spot environmental issues being faced by their clients.

Scott Petty doesn't just go to specific partners to find specific opportunities. He also makes sure that all of his partners know what value he can add to a client. With that in mind, he regularly makes trips to all of his firm's offices, speaking to his partners and generally spreading the word about how his practice can add value to their clients' businesses. "I want to make sure that when they run across something that I can do, they'll know who to call," he says.

The Relationship Partner: Creating Deep Client Infiltration

As a relationship partner for a client, you probably will do some of the legal work for that client. But if you want to grow the client, the legal work is not your primary job regarding that client. Your primary job is to create a state of "deep client infiltration."

What is "deep client infiltration"?

The concept applies where your firm's lawyers have multiple relationships with the client at all levels. When I was practicing law, my firm certainly achieved deep client infiltration with Georgia Power Company, the state's largest electric utility. Although there was a single partner in charge of the entire relationship, dozens of lawyers throughout our firm had close business relationships with big and small players throughout the Company.

But this deep client infiltration didn't happen overnight. It took years of nurturing, carefully listening to the client, and trying to understand its needs at all levels throughout the organization.

So if you're going to achieve deep client infiltration with your big clients, you're going to have to do the same.

In general, it takes three steps to achieve this goal:

(1)   The relationship partner must accept the fact that he or she won't do all the work for the client. For some relationship partners, this is the biggest barrier to growing a client. Unless you're willing to do some client management rather than just the work that leads to billing, you're never going to be able to grow the client.

(2)   You must identify exactly where you want to go within the client's divisions. If you don't know where you're going, you'll never get there.

(3)   You must also address the client's needs as a team. You can do this either formally or informally. As we'll discuss below, the ultimate goal is to create a "client think tank."

Letting Go

An attorney and I were discussing the clients within his firm for which he could cross-sell his services. We honed in on one client and the lawyer said that this client would be perfect for his services.

"But there's a problem," the lawyer told me. "The relationship partner is a jerk. He micromanages every matter."

And that's a shame, because this client will never produce revenue for the firm like it could or probably should. The relationship partner in this case simply can't take the first major step to really growing a client: *letting go*. The first step in growing a client is acknowledging the fact that you're going to have to bring others into the fold and trust them.

For example, if you're a tax lawyer, you're going to have to accept the fact that in order to get the labor work, you're going to have to get your labor group involved.

Indeed, some of the best relationship partners do only a small percentage of the legal work for key clients. A wonderful example was Jim Stokes, former attorney for Alston & Bird, who recently left his environmental practice to become president of the Georgia Conservancy. Stokes was, until recently, the relationship partner who oversaw his firm's representation of UPS in many areas. But Stokes, an environmental lawyer, actually did only a relatively small portion of the environmental legal work himself. What was important was that he did a great job of identifying client needs and marshalling the firm's resources.

Deciding Where You Want to Go

The Cheshire Cat should have been a business developer. In the book *Alice in Wonderland,* Alice comes to a fork in the road and asks the Cheshire Cat which direction to take. The cat asks, "Where do you want to go?" only to be told that Alice didn't know. "Then it doesn't matter," says the cat.

Indeed, the first question you need to ask yourself as a relationship partner for a client is, "Where do you want to go?" Your answer can be found by looking at your client's business.

What other legal needs does the client have? You should catalog all the areas where the client uses outside counsel. Does the client need securities lawyers? Tax lawyers? Intellectual property lawyers? And so on.

Note that I didn't ask whether the client is already using other firms for other specialties. Of course they're using other firms. But that doesn't mean that they love those firms or are committed to them forever. You certainly could get a shot at the work, especially in the case of a potential conflict of interest.

Further, in-house counsel often love giving more of the work to a single firm. And in-house counsel is also very aware of the fact that they can often get good value from a firm that knows many aspects of their business. I know one lawyer who persuaded a client to send most of the legal work to a single firm because having too many law firms handle his firm's business meant that certain issues would inevitably fall through the cracks.

"A team approach can add a lot of value to the client and the law firm," says attorney Bruce Richards, former General Counsel to Certegy and Equifax, "particularly on large projects—for example, a spinoff that involves a number of legal disciplines. And consolidating work with one firm creates pricing leverage, something companies want. But most GCs would rather build the team from multiple firms than sacrifice top quality."

What Do You Do With the Plan?

Once you have the plan, you need to act on it as if you were calling on the client anew. You need to ask your client for the chance to discuss the value you can provide his business.

This is the same process that we discussed in Chapters 10 and 11. If you want to do the client's labor work, you must call the client and ask for the chance to discuss its needs. If you want to do the client's M&A work, you must ask the client for a chance to discuss the company's needs in that area. You need to call for an appointment to discuss how you can add value. Then you must show up for the appointment and try to understand the client's needs.

Why should you do this, even if the client knows that you already handle its labor work? Because the client doesn't spend time thinking about how *it* can help *you*.

Bruce Richards, former General Counsel to Certegy, points out that if you want business from another area, you need to invest time in getting to know a client's needs in that area.

And there are many ways to do that. "How about the law firm proposing to me that they come in and do an audit of our labor and employment practices for free?" Richards suggested. "It gives you a chance to demonstrate expertise, generate value, learn more, and build relationships."

I know a prominent labor lawyer who was being interviewed as the head of the labor and employment practice group for a large Washington, D.C. firm. In the interview he was asked to "describe [your] business plan" for the group. Even though he had thought long and hard about his plan, ultimately his response was pretty simple. "I told them that I was going to look at our clients and determine which ones aren't using us yet for their labor work. Then I'm going to go and meet with them and see how we might help them. It ain't complicated. That's it."

Well said.

Creating Client Team Think Tanks

Ultimately, the relationship partner should be trying to foster a team approach that utilizes a group of partners and associates working together and constantly looking for opportunities to provide value to a particular client.

The client team idea is one that has been used by consulting firms for years. Typically, consultants from across a firm with differing areas of expertise will meet about a client to discuss trends, research, and issues facing that particular client. Often, interesting ideas result from those meetings.

In a sense, these meetings are intended to create a "client team think tank" that is seeking ideas to add value. The consultants then meet with the clients to discuss these ideas and propose solutions.

Ed Schechter instituted a client team approach with consultants at A. T. Kearney and Andersen. Now he's doing the same for Duane Morris, where he is the law firm's chief marketing officer. There the teams consist of three to seven lawyers, focusing on individual clients. There are also ten to twenty lawyers on specific industry teams. The teams are the focus of an on-going discussion of client issues.

"What you're looking for in these discussions are ideas that can create new opportunities to help clients," he said. "You want to be a consultant who is in your clients' 'kitchen cabinet.' While ideally you want to reach them proactively with ideas, you need to be ready, willing and able to help them react to their business needs. Hence, the value of both specific client and industry teams. I hate reinventing the wheel; industry teams should share best practices."

At Alston & Bird, Jim Stokes instituted a very successful client team approach for UPS. Up to twenty lawyers from across the firm would meet every month to discuss UPS and the issues that the company was facing. Topics changed from meeting to meeting and focused on ways of understanding and adding value to the client. One month the lawyers may talk about diversity issues. The next month they may talk about how to provide better value for lower fees.

The cross-pollination of ideas helps maximize the value that the law firm can add to UPS. "The technology folks may say that there is a problem that might be headed toward litigation," Stokes said. Such discussion might alert the chief technology litigators to start working on ways to help UPS avoid or limit exposure.

The Alston & Bird/UPS meetings were well-attended because so much value was being added. "People tend to vote with their feet if there is little or no value in these meetings," Stokes said.

Remember that clients hire lawyers who understand the business and know how to add value. Client teams take that idea and supercharge it by bringing together a group of lawyers who understand the company intimately. When such lawyers discuss the company, they can come up with even better ways to add value.

By any measure, that's a recipe for successful business development.

THE CLIENT SURVEY: A GREAT CROSS-SELLING TOOL

Former New York City Mayor Ed Koch's most famous expression was, "How'm I doing?"

And that's essentially what a good client survey asks. But it does so in a way that allows the firm to ensure that it is providing the best value possible to the client. "I don't know why more clients don't do client surveys," one General Counsel told me.

Indeed, if you want to cross-sell within a client, you had better be confident that the client loves the work you're doing for it already. You can determine this in a client survey or other form of client review. The wonderful thing about the review is that it can often lead to more work for you.

The survey need not be particularly formal. I know one lawyer who makes appointments to spend several hours with each of his clients every December. He reviews every piece of work done for them and discusses the outcome.

Bruce Richards, former General Counsel with Equifax and Certegy, appreciates a regular meeting with his outside counsel to discuss billing issues. And it is during those meetings that he will often discuss potential future matters.

"We take a look at what the potential looks like for more business, how the billings might project out over the next month or couple of months," he said. "We discuss what types of new matters might be coming down the pike, what types of changes in the business might be coming."

This type of big picture conversation with a client is exactly what a relationship partner wants to have as regularly as possible. Such conversations can pinpoint other areas where the firm can be serving the client.

Remember that the key to any business development conversation is to determine which challenges the client is facing and try to help it find solutions. For example:

▶ Is the client planning to expand the business to South America? Why not ask, "What is the biggest challenge you're facing in making the expansion?" Who knows? Maybe they'll need to register trademarks in Brazil.

▶ Does the client have plans to introduce a new financial product? "I'm curious. What is the biggest challenge you're facing in introducing the product?" Who knows? Maybe there are regulatory issues that the company hasn't thought through.

▶ Perhaps the client wants to grow sales next year by 50%. "I'm curious. What is your plan for getting there?" Who knows? Maybe the plan will involve strategic acquisitions.

The client satisfaction review is a perfect chance to learn how the client sees its own challenges. Those challenges will provide you with more business.

Why Don't More Firms Do Client Surveys?

Some people suspect that most law firms don't do client surveys because they're afraid of the results. Such a notion seems a little too cynical.

I suspect the reasons are more mundane. That is, law firms tend to have too little discretionary time, and most lawyers fail to understand why clients hire lawyers, i.e., to find someone who wants to add value. Too many lawyers assume that if they're giving good legal answers, the client must be happy.

Well it just isn't true. If you want to make sure that your client is happy, the best thing you can do, like Mayor Koch, is to ask.

Indeed, many law departments are conducting their own vendor reviews anyway, so you might as well ask what your clients are saying about you. Many Fortune 500 companies evaluate outside counsel after each transaction or lawsuit, some using very formal rating systems, grading their lawyers in several areas, including budgeting accuracy and work product. These evaluations are discussed with outside counsel so that improvements can be made.

Hence, if some clients do their own surveys, consider conducting your own survey and then respond to it in order to add value.

Contents of a Customer Survey

How should a client survey be conducted and what should it contain? You can ask questions in written form or do interviews in person. Allowing the client to answer written questions usually results in more honest answers. If you ask the client to respond in writing, however, you should certainly schedule a time to debrief him.

Here are some typical questions that you can include in your customer survey:

(1) Are you happy with the quality of the legal service you're getting from Smith and Williams? Please explain in detail.

(2) Please explain how our service could have been better in the past year. Be specific.

(3) Please tell us how satisfied you are with the following areas of our service:
   (a) Legal expertise
   (b) Responsiveness to pressing issues

      (c) Help from support staff

      (d) Work product

      (e) Adherence to budget

      (f) General communications

(4) Are you comfortable that the lawyers doing your legal work understand the substantive area of law involved?

(5) Are you comfortable with our firm's understanding of your company's business and industry? In which areas could we improve that understanding?

(6) Do you think that our firm adds sufficient value to your business? Where could we improve in this area?

(7) Would you be comfortable recommending our firm? If so, why? If not, why not?

(8) In what other areas of legal work do you use outside counsel?

(9) If our firm were competent in other areas of legal work, would you feel comfortable giving that work to us? If not, why not?

(10) What are the major legal challenges you see your company facing over the next two years? Would you feel comfortable entrusting our firm with the opportunity to help you with those legal challenges? If not, why not?

(11) What are the major business challenges you see your company facing over the next two years? In what ways could you see our firm helping you with those challenges?

This Ain't Brain Surgery, but It Is Great Customer Service

As you can see from the above questions, there is no magic to a customer survey. All you want is honest answers to the fundamental question that Mayor Koch posed so often: "How'm I doing?"

But the reason that these "How'm I doing?" questions are so valuable is that they lead directly to other questions about ways you can continue to add value to the client's business. And honest answers to those questions are extremely valuable. Possible responses include:

"Well, we are thinking of doing a big expansion of our western office next year. In fact, we're going to have to buy a couple of office buildings." Kaaaa-Ching! Call your real estate partner.

"Well, the biggest challenge we're going to have over the next year is making sure that all these people we're hiring are properly trained." Kaaaa-Ching! Call your labor and employment partner.

"Well, we're very concerned that one of our competitors has started to poach some of our intellectual property. If we can't protect this stuff, we're going down the tubes." Kaaa-Ching! Call your intellectual property litigation partner.

This strategy incorporates what my friend the software salesman told me: "The way to make a sale is just to listen to the clients. They'll tell you how to sell them."

The customer survey is a wonderful chance to listen to the customer.

A FINAL THOUGHT ON CROSS-SELLING

For years, *cross-selling* has seemed to be a mystical procedure that lawyers have expected would magically grow their practices. But for most firms, the promise has been unfulfilled primarily because the partners don't really understand that the key part of "cross-selling" is the word *"selling."* And most lawyers don't really understand what selling is all about.

Selling will always be about identifying decision-makers, understanding the challenges that face a client, and finding solutions for those challenges. More important, selling is about making a client understand that you're capable of adding value in a particular area.

So what if you're doing great M&A work for a client? He's not going to give you labor work unless you show interest in it and show him how you can add value to his business in the labor area. To do that, you're still going to have to meet with him and discuss his labor needs.

So what if you're a great litigator and have done a great job defending a client against a product liability matter? The client is not going to give you his real estate work unless he sees how you can add value there. And he won't understand that unless you ask to meet with him to discuss his business's needs in real estate. Then, once you understand those needs, you're going to have to systematically start showing how you can add value to the business. Over time, maybe they'll give you a little real estate work.

So what if you're writing wonderful patents for the client? It won't give you its big IP litigation unless the partners know you can add value there.

Cross-selling, like all selling, doesn't happen unless you show the client how you can add value in the new area. And to do that you have to meet with the client and have a discussion about the business and how you can solve his problems.

CHAPTER **13**

Planning and the 12/4/5 Rule

UNDERSTANDING THE 12/4/5 RULE

FOLLOW UP WITH THE RULE: STAYING IN TOUCH
Contacts That Add No Value
Contacts That Add Some Value
Contacts That Add Substantial Value

SETTING UP A 12/4/5 PLAN
Selecting the Prospects
Plotting a Path to Each Prospect's Decision-Maker
Follow Up

CREATING YOUR OWN PLAN

PERSISTENCE

ALLOTMENT OF TIME

OTHER BUSINESS DEVELOPMENT PLANS THAT WORK
The Business Niche Plan
Grow a Single Client
Pick Ten Cross-Selling Prospects
Develop a Legal Product and Show It to Prospects

UNDERSTANDING THE 12/4/5 RULE

There is an episode of the old television sitcom "The Beverly Hillbillies" in which a banker learns that Granny Daisy Moses apparently has developed a sure-fire remedy for the common cold. When the banker learns of this remedy, he gets very excited. He's convinced that he's found a diamond in the rough. The banker hatches all sorts of plans for getting rich from Granny's home cure.

At the end of the episode, the banker finally goes to Granny and says something like, "Can you tell me the cure?" Whereupon Granny explains that the cure (which she has apparently worked out after many years of careful trial and error) is to lie in bed for a couple of weeks and drink lots of water.

"It never fails," says Uncle Jed Clampett.

Now, of course the banker was disappointed. He wanted a quick fix. He wanted a pill to take or an herb to make the sniffles stop. But Granny offered no such panacea. Moreover, Granny's cure did indeed work for those who were willing to give it a try. Do what Granny says and your cold will definitely go away.

When we get to the issue of how to plan for business development, I have a similar cure that will work as well as Granny's cure. In fact, this system is the only one that will absolutely guarantee you new business.

It's called the *"12/4/5 Rule."*

Pick *twelve customers* or prospects or firm clients that you want to grow. Then initiate *four "quality contacts"* per year with that prospect over the next *five years*. A quality contact is "touching" or having contact with decision-makers in ways that add value to their business, i.e., meetings, telephone calls, personal letters on key business and legal trends, personal invitations to seminars, personal briefings on key issues, etc. The only rule is that every contact or "touch" must be focused on adding value to the prospect's business.

For the "glass is half empty" crowd (those descendants of the banker in "The Beverly Hillbillies"), this rule might be a little disappointing because it's not a quick fix. Just as Granny's remedy for the common cold really wasn't a true "cure," this rule might not seem like much of a "business development system."

But in the legal services business, which is rife with bad business development advice, I think it's comforting to know that this system actually is going to lead to increases in revenue.

You could sell the most memberships to the local Chamber of Commerce for five years in a row and never have a single piece of business to show for it. But if you follow the 12/4/5 system, you'll get clients. It's a sure thing.

Let's be clear. I'm not saying that this system *"might work."* I'm *guaranteeing* it. I'm saying, *it's a mortal lock.* I'm saying that if you do this, you'll develop substantial amounts of good business. In fact, you'll probably become one of the handful of top business developers in your firm.

A rule of thumb in sales is that you will close half of all potential business deals where you have seven quality contacts with the business. Sales guru Walter Hailey says that you can increase your close ratio to over 90% simply by having fifteen quality contacts with a prospect. That's certainly consistent with my own experience and the experience of dozens of business developers I know. Indeed, most people in business development give up after two or three contacts. But with the 12/4/5 method, your goal is more than fifteen contacts.

So if you want to spend time selling tickets to the symphony, that's fine. I think the arts are wonderful. And if you want to serve your fellow man by volunteering for the American Cancer Society, that too is wonderful. Want to get involved in your church, synagogue, or mosque? More power to you. That's a wonderful way to serve your community. Do all of those things. But don't deceive yourself into thinking that those activities alone will generate revenue.

If you want a system to generate business reliably, then you need to follow the 12/4/5 rule. Do that and you'll have business by the time you're done.

As Uncle Jed would say, "It never fails."

FOLLOW UP WITH THE RULE: STAYING IN TOUCH

I had a meeting with an in-house lawyer recently and asked her, "How often can a lawyer follow up without being considered a pest?" She thought about it for a moment and then said, "You can send me something every quarter and call me a couple of times a year."

That's consistent with what I'd suggest as well. If you want someone's business, you're going to have to stay in their consciousness. The best way to do that is to find some way to touch each contact every quarter. And you want to make sure that each contact hears your voice at least twice a year. Most important, you want to make sure that you're offering something of value every time you connect.

The numbers of ways of staying in touch are limited only by your imagination. What's most important, however, is that you touch the prospect in ways that add value. Of course there are degrees of "value adding."

There are some touches that add lots of value. Other contacts add a little value. And some communications add no value but at least let the client know that you still exist.

Contacts That Add No Value

(1) *Sending a prospect a Christmas card.* Call me Scrooge. But Christmas cards just aren't very good business development tools. They're nice. I like Christmas cards. But they don't add value. If you want to send Christmas cards, that's fine. They alert your clients that you are a person who is still living on the planet. They also spread holiday cheer. Even I send Christmas cards. But don't consider yourself a business developer based on your Christmas card list.

(2) *Sending a prospect a pizza.* Some sales coaches will tell you that it's a great thing to give the client food. "Everybody loves food," goes the theory. So people send doughnuts, or pizzas, or fruit baskets. Sending gourmet food is a nice way to thank an existing client. But if you're trying to establish yourself as a *business* resource, save your money.

(3) *Sending e-mails on general items of interest.* I know one lawyer who loves to send out e-mails that include his favorite political cartoons. I know another lawyer who sends out a newsletter on household tips like how to fix a toilet. I guess these things can be interesting and even useful. And they tell the prospect that you're still alive. But neither would make the prospect see you as a value provider.

(4) *Sending a prospect a pair of tickets to the hockey game.* Once again, this is a nice way to thank a client for business. But it adds no real value to the client's business. Maybe the client will be more inclined to take your next call as a result

of the tickets. But you'd better make sure that the next call adds some value. Otherwise, you'll be firmly established as someone who wants his business but doesn't really know enough about that business to add value.

(5)   *Sending a prospect a gift certificate for a free beauty salon or spa visit.* Some lawyers, in an effort to be gender-neutral, substitute massages or facials or manicures for sports tickets when they are courting women clients for their law firms. Which for some professional women may be welcome indeed. But most of these gifts are "thank you's," not value-adders.

(6)   *Sending a client a copy of his picture in the newspaper.* I hate to be a killjoy, but this just doesn't add any value. It simply establishes that you recognize the person's picture when you see it in the newspaper. Sure, it's a nice thing to do. And as my mom would say, "It's nice to be nice." But few people will give you business because you act as their personal clipping service.

Contacts That Add Some Value

(1)   *Firm brochures.* The only reason that I don't put brochures in the "no value" category is that sending a client the firm brochure sends the implicit message that, "I'm interested in being a value provider." And of course many clients ask for a firm brochure. If they ask for it, send it of course. But every firm has a lovely looking brochure. And although you may think your brochure is fabulous, chances are your client doesn't really care.

(2)   *Firm newsletters.* If the newsletter is relevant to the client's business, then send it along. The problem with these newsletters is that the client knows that they are generic. And most clients think their business is unique. Also, you're not really distinguishing yourself from other firms with newsletters because every major firm produces them.

(3)   *Memoranda on new law.* When the Sarbanes-Oxley Law came out, general counsels across the country were flooded with memos summarizing the impact of the law. No doubt

most of the memos were well-written. Unfortunately, few of the memos really analyzed the specific issues of the prospect company in light of the new law. Such memoranda do not convince prospects that you're really thinking about their businesses.

Contacts That Add Substantial Value

(1) *Clip and send articles about legal issues that are impacting the client's industry.* If you're trying to get the business of a chemical manufacturer and you send the general counsel an article on a forthcoming environmental law issue for chemical manufacturers, you're stepping into the realm of value provider. Why? Because such an article shows that you're thinking specifically about this prospect's business. Put another way, the client can't just throw away the article thinking, "He sent that to all his clients." You add extra value if you include a brief note with your comments on the law and how it might apply to the client's business.

(2) *Clip and send articles about business trends in the client's industry with a personal legal comment from you.* Write five sentences on the legal implications of the business trend. This implies that you're thinking specifically about the client's business. That's adding value.

(3) *Send a copy of your firm newsletter with additional analysis for the prospect's business.* This is a good way to make the firm newsletter "non-generic." All you need is a couple of paragraphs on your letterhead that show you're thinking about ways to help the prospect's business.

(4) *Send a copy of an article that you've written with additional analysis for the prospect's business.* Once again, the goal is to tailor a "generic" piece to the client's business.

(5) *Send personal letters updating the prospect on how you think a court decision will impact the client's business.* Again, anything that is personally tailored to the client's business is a great touch. Make this kind of gesture often and you're going to make a lot of money.

(6) *Connect the prospect with his business prospects.* This is a master stroke and isn't hard to do. You don't have to actually land the business for the prospect's business. You just have to make the introduction. I know a lawyer who is trying to get the business of a large New York investment bank. To get the business, he passes along information about companies that are considering making initial public offerings. As another example, do you want to win the business of a large construction company? Arrange for the key players at your prospect to meet the construction manager of a large college in your area.

(7) *Personally invite your prospect to a firm seminar.* The fact that you are informed enough about the client's business to know that an upcoming labor relations seminar is going to be valuable to the prospect demonstrates that you're thinking about the specific business. That's adding value. And for goodness sake, *make the call personally.* Don't rely on a mailed invitation. Even if the client can't come, that personal call shows that you're willing to work hard to get the business. It's a non-threatening way to build the relationship.

(8) *Offer to do a one-hour presentation for the client on a new legal issue.* "I think that outside counsels fail to understand how much we appreciate free legal advice," one in-house lawyer told me. Once again, the personal invitation gives you a good deal of credibility. If you make the presentation highly interactive, you're going to ensure that the presentation is highly relevant to this client's business. And as a bonus, the time you spend with the client will give you a lot of valuable information that you can use as future follow-up fodder.

(9) *Offer to co-write an article with a prospect.* Many in-house lawyers are interested in building their reputation through publishing. Build the prospect's reputation and you add value to his business.

(10) *Invite a prospect to hear you speak on an issue that affects his business.* If you're going to be giving a presentation to a bar meeting or CLE conference on a legal issue that is

relevant to the prospect's business, call the prospect and personally invite him to attend. If he shows up, make sure that you tailor the presentation somewhat to his company's specific needs. Once again, it shows that you're thinking about his business.

(11) *Invite a prospect to speak at your firm.* I know one lawyer who did this with a big prospect and ended up building a strong relationship and eventually getting some business. Once again, building your prospect's reputation builds value into his business.

(12) *Invite a prospect for a personal dinner with an industry leader.* If you're an environmental lawyer, organize a dinner with a key player at the EPA and a prospect who is in a manufacturing business. Your prospect will appreciate the chance to rub shoulders with someone who can impact his business. And you'll be a hero for adding value to his business.

(13) *Send the prospect a personal book review of a book relating to his industry.* If you're reading the book anyway, why not write a brief letter to the client with your reaction to the book. Then send the book to the client, along with your "review." It shows you as a thoughtful reader in both his and your businesses.

(14) *Invite a prospect to speak to a trade association.* Once again, you're building the prospect's business value by building the reputation of the decision-maker.

(15) *Create a regulatory compliance matrix for a client and show him how to administer it.* When the Sarbanes-Oxley law was enacted, figuring out how to comply with it was complicated. Many lawyers wrote memos. But it would have been extremely valuable to many General Counsels to have some sort of spreadsheet/matrix that they could use to ensure compliance with all different aspects of the law. If the prospect is interested in the matrix, offer to walk him through it to assure he knows how to use it with his business.

(16) *Offer to audit the prospect's regulatory compliance.* If you want the prospect's labor and employment work, offer to

audit some aspect of the prospect's labor and employment practices. It may take you a couple of hours of work. But you'll gain an incredible amount of information about the prospect's company. And you'll be adding value.

(17) *Send legal analyses of issues facing the prospect's competition.* Once again, the foregoing action can convince a client that you are showing true interest in the client's business. Explaining your reaction to challenges facing the business's competition is certainly adding value.

SETTING UP A 12/4/5 PLAN

Now that we've discussed follow-up issues, we can move on to create a business development plan as follows.

Selecting the Twelve Prospects

Relationship partners should select some or all of their new "prospects" from within an existing firm client. For example, if the firm already does the firm's employment work, you may wish to seek the firm's tax work, mergers and acquisitions work, and environmental work. Where you're confident of the value you can add, select some new clients as well.

Value adding partners should also select some or all of their new "prospects" from the firm's client list. Where these partners are confident of the value they can add, they should also select some new clients.

Plotting a Path to Each Prospect's Decision-Maker

You're never going to win the business of a prospect if you can't speak directly to the decision-maker. So the first part of any business development plan with a specific prospect is to arrange a meeting with the key decision-maker. There are usually four steps involved:

(1) *Identify the key decision-maker.* In most large companies, the decision-maker will be someone in the General Counsel's office. But with smaller companies, the CEO, CFO, or other key manager may have hiring power. Do the necessary research to identify the key decision-maker.

(2) *Research the key issues facing the business.* Read the 10-K. Read what the analysts say about the company on the Internet. If the company is privately held, read the web site and any articles you can find. You're trying to discover the challenges that the company is facing.

(3) *Find a connection with the company.* Chances are that you don't yet know the key decision-maker. But it shouldn't be too hard to find a connection with someone in the company. One lawyer wanted to get a meeting with the General Counsel at Georgia-Pacific. His first meeting was with his cousin, an attorney who worked in the GC's office.

(4) *Get a meeting with the decision-maker.* Meeting with your connection, together with your company research, should produce a hook for calling your decision-maker. Use that hook and make the call to get a meeting with the decision-maker. For example, "I spoke with Fred Smith in your office last week and he told me that you're interested in ways to reduce your environmental litigation risk. I have some ideas and I'd love to discuss them with you." This is one of those critical steps that you have to take. So pick up the telephone and make the call. Try several times if necessary, leaving messages over a couple of weeks.

If the above four steps are unsuccessful, don't give up. That is:

(5) *If you don't get a meeting, keeping trying.* Just because the first call doesn't produce a meeting (it may not) doesn't mean that you should give up. Rejection is part of the sales process. How you handle that rejection will determine whether you ultimately succeed. So what do you do next? You keep plugging away in other ways.

For example, meet with others at the company and try again to finagle a meeting with a new angle, making another call in a couple of months. Then:

▶ Correspond with the decision-maker, providing personal value-added information;

▶ Invite him or her to value-adding events at your firm;

> ▶ Invite him or her to hear you speak on a topic that you
>   know he/she will find interesting; or
> ▶ Invite him or her to speak at a firm function.

Follow Up

Communicate with the prospect directly or indirectly every quarter in
some way that adds value. And be sure to speak to the prospect at
least twice a year. Hence, if you send a prospect a letter during one
quarter, call him on the telephone the next quarter to invite him to a
firm function.

Og Mandino is the author of a tiny book first published in 1968
entitled *The Greatest Salesman in the World*. The book contains a
powerful piece of advice in the form of a mantra that Mandino
advises salesmen to follow. The mantra is, "I will persist until I
succeed." At first this mantra seemed like corny advice to me. A little
simplistic, I thought.

But the advice has proven to be of great value to me and to many
other lawyers in getting business. If you have the attitude that you will
simply persist with a client until you get the business, you'll be
surprised at how much business you'll win. To be sure, this attitude is
a long-term strategy. But if you believe that a slow, steady stream of
value-providing contact is the best way to win business (*and it is*),
then you will eventually win that business.

CREATING YOUR OWN PLAN

Following is a business development planning tool or table to track your
progress in pursuing your prospects. Part I is your *Prospect Approach
Plan*. Part II is your *Follow-Up Plan*. The total plan works as follows:

For Part I, fill in all your prospects and the key decision-maker for
each along the left-hand side. The key steps for getting the first
meeting with each key decision-maker are indicated across the top of
the table. Check off each box as you work your way across the grid.

Once you've gotten the first meeting with each prospect, transfer
that person to Part II, the Follow-Up Plan. Once again, you should
begin working your way across the chart, checking off the boxes as
you repeatedly communicate with the prospect.

SAMPLE PROGRESS CHART

	PROSPECT AND APPROACH		
Prospects		**Activities to Get Meeting with Decision-Maker**	**Meeting with Decision-Maker**
1. Company -- Decision-Maker ---------------------------------- Phone # ---			
2. Company -- Decision-Maker ---------------------------------- Phone # ---			
3. Company -- Decision-Maker ---------------------------------- Phone # ---			
4. Company -- Decision-Maker ---------------------------------- Phone # ---			
5. Company -- Decision-Maker ---------------------------------- Phone # ---			
6. Company -- Decision-Maker ---------------------------------- Phone # ---			
7. Company -- Decision-Maker ---------------------------------- Phone # ---			
8. Company -- Decision-Maker ---------------------------------- Phone # ---			
9. Company -- Decision-Maker ---------------------------------- Phone # ---			
10. Company -- Decision-Maker ---------------------------------- Phone # ---			
11. Company -- Decision-Maker ---------------------------------- Phone # ---			
12. Company -- Decision-Maker ---------------------------------- Phone # ---			

SAMPLE PROGRESS CHART

Follow-Up Year 1–Q1	Year 1–Q2	Year 1–Q3	Year 1–Q4	Year 2–Q1	Year 2–Q2	Year 2–Q3	Year 2–Q4

PERSISTENCE

Sales trainers constantly tell their students that "sales is a numbers game." And this is true, especially in businesses where having a great many prospects is important. However, even though business development for lawyers is a numbers game to some extent, it's more important for lawyers to think of business development as a "persistence game."

"Sales is a numbers game" derives from businesses where huge numbers of prospects are critical for success. I went to law school with a former stockbroker who told me that his firm's prospecting ratio was 200 to 10 to 1. In other words, he needed to make 200 prospecting calls (cold calls) to get a single qualified prospect who would meet with him. He then had to go to ten meetings to get one paying client. "There were days when that telephone receiver felt like it weighed a ton," he told me. (No wonder you get so many cold calls from stockbrokers.)

In fact, sales is not a numbers game for many businesses that focus sales efforts on very small numbers of prospects and work very hard at getting to know their businesses and adding value. For example, I know a salesman for a large computer company that has only one prospect: Delta Airlines. His job is to penetrate that company in any way possible. He does it by learning as much as possible about the company and its needs.

Similarly, I would rather lawyers focus on a smaller number of key prospects and activities and be very persistent over a long period of time to show the value that they can provide. If you do this with a pool of ten to twelve high-quality prospects, you're much more likely to have success than if you spread yourself too thin and try to connect with many more prospects, none of whom will get to know you very well.

ALLOTMENT OF TIME

One of the most common questions I am asked is, "How much time must I spend on business development?" Instead of focusing on numbers of hours, it is wiser and more efficient to make "an advance a week." In other words, advance the relationship of one client every week. Hence:

- ▶ If you haven't had an initial meeting yet, then call up and get the meeting.
- ▶ If you have already had a meeting, then send a value added e-mail.
- ▶ If you didn't speak with the prospect last quarter, come up with an excuse to call the prospect and invite him to a firm function that he would find interesting.

If you have twelve promising prospects, you can make an advance for each prospect once a quarter. That's about all most people can handle and still practice law.

But there are some lawyers who are pressured to quantify the amount of time they spend on prospecting each week in terms of hours. I suppose this is because lawyers are generally required to view their work days in terms of *billable* hours.

I don't like suggesting any specific "time per week" because quality counts more than quantity with business development. When I was practicing law, my firm's billing system had a billing file in which we were encouraged to record our "business development" time. And many lawyers would bill to the "business development" account all sort of things that, by themselves, don't lead to business: volunteer work, time spent writing articles, time spent preparing speeches, etc. None of this leads to business unless the lawyer follows up with the prospects whom he meets at these activities.

I also hesitate to give a number because no one number works for everyone. But if you must have a number, then how's this? *Two hours a week.*

- ▶ Two hours is about how long it takes to call someone on the telephone and then attend a meeting.
- ▶ Two hours is about how long it takes to invite someone to your speech and then deliver the actual speech.

> ▶ Two hours is about how long it takes to write a personal letter to a prospect with a personal analysis of how a new law might impact his business.

> ▶ Two hours is about how long it will take to set up and deliver a free seminar on a new labor regulation to a prospect.

Two hours of high-quality business development work a week should be plenty. And don't tell me that you don't have two hours a week. I used to practice law. And I used to bill 2,000 hours a year. I easily wasted two hours a week.

You've got the two hours. Now you just have to use them wisely.

OTHER BUSINESS DEVELOPMENT PLANS THAT WORK

Of course, 12/4/5 isn't the only plan that will get you business. There is no single best way to develop business. But some business development plans are better than others. The best business development plans focus on a limited number of prospects and are aimed at getting the key decision-makers in that market to see how you or your firm can add value to their business.

Here are four other plans that I have seen work:

The Business Niche Plan

In this plan, the lawyer focuses on a particular niche of business and gets to know as many of the key players in that niche as possible. For example, a litigator might decide that he wants to focus on media companies. By focusing on a narrow niche, a lawyer can understand key issues facing that business and thereby become known as a true value provider.

STEP 1: Pick a niche. Examples include affordable housing, automobile dealers, the airline industry, nursing homes, software businesses, etc.

STEP 2: Identify the key trade groups and begin working to become a leader in one of the groups.

STEP 3: Set a goal to meet with a key decision-maker in the niche at least once a month.

STEP 4: Develop a presentation on industry legal trends and offer it at trade shows and in private meetings with clients and prospects.

STEP 5: Send out industry updates on legal issues facing the niche.

Grow a Single Client

If you have a small piece of a big client, a great plan is to get more of that client's business. However, most lawyers cannot grow a client alone. They will need the help of partners with different legal expertise.

STEP 1: Conduct a client satisfaction survey with the client. You won't be able to grow the client unless the client loves your work. The survey needn't be in writing. You can just take the general counsel to a "How'm I doing?" lunch.

STEP 2: Assuming that you're sure of the client's confidence in your work, identify specifically what areas of work that your firm is not currently providing to the client.

STEP 3: Based on your knowledge of your firm, decide which area is the most likely area where your firm could help the client (and where you're not helping it already). For example, based on your understanding of the company's plans to expand overseas, you're pretty sure that the company could use your help protecting intellectual property abroad.

STEP 4: Sit down with a partner and discuss ideas for helping the client. For example, discuss with your intellectual property partner how to help the client protect intellectual property abroad.

STEP 5: Set up a meeting with your partner, yourself, and a key decision-maker to discuss how to help the client in the new area. For instance, a telephone call to the client contact might begin with, "I'd like you to come over and let me introduce you to my partner Fred Smith. He has expertise in protecting intellectual property abroad. He might be a resource for you at some point as you expand overseas."

Pick Ten Cross-Selling Prospects

The biggest and best reservoir of good prospects for any law firm is the firm's existing client list. The best cross-sellers constantly revisit their firms' client lists, looking for ways to sell other services.

STEP 1: Get a list of the firm's top 100 clients from the past year.

Step 2: Look through the list and pick ten that you think might need your type of legal expertise. For example, if you're an immigration lawyer, pick ten clients that you think might need immigration work. Don't *"overthink"* this. Just use your judgment to determine ten good prospects.

Step 3: Set up meetings with each prospect's "relationship partner." During the meetings, discuss the client and strategize how you might be able to work with the client.

Step 4: Go with the relationship partner to a meeting with the client to discuss its needs.

Develop a Legal Product and Show It to Prospects

A very powerful way to develop business is to create a free product and "sell" it. For example, tax lawyers can create a tool to audit a prospect's tax compliance procedures. If the product is compelling, it's a great way to gain access to many prospects. You need not charge for the use of the product. Give it away in hopes of getting more substantial business opportunities.

Step 1: Create the product and give it a name. For example, call it "The Smith and Williams Tax Law Compliance Audit." At the same time, create a presentation to discuss and describe the product.

Step 2: Compile a list of prospects that might be interested in the product. This can be a list taken from the firm's existing client list (cross-selling opportunities). It can be completely new prospects. Or it can be a combination of cross-selling and new prospects.

Step 3: Offer the product to the prospects. You can do this through a letter or direct telephone contact. The telephone call would sound something like this: "We've developed a Tax Compliance Audit that is designed to ensure that you're complying with the changes in the tax code. If you're interested, I'd be happy to come to your office and give you a brief presentation on how to use it. Are you interested?" You can also sponsor an event in which you invite clients and prospects to the presentation.

There are a million variations on these plans. Frankly, I don't think it really matters which one you choose. But you must do *something*. So pick a plan and get going. Two years from now, if you stick with it, you'll have plenty of business.

PART TWO
Communication Skills

CHAPTER **14**

Overview of
Communication Skills

HOW IS SPOKEN COMMUNICATION LIKE THE SCHRADIN ROAD BRIDGE?

SPOKEN COMMUNICATION IS A LIMITED MEDIUM THAT ACCOMPLISHES SOME THINGS WELL AND OTHER THINGS ABYSMALLY

What Does the Spoken Word Do Well?

Listener-Value Statements

Big Picture Explanations

Telling Two or Three Main Ideas

Telling Stories

Conveying Passion and Influencing with Personal Style

What Does the Spoken Word Do Badly? Convey Complex Detail and Reasoning

IGNORE THESE PRINCIPLES AT YOUR PERIL

HOW IS SPOKEN COMMUNICATION LIKE THE SCHRADIN ROAD BRIDGE?

To be a great communicator, you need not be a great orator. Nor must you be eloquent or clever. You don't even need to be charismatic. To be a great communicator, all you must do is *connect with the listener.* In speaking with clients, that usually means you should avoid concentrating on legal technicalities and instead focus on the practical business impact.

In some respects, in order to understand how to communicate effectively with the spoken word, you must understand bridge engineering. For example, if you're ever driving in Morgan Township, Ohio, in the southwest corner of the state, look for the Schradin Road Bridge on County Road 219. It's a perfectly good bridge if used correctly, paved over a reinforced concrete culvert. I could drive my 2004 Honda Accord over it with no problem. But if I were to drive an eighteen-wheeler over it carrying fifteen tons of cargo, there's a good chance the Schradin Road Bridge would collapse because the bridge has a posted weight limit of ten tons.

How is this connected to communication skills? Great communicators understand that spoken communication is a lot like a bridge with a posted weight limit. Spoken communication can handle certain things well: big ideas, stories, and well-focused messages. But if you burden spoken communication with too much baggage, it will "collapse." If you try to crowd too much information into a spoken message, you'll almost certainly fail to connect with the listener.

What makes spoken communication collapse? *Details. Numbers. Complex legal explanations.* Anything with more than three or four main ideas.

Therefore, if you want to be a great communicator, always remember to embrace only a single idea at a time.

Spoken Communication Is a Limited Medium That Accomplishes Some Things Well and Other Things Abysmally

That is, if you want to be a great communicator with the spoken word, you must understand what the spoken word does well and what it does poorly.

What Does the Spoken Word Do Well?

Listener-Value Statements

Explaining the law can be very complicated. Explaining the impact of the law on the client is usually pretty simple. With that in mind, great communicators usually start interacting with a client by focusing on the client impact.

Let's say that your client reads in the newspaper about a big legal decision deciding that certain types of tax shelters are no longer lawful. He calls you up and says, "What's the meaning of this tax law decision I just read about?"

You have a decision to make. You can respond by giving your client a complex legal explanation of the court's decision. Or you can give a simple explanation of the impact of that decision on the client's business:

> *"We're going to have to change the tax treatment of one of your tax shelters. It will probably cost you some money in taxes. But it will save you from being audited."*

If the client wants a more technical legal explanation, he or she will ask for it. But the best communicators generally assume that clients are most concerned about the impact on their businesses. And that is usually an accurate assumption.

Big Picture Explanations

Spoken communication describes the "big picture" far better than the dirty details. Suppose a client asked, "What's wrong with non-compete agreements?" A reasonable spoken answer might be:

> *"Courts don't like non-compete agreements because they restrain trade and otherwise seem un-American. That's not to say that they are never enforceable. If you limit the scope of the non-compete agreement, the courts will sometimes honor it. It just depends on the circumstances."*

That's not a bad "big picture" explanation. But if you try to quickly describe all the detailed circumstances where non-compete agreements are deemed "reasonable," the communication may well fail. That is, you won't connect with your listener (the bridge will collapse).

As a result, great communicators prefer to explain the big picture. The Formulas for such explanations that I will detail in this section will constantly encourage you to focus on big picture issues that most concern the client, not the details that could confuse that client.

Telling Two or Three Main Ideas

Listeners cannot retain more than two or three ideas when those ideas are delivered to them by the spoken word. Ten or twelve ideas are too much.

Think about this flawed process that we call "speaking." You are sending sounds through the air that your listener must capture and decipher in real time despite constant distractions.

Think about it. You're trying to make your listeners understand tax law. But your listeners are battling a constant stream of internal distractions such as sex, snacks, and the Sopranos.

With that in mind, great communicators constantly try to boil down their messages to two or three main ideas. The Formulas that we will discuss in this section will continually require that you focus on only two or three main ideas.

Telling Stories

The spoken word is a great medium for stories. Why? Nobody knows. We just know this is true, and here is the proof. Try to memorize a list of the following words after one reading:

> *wallpaper mountain skirt cone scissors nail watch*

Read the list quickly, then cover it up, and try to write down all the words from memory.

Not easy, is it?

Now let's try again. But this time I'm going to give you a story. Read it out loud slowly with lots of expression (like you're telling a story to a fascinated child). Try to imagine the following strange scene:

> *On the wall is a gorgeous piece of **wallpaper**. In fact, the wallpaper has on it a painting of a beautiful snow-capped **mountain**. The mountain is wearing a **skirt**. You take a piece of string and tie it around the base of the skirt so that it forms a **cone**. Then you take a pair of **scissors** and cut off the base of the cone.*

*Then you take the scissors and hang them on a **nail**. Also hanging on the nail is a beautiful gold **watch**.*

The story (an admittedly silly story) makes remembering disconnected words relatively easy. Facts stick to stories like Velcro. Great communicators understand that stories have impact, and are constantly using stories to bring to life the actual business impact of legal issues.

If a great communicator needs to explain the value of a "merger clause" in a contract, he might tell how a merger clause saved a client from a lawsuit:

> "I had a client who had been doing business with a vendor for years, and they had entered into dozens of agreements. When the vendor tried to sue the client for violation of one of the old agreements, all we had to do was point to the merger clause in the most recent agreement which stated that this agreement was the final controlling agreement and that all prior agreements were irrelevant."

Usually, a story will get a point across better than a technical legal explanation. As a result, the best communicators are constantly relying on stories to help them explain legal concepts.

Conveying Passion and Influencing with Personal Style

The spoken word is a great medium for conveying passion and attempting to influence the listener with personal style. Whether or not we like it, people judge what we say based on how we look and sound. They judge what we say based on our body language, our facial expressions, and the energy in our voices. The best communicators embrace this fact and understand that the spoken word is a wonderful medium for influencing with style.

Indeed, when you tell a client that she must comply with a new ERISA regulation, whether you say it enthusiastically or with boredom will have a significant impact on how the listener reacts and responds. Great communicators work to develop a personal style that influences beyond the words.

What Does the Spoken Word Do Badly? Convey Complex Detail and Reasoning

Complex legal logic is virtually impossible to communicate effectively to someone who is not actively participating in the conversation through questions and answers. And few clients really care about the legal reasoning involved.

Yet so many lawyers try to connect with clients about complex legal rationales. We lawyers love to detail our logic *ad nauseum*. It makes sense that we would. We went to law school for three years to learn this stuff. When we think of a particularly strong legal idea, we usually love to show how we've logically arrived at the idea.

Unfortunately, this legal reasoning doesn't work particularly well in spoken communication. You can describe your complex legal concept until you're blue in the face. But there's little chance that you'll really connect with the audience about the concept.

This doesn't mean that you should never describe complex ideas to an audience. But it does mean that if the ideas are complex, it's better to try to connect through a question and answer format rather than through a lecture.

IGNORE THESE PRINCIPLES AT YOUR PERIL

These principles are not without exceptions. You will at times have to convey complex circumstances with the spoken word. But when that day comes, you'll be wise to keep in mind the basic principle that the spoken word is a limited medium that is most effective when it is not overburdened. You'll also be wise to remember that the spoken word works best when it is delivered with passion.

The chapters in this Part will provide you with some Formulas and other principles that you can use as a guide for connecting with listeners. After all, you don't want your communication bridge to collapse every time you try to drive over it. You want to arrive on the other side with a strong connection to the listener.

CHAPTER **15**

Organizing a Message

You're in your office writing a brief when the telephone rings. It's Big Johnny, a Senior Vice President at your client Huge Electron, a large electric utility. Big Johnny wants you to prepare a presentation to Huge Electron's top management on how to avoid antitrust liability.

Then comes the kicker. Big Johnny says, "We can get them all together for breakfast next week. Will twenty minutes be enough time? We don't want to spend too much time on this."

A hot rush of panic spreads through your chest. You want to scream, "Twenty minutes? How can I cover antitrust law in twenty minutes? Do you guys really want to avoid liability? Do you really care about how this could potentially ruin your business? Do you care about jail? You guys need at least a whole day on this subject! Maybe more if you're going to really keep your company safe and stay out of jail!"

But instead you take a deep breath. Before you answer, you remember that electric utilities tend to be very good clients. You remember that electric utilities tend to pay their VERY LARGE legal bills on time. And you remember that Huge Electron is no exception. So if you have any sense at all you respond with the following, more measured statement: "No problem. What time do you want me there?" And you say it with a confident tone, as if what Big Johnny wants really is no problem.

You hang up the telephone and begin to sweat. "Well, let's see. I have spent the last ten years learning antitrust law. This is going to be a disaster. What are the key cases I need to tell them about? What are the key statutes? Where have the courts looked at electric utility activity?"

This chapter is about how to put together a presentation that not only makes Big Johnny happy, but shows you off as a great, and valuable, lawyer to your client.

NAIL YOUR PRESENTATION USING KEY COMMUNICATION PRINCIPLES AND A FORMULA

Great communicators know that this is not going to be difficult. You have an inherent understanding of the four Key Communication Principles:

(1) Focus on the issues that the listener values.

(2) Keep the presentation Big Picture.

(3) Make only two or three main points.

(4) Tell stories.

And with those principles in mind, you quickly fly into action, focusing on how to simply communicate to these executives what they must know regarding antitrust liability.

A FORMULA FOR QUICKLY ORGANIZING A STRONG PRESENTATION

Start with a process. In our workshops we teach a simple Formula for organizing a presentation that puts into action the four *Key Communication Principles*. You can use this formula and variations of it to handle virtually any communication situation. This Formula (and variations of it) will enable you to:

▸ Give a great antitrust presentation to a client.

▸ Persuade your partners to change your firm's compensation structure.

▸ Win the Coca-Cola Company beauty contest.

▸ Handle questions from any audience, including judges.

▸ Speak effectively "off the cuff" when the President asks you, "Why should I sign this deal?"

Here is the Formula.

OVERVIEW OF THE FORMULA

The basics of great communication are all contained within this simple formula. Master it (and all of its variations) and I guarantee that you will become a highly successful lawyer. You'll have become a great communicator on legal issues.

As you will see, there are five steps:

STEP 1: Create a message objective (MO). This is the cornerstone of a clear message.

The Formula©

STEP 2: Use no more than three points in support of your MO. Three points ensure that your presentation is crisp and easy to follow.

STEP 3: Determine what evidence supports your three points and subpoints. Deft use of stories is the quickest way to become a top-notch communicator. Everyone loves stories.

STEP 4: Determine your "hook." Although this comes near the beginning of the presentation, wait until you've created the core of your presentation before trying to create the hook, which can be tricky.

STEP 5: Determine your wrap-up. Always end with a call to action.

Step 1: Create a Message Objective (MO)

"WYP?"

"What's your point?" If you are asked that question during a presentation, you've been WYP'd. (And if it's an important presentation, you should be whipped for being WYP'd.)

Whether you're speaking at a presentation or in a meeting, if you get WYP'd you're not communicating well. *Great communicators never get WYP'd.* That's because they always state a simple point coupled with a clear reason why the listener should care.

To avoid getting WYP'd during a presentation, always make sure that you have a clear Message Objective (MO). A clear MO is the cornerstone of great communication because it assures that you begin by bringing together the two most important parts of any spoken communication:

(1) What you want from the audience.

(2) What's "in it" for the listener.

MO Part 1: What You Want from the Audience

When you sit down to create a message, your first question should be: What do you want from the presentation? That is, what do you want the audience to do in response to your presentation?

▶ If you're speaking to your partners about whether to promote an associate to partner, tell them what you want: "I want you to make Frank a partner."

▶ If you're speaking to a client about whether to adopt a new hiring policy, tell the client what you want: "I think you need to consider changing this policy."

> ▶ If you're speaking to a prospective client in a beauty contest presentation, tell them what you want: "I want you to hire us."

My grandfather's advice as a master jewelry salesman applies to lawyers who are trying to become strong communicators. Grandpa always asked for the order. Or, as he liked to put it, "You don't ask, you don't get."

MO Part 2: WII-FM

We've all seen a headset-wearing teenager, grooving to her favorite radio station on the subway, haven't we? The listeners to your presentation have something in common with that teenager. They're tuned to their favorite radio station. But unlike the teenager, the favorite radio station of your listener is WII-FM: *"What's in it for me."* Regardless of what you want from them, your listeners are wondering what they're going to get from you.

In business, the WII-FM of any presentation should almost always relate to the success of the company or the personal success of the people in the room. When you speak to clients, you should be addressing *their need to make the business succeed.* When you speak to your partners, you must address their need to make the law firm succeed. Tell the listeners to your presentation how your ideas will make them richer or smarter or otherwise more successful.

Formulate the MO by Bringing the Two Parts Together

A strong MO in a presentation clearly brings together your goal for the presentation with a WII-FM for the audience. Formulate your MO by bringing these two elements together into an "If/then" statement: "If _____, then _____." If [you do what I want], then [you get what you want].

Here are a few examples:

> ▶ If we make Frank a partner of this firm, then he's going to attract many clients.
> ▶ If we change how we hire associates, then we're going to do a better job of attracting qualified applicants.

▶ If you adopt this new tax strategy, then your business can save a lot of money.

▶ If you hire our firm to do your patent work, then your business will be more successful at making money from its inventions.

MO Sidenote: Education vs. Persuasion

"What if I just want to educate the client and don't want them to DO anything—such as adopt a specific policy?"

That's a common question in our workshops.

But you need a clear MO even if you're "merely" educating a client.

In an educational presentation, the first part of the MO is a simple plea for the audience's attention and the use of your ideas. The second part of the MO is the WII-FM.

Here are a few examples:

▶ Use these ideas next time you write a contract and you'll save your clients a lot of time and money.

▶ Follow these simple rules when you meet with competitors and you'll avoid antitrust liability.

▶ Learn these simple ideas about trade secrets, and you'll be able to keep your company's key information out of the hands of your competitors.

Second and Final MO Sidenote: MOs Aren't Just for Presentations

You need to be thinking, "What's my MO?" every time you open your mouth.

Every time!

That's what great communicators do.

Every time a client asks a question, great communicators pause before answering and think, "What's my MO?"[1]

Every time great communicators stand before a prospect to pitch business, they pause before they speak and think, "What's my MO?"

---

[1] Or if they haven't read this book they ask, "What's my point and why should my listener care?"

Every time they are asked to discuss an issue with their partners, great communicators pause and think, "What's my MO?"

Why? Because they want to make sure that their main point is clear and that the listener understands why it matters to them.

They don't want to get WYP'd.

Step 2: Use No More Than Three Points in Support of Your MO

I was recently working with a lawyer named Kate who had shown me a presentation that she planned to give to a client. The presentation was on immigration law and how to hire people from other countries. There were fifteen different points in the presentation.

After flipping through Kate's PowerPoint, I said to her, "Kate, I think you need to start this presentation with the fundamental realization that your client is not going to remember virtually anything you say."

I didn't take this approach because the topic was uninteresting. But study after study shows that audiences remember only about 15% of what they hear. And I think that figure is too high.

Kate laughed because she knew that she rarely remembered much from the presentations that she attended.

"With that in mind," I continued, "you need to ask yourself, what would you be happy having your client remember? Put another way, if your listeners were to walk out with only three main ideas, what would you like them to be?"

Indeed, one of the most important key communication principles is to limit your points to three.

People won't remember the great majority of what you say. So you might as well be in control of what they do remember.

Three Points Have Impact That Will Be Remembered!

I know a lawyer who lobbies regulators on behalf of a large gas utility. The kinds of legal and regulatory issues he discusses are exceptionally complex. For example, he must try to explain to politicians with no regulatory accounting background why they should support a plan to change how a gas utility does its accounting.

My friend says the secret of his success is that he limits his appeals to three major points.

For example, he might say that the new accounting is needed for three reasons:

(1) *It's good for rate-payers* (that's what politicians care most about). He then details how gas rates will decrease as a result of the accounting change.

(2) *It's good for the utility* (politicians want a healthy utility). He then explains, also in some detail, how the new system will ensure a healthy balance sheet for the utility.

(3) *It's good for the state* (politicians want a healthy state). Finally, he will explain specifically how the new accounting system will benefit the state's economy by keeping down rates and attracting industry to the area.

Three Points Doesn't Mean You Can't Say More Than Three Things: Subpoints

Note that just because you have three main ideas as part of your presentation doesn't mean that you can speak about only those three things. You can say fifty things so long as they are grouped under three "umbrellas." Introduce as many subpoints as you want.

I worked recently with a health care lawyer who was asked to summarize for a client (a company that processes data for hospitals, pharmacies, and doctors' offices) a major federal healthcare law that had recently been enacted. His main point was that the healthcare law offers some substantial money-making opportunities for the client. In summarizing the bill, however, he also characterized the law in three main categories:

(1) *The Good:* He explained several of the main sections of the law that provided the most benefit to the client.

(2) *The Bad:* He discussed the regulations that would probably make it more difficult to make money.

(3) *And the Ugly:* He pointed out the new rules that were neither good nor bad, but for which compliance was going to be complex and troublesome.

He made multiple points under each main idea. But he gave this potentially complex presentation a nice simple structure by keeping it to three points.

If You Don't Believe Me, Just Ask Bill Nye, the Science Guy

Okay, Bill Nye, the "Science Guy," is not a lawyer. But Nye knows something about how to make audiences remember things about a complex subject matter. So I thought we lawyers could learn something from him.

For years Nye produced a popular program on public television in which he explained the complexities of science to children. And what was his secret?

"The key to explaining things on my show," Nye told me, "has been to distill the ideas to get to the fundamental notions and to exclude the other interesting but not-so-focused information. . . . On the dinosaur show, we make two points. These are called 'learning objectives' in the education industry. A learning objective is something you can test the viewer, reader, listener, or student on."

So on the dinosaur show, his two points were:

▶ We know that dinosaurs once lived because we find their fossil bones.

▶ Dinosaurs and humans did not live at the same time.

Similarly, I often ask lawyers, "Assuming that your client won't remember much from your presentation, what two or three things would you like him or her to remember?" The answer to that question is usually pretty close to your three points.

Recently I worked with a corporate lawyer who told me that when he speaks to his clients about non-disclosure agreements with contract employees, he wants them to remember only three things. And that's where we focused his presentation:

▶ *Don't start negotiations without one.* Too often clients begin negotiating and then try to get an agreement signed mid-negotiation. That can lead to problems.

▶ *Use the right agreement.* Don't just take the same non-disclosure agreement and re-use it over and over regardless of the circumstances. Different situations call for different agreements.

> ▶ *When in doubt, call us.* It won't cost much to get us
> involved early in negotiations. The little you spend on our
> help early in the process can save you from spending
> much more on subsequent litigation.

But What About All the Legal Details?

"But what about all the law? The cases? The statutes? The regulations?
I'm a lawyer man. I need to tell them about the law." Is that your
standard reaction? That's what many of *my* clients tell *me.*

But keep in mind that clients hire you to help them make money
and run their businesses more effectively. They don't want to hear you
drone on about cases and statutes.

When I was practicing I sat in on a three-hour antitrust presentation
given by a lawyer (from another law firm) to a room of about fifty utility
professionals. The lawyer cited case after case and referred repeatedly
to the key antitrust statutes. It was painful. And looking around the
room, I could see that almost no one was paying attention. Instead, I
saw plenty of people working their Blackberry pagers under their desks.

These utility guys just needed to be told what to do to stay out of
trouble. Three key points would have been fine. If they want to know
lots of detailed law, let them ask about it in the question and answer
period.

That's not to say that you'll never cite statutes or cases. Sometimes
you'll make a presentation to fellow lawyers who want to know the
details of the law (though often less than you might think). But most
clients just want to know key things to do to stay out of trouble.

Some Three-Point Standards for Tricky Presentations

Sometimes the presentation doesn't naturally break down into three
simple points. So there are some standards that you can use whenever
you need to break down your complex topic into three key ideas.

Chronological Overview

> ▶ *Past:* In the past we've always been guided by a set of
> simple regulations.
> ▶ *Present:* But now the law has changed and become more
> complex.

> *Future:* So in the future we're going to focus on a couple of key "safe harbor" activities to ensure that we don't run afoul of the new regulations.

Weighing the Pros and Cons

> *Advantages:* The advantages of changing our standard form agreement are as follows.
> *Disadvantages:* The disadvantages of changing our standard form agreement are as follows.
> *Recommendation:* We must change the agreement to ensure that we make more money.

Selling a New Idea by Illuminating the Problem and Then the Solution

Whenever you're trying to sell a client or colleagues on changing a policy or taking a new course, this method works wonders.

> *Situation:* The *status quo* is as follows.
> *Challenge:* If we don't change the *status quo*, we are subject to the following parade of horribles.
> *Solution:* Following is a solution that will correct or improve on the situation and avoid the challenges.

Step 3: Determine the Evidence to Support Your Three Points and Subpoints

Clothes, they say, may make the man. But evidence makes a great communicator.

Strong evidence can make a presentation sing and make you look wonderful to your client. Weak evidence makes your presentation seem boring, pompous, or (worst of all) lawyer-like.

The most powerful and interesting type of evidence in a presentation is a relevant story. But you can also use personal examples, expert testimony, analogies, quotes, statistics, or other facts.

People who make broad statements without supporting them with evidence are called "blowhards." And none of us need to be reminded that the legal profession has plenty of those. We tell our clients that unsupported statements are nothing but "wandering blah, blah." Great communicators never speak with "wandering blah, blah."

The Power of Stories

The Speechworks Effective Communication Code, Section 4, reads as follows:

> *Presenters shall strive to find relevant, interesting stories, business examples, and otherwise illustrative fables to illuminate their points. Such stories are as necessary as they are interesting, thereby rendering the presentation memorable. Presenters who consistently use interesting, relevant stories to illustrate their presentations shall be considered to be excellent communicators, and will attain great success in the legal profession.*

Indeed, one of the true marks of a great communicator is the deft use of stories. We noted earlier that spoken communication is a limited medium that does certain things well and other things poorly. For example, the spoken word isn't a great medium for conveying detailed instructions, technical information, or statistics. Our brains just don't seem to retain that data very well when it's told to us. But the spoken word is wonderful for conveying information through stories. Listeners tend to remember stories.

We lawyers can take a lesson from Don Hewitt, the producer of "60 Minutes," one of the most successful television programs in history. When asked to account for the success of his program, Hewitt said, "Four words. Tell me a story."

Lawyers often have plenty of great stories to illustrate ideas. But we need to use them!

Consider the lawyer/client who gave a presentation on non-disclosure agreements. To illustrate his point that negotiations shouldn't start without one, he told the following story:

> *"Don't start a negotiation without a non-disclosure agreement. If you do, bad things can happen. Let me give you an example. Recently a client of mine, let's call him Fred, ignored this advice. Fred owned a string of dry cleaners and started negotiations to buy another chain of dry cleaners.*
>
> *"The first negotiation meeting was a lunch between Fred and his counterpart, let's call him Jim. They started talking in detail*

about their businesses. Jim and Fred had built a strong bond and the deal was looking good. But Fred felt that he had revealed too much. He then had to go back and ask Jim to sign a non-disclosure agreement.

"Going back and seeking the agreement was awkward and could have been disastrous. As it happens, this deal actually took place. But the deal definitely stalled when the two sides had to go back and clarify exactly what information had been exchanged. It all could have been avoided with a simple non-disclosure agreement up front."

The above is a simple story that emphasizes the point. Nice job.

What Makes a Good Story?

The best stories do three things. Such stories are:

Detailed

Notice that the above story is about a specific deal involving dry cleaners. To protect confidentiality, the storyteller changed the parties' names.[2]

But he did use names. Those details give the story a richer feeling than if he had just said, "It was a small business buying another small business." Maybe the fact that the parties were dry cleaners isn't particularly relevant. But it adds to the story and therefore helps your listener remember it.

Relevant to the Listener's Situation

Relevance to the listener is always necessary; this should go without saying. But let me say it anyway. You want the listener to be able to put himself into the shoes of the story's protagonist. If you're talking about non-disclosure agreements in the context of business acquisitions, don't tell a story about the value of non-disclosure agreements when hiring contract employees.

---

[2] The client you're speaking to will respect your zealous protection of another client's confidentiality.

Short

The best stories are short and to the point. Too often presenters will latch onto a good story and embellish it too much. Lawyers can be especially guilty of this. Sometimes we fancy ourselves as old-time raconteurs. But listeners generally want a story that makes a point and makes it quickly. Don't drag it out.

Stories II: Personal Examples

Along with stories, personal examples are the best type of evidence. Personal examples are not only interesting, they add to the speaker's credibility.

I worked with a lawyer named Gary who spoke on how to deal with difficult opposing counsel in litigation. One key, he said, was to stay professional and focused on the case, gathering information through discovery rather than stooping to underhanded methods and sharp tactics.

To illustrate, he told a personal story:

> *"I dealt with a lawyer who pulled every dirty trick in the book. We'd get into a deposition and he'd start yelling at me as I questioned his client. He was a jerk. But we just focused on gathering information about their client's wrongdoing. We didn't stoop to his level. After three months and several very strong depositions, the blowhard and his client just folded up and dropped the case. They just went away! You beat blowhards by out-lawyering them."*

Expert Testimony

The expert testimony that I recommend is not the expert testimony we use in a courtroom. That is, you should strengthen your presentation by citing experts in support of your point. Expert testimony is, broadly speaking, any external source of information. It can be a published study, an article in a magazine, or a quote from a client.

I worked recently with the head of marketing for a law firm who wanted to build support for some humorous firm advertisements. To show that humor was a great advertising method, she cited a study that claimed that humor makes advertising more memorable. The study was her expert testimony.

Expert testimony can be valuable if you want to win new business. In "beauty contest" presentations, lawyers often refer to their own awards, such as being listed in local magazines as one of the city's top lawyers.

Analogies

If you're trying to explain something that is complicated, nothing helps like an analogy. Property law professors for years have relied on the "bundle of sticks" analogy to explain the concept of property rights. Just as you can give away some sticks from the bundle and keep the rest for yourself—the professors all say—you can give away some property rights and keep the rest for yourself. That's not a bad analogy.

One of my professors used to say that the Bill of Rights was a "constitutional leash on the great dog of government."

Analogy-Generating Machine

Here's an analogy-creation technique that works:

(1) Gather two or three colleagues in a conference room for a twenty-minute brainstorming session.
(2) Write down the legal concept that you're trying to clarify, such as "due process."
(3) Write down five commonplace items or services. For example:
    (a) Accordion
    (b) Cotton candy
    (c) Chameleon
    (d) Castor oil
    (e) Insurance
(4) List five ways in which your legal concept is like each of the above terms. For example, "due process is like . . ."
    (a) "An accordion because it can expand or contract depending on the circumstances."
    (b) "Cotton candy, because although it may look substantive, due process is actually very light, fluffy, and hard to define."

    (c) "A chameleon because it changes based on the circumstances."

    (d) "Castor oil since it can taste horrible, but can be necessary for health."

    (e) "Insurance because the more that's at stake, the more due process you need."

Now, all of these analogies may not be especially good ones. But if you sift through a few ideas, you'll come up with a couple of nice analogies.

And be forgiving with an analogy. It need not be perfect so long as it conveys an idea.

Killer Quotes

Sometimes a quote is a great way to make a point. But make sure the quote is memorable or at least interesting. Don't just quote someone for the sake of a quote.

When someone asked FDR the keys to a great speech he said, *"Be sincere. Be brief. Be seated."* That's a nice memorable quote. It's pithy. It's profound. It's clever. And it's even a little funny.

But too often we see presenters with long mundane quotes that would be better paraphrased by the presenter. The following is typical of the wrong way to use a quote. A presenter who is trying to explain different ways to create a strong international culture within a corporation projects a quote from Jack Welch, GE's former chief, on a screen:

> *"Many outsiders often asked me, 'How can the GE culture possibly work in various cultures across the world?' The answer to that question was always the same: Treat people with dignity and given them a voice. That's a message that translates across the globe."*

Okay, what Welch said is true and may well be strong management advice. It may even be worth describing as Welch's philosophy.

But it's not a strong quote. It's not pithy, funny, clever, or otherwise memorable. If it's not an interesting quote, say it in your own words and attribute the sentiment or idea to the person who came up with it. But don't quote just for the sake of having a quote. It's doesn't add to the presentation. And it makes you look dull.

Statistics

When we talk about statistics, remember the core idea for great spoken communication:

> *Spoken communication is a limited medium that does some things well and other things horribly.*

With that in mind, we need to watch for those things that spoken communication does poorly. And the thing that spoken communication does worse than anything else is: *Statistics, Numbers, and Data.* The spoken word doesn't communicate these things well. Listeners are just not good at remembering figures. So trying to deliver a lot of data with the spoken word is usually a waste of time.

Fortunately, most lawyers don't have to deal with numbers too often (otherwise we would have become accountants). But even we lawyers need to communicate numbers occasionally. I even took an accounting course in law school.

Great communicators usually even find a way to make numbers and statistics interesting. Here are a few rules to keep in mind when you have to use numbers in your presentation.

(1) *Focus on one or two key numbers rather than an entire spreadsheet.* Here's the scene. A presenter clicks to the next slide and it's a spreadsheet with dozens of small numbers. A quick view of the audience and you can see the eyes already starting to glaze over. Instead of discussing an entire spreadsheet, zero in on one key figure. "I'd like everyone to focus on our firm's revenue figure for last month. Let me discuss that figure in detail."

(2) *Tell the story behind the numbers.* I was working with an accountant who told me that he likes numbers because he sees them as the end point in a process. In other words, he likes numbers because he understands the story behind the numbers. And that's the key to making numbers come to life for listeners. For example, you might say, "Let me explain why the firm's revenues spiked last month. If you'll notice, we had

three huge banking deals all close within two weeks of each other. The billings on those deals were all three times the size of most deals. So we did well that month but we can't expect the trend to continue."

(3) *Keep the number portion brief and take questions.* A real trick is simply to give a very short treatment of the numbers and let the audience tell you what they're interested in. If they're really confused or interested, they'll let you know by the questions they ask.

Step 4: Determine Your Hook

Every good presentation begins with something that quickly grabs the listener's attention. It can be a clever quote, a story, or even a nifty fact. It doesn't have to be fancy. It can be a simple statement. Most important, it should be quick and relevant.

If you're giving a presentation to show a business how to protect its intellectual property, you might begin with a simple analogy:

"If you could come to my house and tour my basement, you'd see I have stored tons of stuff. There's an old lawnmower, a couple of old computers, books, furniture, appliances, luggage, and who knows what else. Well, we have learned that many business patent portfolios are like my basement. They are filled with useful stuff, but desperately in need of a housecleaning."

From there you can explain how your firm can help the client better manage its patent portfolio.

Or you might consider telling a story:

"I have a client that has been selling software for twenty years. This firm has had dozens of salespeople, all of whom have signed non-compete agreements. Now, over the years, those salespeople have come and gone. And in the entire twenty-year history of the firm, no one has ever challenged the non-compete agreement. But we would review the agreement every couple of years anyway. Six months ago the agreement was finally challenged. And we had to go to court to enjoin this salesperson from improperly competing against my client. We won."

Then you could explain the important points that a business person must remember about non-compete agreements. Or you could start with a simple, straightforward statement:

> *"The vast majority of the non-compete agreements that you will have your clients sign will be filed away and never seen again. But some day you're going to have to enforce this agreement. And we're going to talk today about how you can be confident that the agreement will stand up when that day finally comes."*

Can I Use a Joke as My Hook? Almost Never

Every once in a while I meet a lawyer who wants to be funny. That's okay. The best way to use humor is to poke fun at yourself with stories. (The use of self-deprecating humor shows confidence.) However, starting a presentation with a joke is usually a bad idea.

For example, I heard a lawyer use a joke during a CLE presentation on ERISA law. The lawyer stood at the podium in front of a room of fellow tax lawyers. After he was introduced he stated the following:

> *"Thank you for having me here today. I'm going to tell you what Elizabeth Taylor tells all her husbands. 'This won't take long.'"*

I have developed a four-pronged test for using jokes at the beginning of a presentation. Let's apply the test to the ERISA lawyer's joke.

Prong 1

The joke should be funny. That is, the joke should prompt at least some people to laugh out loud. This cuts out most opening jokes. Certainly no one laughed at the Elizabeth Taylor joke. At best the joke was an "eye roller" or a "groaner."

Prong 2

The joke should be relevant to the presentation. Certainly, the Elizabeth Taylor joke failed to meet this test. The lawyer was speaking on ERISA law, for Pete's sake!

Some people justify irrelevant jokes on the ground that they are "ice breakers." I don't buy this argument. How does a bad, irrelevant joke "break the ice"? To the contrary, I think it "thickens" the ice by making the audience think, "Oh brother! Another stupid joke at the beginning of a presentation. I hope that this isn't going to be as bad as the last presentation we had to sit through this morning."

Prong 3

The joke shouldn't be even remotely offensive. Don't dismiss this test too quickly. People get offended at some pretty innocuous things. Is the Elizabeth Taylor joke offensive? I've had many people tell me that they don't see how anyone could be offended by this joke. But I've also had other people tell me that they don't think jokes about divorce are ever funny. Also, what if there were a loyal Elizabeth Taylor fan among those tax lawyers? Is it worth annoying that person just to tell a stupid joke? Obviously not.

Prong 4

Don't start with a joke unless you are a funny person! Here's why. Let's assume that you've met the first three prongs of this joke test with a funny, relevant, inoffensive joke. Congratulations! You've gotten your presentation off to a roaring start! Your audience is riveted and laughing. But there is a problem. You've started off the presentation by getting your audience to do everyone's favorite thing: laugh. Now everyone is pumped about your ERISA presentation. They're thinking "Wow! This presentation is going to be funny." In other words, unless you have more good humor lined up, your presentation has already peaked and you have barely started. Better to build humor into the presentation with some funny, self-deprecating stories.

But If the Joke Works and Feels Right, Go for It!

If you can successfully tell a joke at the beginning of a presentation (I certainly can't), more power to you. I worked with a lawyer whose client was a large food company. He was speaking to managers in the company's marketing department about the importance of bringing deals to the lawyers early in the process. Like managers in many marketing departments, a number of the top managers in this lawyer's company had decided that lawyers were a pain in the neck who always screwed up their deals. As a result, the marketing managers had stopped consulting the lawyers. In trying to change this attitude, my client started a presentation with the following joke:

> *"A vice president of a large company picks up the telephone and calls his lawyer. The receptionist picks up the telephone and says 'This is Jones, Smith, and Russell. How can I direct your call?'*
>
> *"'I'd like to speak with Mr. Jones.'*
>
> *"The receptionist hesitates and says, 'I'm sorry but Mr. Jones died last week.'*
>
> *"'I'm sorry,' the VP says, and hangs up.*
>
> *"Five minutes later the VP dials the law firm again.*
>
> *"'This is Jones, Smith and Russell. How can I direct your call?'*
>
> *"The VP says, 'I'd like to speak with Mr. Jones.'*
>
> *"The receptionist hesitates a little more this time, but repeats, 'I'm sorry but Mr. Jones died last week.'*
>
> *"'I'm sorry,' the VP says again and hangs up.*
>
> *"The VP calls a third time and repeats, 'I'd like to speak with Mr. Jones.'*
>
> *"This time the receptionist is ready and says, 'Listen, Mister. I know that you've called twice in the last ten minutes. You know Mr. Jones is dead. Why do you keep calling?'*
>
> *"The VP responds, 'I just like hearing you say it.'"*

The lawyer (my client) then said that although many clients grow tired of their lawyers, he doesn't want to be seen as the enemy. Next he explained how he and his colleagues could actually help the deals close faster if they were consulted early in the process.

Did this joke meet the four-pronged test? I think so. It was funny and relevant. Offensive? Probably not to a room of non-lawyers (but never tell a lawyer joke to a room of lawyers). Indeed, in context I would put this joke in the category of self-deprecating humor. As for the fourth prong, this particular lawyer happened to be a funny person who had a very light tone to all of his presentations. The joke worked.

Final Point on Hooks: Skip the "Thank You's"

A lot of people like to start their presentations by thanking members of the audience. I think it's a bad idea. Better to just start your presentation. If you have to thank someone, quickly thank the person who introduced you, pause for a two or three seconds, and begin.

I may sound like a curmudgeon here. But who cares about the "thank you's"? Really. The people who are getting thanked certainly don't. Their best thanks will be a great presentation. I recently heard a top bar official take the first five minutes of his presentation to thank people in the audience. Five minutes! His thirty-minute presentation was terrible. I looked around the room and noticed that no one was paying attention. (By the way, I was one of the people he thanked. He wasn't thanking me for helping him with his presentation because I had nothing to do with it. I would have gladly traded my "thank you" for my thirty minutes back.)

Dump the thank you's. It's wasted breath. Just begin.

Step 5: Determine Your Wrap-Up

The wrap-up is the call to action at the end of your presentation. You can throw in an extra piece of evidence such as a story or a nice statistic. But remember that great communication is about connection and persuasion. You've just spent your presentation selling your listeners on something—be it the need to comply with a regulation, sign a contract, or adopt a legal strategy. As you wrap up, you must urge your clients to take action.

A wrap-up might sound something like this:

> "We've just talked about how to write contracts that comply with the new healthcare regulations. I'd like to urge everyone here to take the form agreements that I've handed out and start using them immediately. If you do that, your deals will be stronger, the regulators will be happy, and most important, your customers will love you."

I worked recently with a general counsel of a large bank who was preparing a presentation to his bank's board of directors. The presentation stressed the need to terminate a contract with a particular vendor because of business risk. The counsel gave a wonderful presentation, but after laying out the problem he just stopped. I told him that he needed one more element: a call to action.

He had to tell the board what he wanted from them. Did he want them to make a decision about the vendor? Or did he simply want them to keep the information in mind and be prepared to make a decision in the future? Either would have been fine. But he had to tell them what they were expected to do next.

ASSEMBLING YOUR PRESENTATION USING THE FORMULA

Now that you have all the pieces, you must assemble your presentation. Good presentations follow Socrates' old rule that you should "Tell 'em what you're going to tell 'em. Tell 'em. And then tell 'em what you told 'em."

Indeed, great communicators intuitively understand Socrates' idea of repetition. Don't forget that spoken communication is a limited medium. To make this medium work, the number of ideas must be limited and then repeated to ensure that the audience gets the idea.

With that in mind, we will break the presentation down into three parts.

Preview

This comes first. You state your Hook and your MO, and then quickly summarize your three points. When done effectively, the preview acts as a clear "road map" for your listeners.

Body of the Presentation

This is the "meat" of the presentation where you go into detail with each of your three points, telling stories, using analogies, quotes, etc.

Recap and Wrap

This is where you restate your MO and three points. Remember that spoken communication is a notoriously flawed and inefficient medium. Redundancy ensures that your points are remembered. After recapping, you call your listeners to action with your wrap.

Your Great Communicator Presentation Form

Use this form to organize your presentation.

Preview (Tell 'Em What You're Going to Tell 'Em)

Hook:

_____

_____

Message Objective:

If you _____

Then you will _____

Three Points:

(1) _____

(2) _____

(3) _____

Body of the Presentation (Tell 'Em)

Point 1. _____

Evidence: _____

_____

_____.

Point 2. _____

Evidence: _____

_____

_____.

Point 3. _____

Evidence: _____

_____

_____.

Recap and Wrap (Tell 'Em What You Told 'Em)

Message Objective:

If you _____

Then you will _____

Three Points:

(1) _____

(2) _____

(3) _____

Wrap: _____

_____

_____.

THE FORMULA IN ACTION

I recently worked with an antitrust lawyer who was asked to help managers of his large food company client understand and comply with antitrust laws. It is important that any lawyer who is teaching about the law focus more on helping the client learn *what to do*, rather than focusing on *what the law says*. So that's what we urged the antitrust lawyer to do in his presentation.

Preview

Hook (Attention Grabber)

"I saw a New Yorker Magazine cover recently that showed what was clearly one of those stodgy gentlemen's clubs. There were overstuffed leather chairs, imported carpets, hunting prints on the walls. And there were lots of balding old businessmen walking around in three-piece suits, holding martinis, smoking big cigars. The only thing odd about this picture was that after a while you noticed that all these nicely dressed, smiling businessmen were wearing handcuffs!

"And as an antitrust lawyer, I realized that this was my worst nightmare. Many of you may not know it, but some of the activity that goes on in a place like this business can lead you to jail if you're not careful. And believe me, the jails are not fine gentlemen's clubs like the one on the cover of The New Yorker."

Message Objective ("If/Then" Statement)

"I'm here today to discuss with you the essentials of antitrust law. And if you follow the guidelines I give you today, you will stay *out of jail and avoid having your company potentially assessed millions of dollars in penalties."*

Three Points

"I'm going to talk to you today about three things:

- *"(1) Dealing with competitors.*
- *"(2) Factors to consider when you're doing something that will seriously harm a competitor.*
- *"(3) Issues surrounding what you put in documents."*

Body of the Presentation

Point 1: Dealing with Competitors

Subjects to avoid during discussions:

- ▸ Price, bids, volumes, plans for customers.
- ▸ Story about Archer Daniels Midland, whose managers and officers met with competitors in hotel rooms and conference rooms around the world to divide the market. They were caught by the FBI on videotape and prosecuted. People went to jail.
- ▸ Trade association concerns. When you're in associations where you meet with competitors, you must be careful. Discussions of subjects such as lobbying and industry legislation at trade associations are legitimate.
- ▸ A "conspiracy" can be implied from small things, even if there is no formal agreement with competitors. So be careful. Remember the story about the ADM executive who wrote, "The competitor is our friend. The customer is our enemy." That statement was considered to be evidence of a conspiracy.

Point 2: Actions That Have Adverse Impact on Competition

There is nothing inherently wrong with competing vigorously in the marketplace. That's what you're supposed to do. But certain activities require consultation with counsel:

▶ *Predatory pricing.* If you're planning to sell a product at below cost, that could suggest antitrust activity. So before you do something like that, call the lawyers in for consultation.

▶ *Exclusivity agreements.* If you're about to sign a huge deal with a customer that will displace a rival, be careful. Consult with the lawyers. Remember how Microsoft tried to get computer makers to include Microsoft Explorer pre-installed on computers rather than Netscape. This was one of the activities that led to the unprecedented antitrust case against Microsoft.

▶ *Tying arrangements.* Be careful about requiring a customer to buy a second product as a condition of getting a first product. Example: If Microsoft would not let you buy Windows if you didn't also buy PowerPoint, that would be tying.

Point 3: Issues Surrounding What You Put in Documents

Remember that everything you say or write can come back to haunt you. But what you write can be especially troublesome. So be careful.

▶ Be careful what you write in e-mail. For example, an e-mail from an alleged monopolist that said "We're going to cut off their oxygen" might sound like unfair trade practices.

▶ Avoid inflammatory phrases such as, "We're going to dominate," "Squish the competition like a bug," "Put a lid on the competition," or "Squeeze them until they scream."

Recap and Wrap

If you follow these basic guidelines, you will keep yourself and your business out of trouble:

▶ When dealing with competitors, stay away from talk about prices, dividing up the market, what your plans are, etc.

▶ When you're considering activities that might be construed as predatory pricing, tying, or exclusivity agreements, be careful. Call the lawyers before completing the deal.

▶ And be careful what you put in documents.

So keep these basics in mind and you'll keep the company out of trouble. You'll also keep yourself out of jail.

Post-Presentation Analysis

So what did this presentation do well? It focused on simple things that the client needed to do, such as: (1) don't discuss prices with the competitor; (2) call the lawyers when you're thinking about doing things that will cause extreme pain to the competitor; and (3) be careful what you put in writing because it can come back to haunt you. The presentation then brought the concepts to life with simple, easy-to-relate-to examples.

Just as important is what the speaker left out of the presentation. The presentation omitted complex legal policy issues and debates, didn't give any detailed analysis of legal issues, and didn't cite case names. Very few lawyers understand how little their clients care about legal details. (I've even heard presentations to clients where statute numbers and case citations were included.) Most clients don't care about this stuff. They just want to know what to do to stay out of trouble and help their businesses grow.

SOME FINAL CONCERNS

Transitions or Presentation Mile-Markers

If you're like me, you love mile markers when you drive on long trips. For some reason, I find it comforting and orienting to know when I have 92 miles left on a drive to New York City. And thirty minutes later I get the same feeling when I learn that New York City is then only 56 miles away.

For your listeners, transitions are the mile markers of your presentation. Every once in a while you must remind your audience how much they've learned and how close they are to the end. This is especially true when you're speaking about complex topics like the law.

You accomplish this orienting process with clear transitions. A clear transition has three elements:

(1) A brief recap of the first point.

(2) An indication that the first point is finished, whether this is implicit or explicit.

(3) An indication that we're now moving on to the next point.

This need not be complicated. Remember that the sole goal of the transition is to give the listener a mental cue as to where we are in the presentation. It can sound like this:

> "We're now done with the first point, what our policy has been in the past. I'd like to move now to the second point, what the policy is now."

Or you could try to be a little smoother:

> "Okay, we've talked about what this tax law says today; now let's move to point two: what will happen if the law isn't changed?"

Smooth or clunky doesn't matter. What's important is that all you're really doing is posting mile markers for your listeners. They're on a journey with you and need to know how far it is to the finish line.

A Note on Jargon: Dump It

Jargon can cost you money. A *Forbes* report stated that 30% of technology projects in the U.S. are canceled before completion. The cost: $75 billion a year. The report stated that *low-tech* executives cancel projects when they fail to understand *high-tech* consultants' "geek speak." Certainly we attorneys are no less guilty of frustrating our clients with excess legalese.

The fact is that jargon is usually not necessary and can often frustrate your listeners. When I was practicing law, I was negotiating an agreement with opposing counsel who kept referring to an "NDA." I didn't know what he was talking about. "What is an NDA?" I said. He looked at me like I was an idiot. "A non-disclosure agreement," he said.

By this time I had spent five years drafting the very documents that he so cavalierly called "NDAs." I knew so-called "NDAs" better than he did. I just had never used that term. I used the boring old "confidentiality agreement," a jargon-free term that did a pretty good job of conveying what the document actually accomplished. The opposing counsel's NDA jargon accomplished nothing other than to antagonize me.

Scrubbing your presentations free of jargon is especially important if you want to connect with clients. A lawyer for a large investment firm had to give a presentation on legal developments to the investment advisors who sold her company's products. Rather than talking about the SEC ruling that prohibits the use of "soft dollar arrangements," she connected with her audience's interests by explaining that the new ruling prohibited "waiving commissions in exchange for new business referrals." Her presentation was a hit because she dumped the jargon and used the language of her listeners.

Mark Twain said, "If you can catch an adverb, kill it." A corollary could be, "If you can catch some jargon, strangle it."

Quick Presentation Checklist

Like all people in business, lawyers spend too much time writing presentations and too little time practicing delivery of the presentation. This page is designed to give you a quick checklist for creating your message in half the usual time so that you can concentrate on the latter. For your next presentation, turn to this page and simply check off each part of your presentation. When you've checked off everything, and assembled your message, start practicing. With enough practice, almost anyone can give a great presentation.

☑ *Message Objective*

▸ The presentation has a clear MO.

"If you [do what I recommend], then you will [get what you want]."

▸ The MO explicitly states that the listener's goals will be achieved by doing what the presenter proposes or argues for during the presentation.

"If you approve this new tax treatment, you will protect your business from tax liability."

☑ *Three Points*

The presentation has no more than three points in support of the MO:

> *"I'd like to talk about three things today:*
>
> *"(1) Why we need to change our hiring policy.*
>
> *"(2) What we must do to comply with the new law.*
>
> *"(3) The penalties and risks of failing to comply with the law."*

☑ *Evidence*

Each point is supported by evidence:

▸ The presentation includes detailed stories and business examples as illustrations.

> *"Let me tell you a story about what happens when we fail to comply with OSHA safety standards."*

▸ Statistics are kept to a minimum and explained in a way that helps the listener see the significance of a few key numbers.

> *"The most important thing you need to know about this line of business is that it is high-risk. We make only $2 million a year but have potential liability of $2 million a day."*

▸ The presentation contains personal examples.

> *"Recently one of my clients adopted a new hiring policy. Let me tell you how they made the change successfully. . . ."*

☑ *Hook*

The presentation grabs the listener with a "gee-whiz" fact, a relevant story, or a compelling question:

> *"The Crown Jewels of England are kept under guard in the Tower of London. Our company has far more valuable treasures*

which are largely unprotected. I'm talking about some of our most important trade secrets. I'd like to talk today about how to keep our company's treasures as safe as the Crown Jewels of England."

 Recap

The presentation concludes by recapping the message object and the three supporting points.

 Wrap

The presentation contains a final motivating wrap-up story or call to action:

"I've talked today about how we can protect this firm from serious litigation. Let's begin implementing my plan immediately."

CHAPTER **16**

Communicating with a Style That Connects

INTRODUCTION

WHY ARE LAWYERS SUSPICIOUS OF GOOD PRESENTATION SKILLS?

HOW WE LOOK AND SOUND IS JUST AS CRITICAL FOR LAWYERS AS FOR OTHERS

DEVELOPING STYLE: FINDING MAXIMUM YOU

MASTERING FILLER WORDS

YOU DON'T SPEAK TOO FAST, BUT YOU PROBABLY DON'T PAUSE

EYE CONTACT

NOW IT'S TIME TO SMILE; NO, I'M SERIOUS. IT'S TIME TO SMILE!

GESTURES AND MOVEMENT

A CONFIDENT PRESENCE: WEAR THOSE BOOTS AND SPURS

PICK A SKILL AND WORK ON IT FOR A MONTH

REHEARSAL: IT'S THE KEY TO BEING GREAT

INTRODUCTION

I was working with an associate at a large commercial law firm on a presentation that she was planning to give to the partners of a German accounting firm. The associate's presentation was going to explain how best to incorporate a business in the United States.

As she was rehearsing, I kept saying the same thing, over and over: "Speak with more passion. You don't sound like you enjoy this stuff. You need to get excited."

But no matter how hard I pushed, the associate would not let loose and speak with passion. Finally, she looked at me, exasperated. "Most lawyers don't speak with that kind of excitement," she said.

"I know," I said. "The problem with that argument, however, is that most lawyers stink."

With regard to passion and personal style, lawyers as a group are clueless. To be sure, there are exceptions. A few lawyers have learned how to communicate with the kind of personal style that conveys passion and connects with listeners.

In this section, you will learn how to develop and hone a personal communication style that will allow you to connect with your listeners. The goal is not to become "slick." Rather, it is to find ways to connect rather than appear to be another nerdy, overly serious lawyer.

We will discuss how to:

▶ Develop a style we call "Maximum You."
▶ Have great voice energy.
▶ Move and gesture effectively during presentations.
▶ Have the kind of facial energy that connects with listeners.

WHY ARE LAWYERS SUSPICIOUS OF GOOD PRESENTATION SKILLS?

When I stopped practicing law to enter the communication skills training business, I soon started hearing rumors about how difficult it was to work with lawyers. "Get ready for a tough day, they're lawyers," would be the common complaint of a trainer preparing to work with lawyers. As an attorney, I was skeptical. "Everyone loves to hate lawyers," I thought.

But when I first began working with lawyers, I also found them to be tough to train, especially with regard to the fluffier "presentation skills" of communication skills coaching. We lawyers are trained to question. And our minds are rigorous. We tend to look at the fluffier side of training with a healthy dose of skepticism.

When I work with lawyers and try to encourage them to communicate with more passion and less stoicism, following are some typical excuses (and my responses):

- ▶ *"Our firm has a more serious culture than others."* I hear this from people in almost all firms (and businesses for that matter). Everyone thinks his or her business or firm has a serious culture. But I can almost always find a few communicators in any business who don't fit this mold. These great communicators prove that passion works even in a law firm culture.

- ▶ *"Speaking with passion and excitement about such a serious subject doesn't seem proper to me."* We aren't funeral directors. We're lawyers. And if you can't be passionate about the law, matters of justice, and helping businesses succeed, then you should look for another profession. (And no doubt, many lawyers need to quit the business. But that's another book.)

- ▶ *"I never get excited."* This is ridiculous and is usually a disingenuous excuse. Of course you get excited. You get excited when you go home and speak to your husband or wife about the crazy thing that happened at work that day. Now, we just need to find a way for you to get excited when you're working.

- ▶ *"What you're asking me to do doesn't feel natural."* So what? Many things feel unnatural the first time you do them. That doesn't make them wrong. The first time you swing a golf club correctly it doesn't feel natural. It's through practice that things start to feel natural.

> *"I went to law school to practice law, not to be a salesman."* I give this answer credit for honesty. Lawyers can be cerebral and inward-looking. And that's good. We also tend to discount the value of non-substantive things such as how we look and sound. But just because something such as appearance is non-substantive doesn't mean it's not critically important.

HOW WE LOOK AND SOUND IS JUST AS CRITICAL FOR LAWYERS AS FOR OTHERS

The law is a brainy business. You don't get through *Pennoyer v. Neff* without having a lot of smarts. But great communicators know that how they look and sound has a major impact on how well they connect with clients.

There is research that supports this idea that *how* you say something matters as much as or more than *what* you say. Some years ago Dr. Albert Mehrabian of UCLA pioneered a study of how we communicate, and lawyers should heed what he found if we want to communicate effectively.[1]

One of Mehrabian's studies included the following statistics:

> Fifty-five percent (55%) of the impression we make when we communicate is based on how we look. Included in this percentage is how we stand, our gestures, eye contact, facial expression, and overall body language.

> Thirty-eight percent (38%) of the impression we make when we communicate is based on how we sound. When we speak, do our voices convey passion and excitement? Or do we sound like we are bored?

> Seven percent (7%) (yes, it's true) of the impression we make when we communicate is based on the actual content of what we say.

So what do we lawyers make of a study that says style matters more than substance? When I tell lawyers about this study, I usually

---

[1] A. Mehrabian, *Silent Messages* (Belmont, CA: Wadsworth, 1981).

get disbelieving looks. But one thing lawyers certainly can agree on is that people (clients included) make important judgments based on non-substantive reasons.

When lawyers complain that focusing too much on style is offensive, I tell them about a big-firm lawyer who was deciding which accounting expert to hire as a testifying expert in a major litigation case. In turning down one highly qualified expert, the deciding lawyer told the accountant some time later, "You didn't have enough gray hair." And he wasn't joking!

The fact of the matter is, whether you agree with the Mehrabian study or not, you can't deny that how you look and sound is a critical part of whether you communicate effectively. After all, the listener can't look into your brain and see all that intelligence like some brimming fuel tank. All that your listener sees is how you look and sound combined with what you say.

So like it or not, if you want to be the kind of communicator who connects with clients, you're going to have to pay attention to the passion in your voice, the smile on your face, and the way you make eye contact. That's what the great communicators do.

DEVELOPING STYLE: FINDING MAXIMUM YOU

"I don't want to seem like a huckster."

That's the complaint I get over and over again from lawyers who resist shedding the boring, stoic, stereotypical image of our profession. "I don't want you to *be* a huckster," I respond. "But I do want you to be yourself. And you can't tell me that Maximum You is this dull."

That's right. I want you to communicate like the "Maximum You." As you go through this section on presentation skills, every specific tip—from how to energize your voice to how to connect with your eyes—is aimed at helping develop the stylistic goal of Maximum You.

What Is Maximum You?

Maximum You is how you naturally communicate when you're excited. It's how you communicate when you're boasting to a close friend about your top-ranked college basketball team. It's how you communicate when you're complaining to your spouse about "what those idiots at the office did today." It's how you communicate when you're speaking passionately to friends about something you care about.

Finding Maximum Jack

I was working with a healthcare lawyer named Jack, trying to get him to speak with more passion. We were doing exercises where I had him describe his most current deal. Every time he spoke, his eyes took on a blank, inward look. It was almost as if he were carefully weighing each word and proofreading on some sort of internal computer screen before spitting it out. His voice had a flat, lawyer-like monotone. He sounded like a caricature of a stoic lawyer.

I said "Jack, tell me something you feel passionate about." He thought about it for a moment and starting talking about how he is an accomplished automobile mechanic and used to work fixing cars. Then he went on to discuss how he had bought an old Corvette for his son and that they were working on it together. As he spoke, suddenly his eyes lit up and he was smiling.

He described how his son loves the car and loves taking apart the carburetor, cleaning it, and putting it back together again. His voice was a roller coaster of excitement, getting alternatively loud, soft, speeding up, and then slowing down.

"That's it," I said. "That's Maximum Jack. That's how I want you to speak about your latest deal. I want you to fix in your mind right now exactly how you're communicating. How it feels. How your voice sounds."

He paused for a moment as if trying to take a snapshot in his mind.

"Now, I want you to go back and describe the deal for me with the same energy."

And he did much better! He still reverted somewhat to the more stoic style. But he certainly understood that he had to seem more connected to the listener.

Now, was I coercing Jack into communicating like a stereotypical used car salesman? No! I was merely trying to get him to communicate like he commonly does when he's relaxed and speaking of something about which he's passionate.

That's what Maximum You is all about.

It's Sort of Like Michelangelo's David

Finding Maximum You is a lot like the process that Michelangelo reportedly used when he sculpted his famous statue *David*. According to the story, when someone asked the great artist how he decided to create his beautiful sculpture, Michelangelo famously replied that he imagined the figure within the stone and simply carved away everything that didn't belong, that "wasn't *David*."

Finding Maximum You is a similar process. Just strip away everything that isn't you and bring what's left to your next presentation. Here are some steps to help:

(1) *Use a self-rating system to find Maximum You.* Rate your communication style throughout the day on a scale of 1 to 10. A "1" is the low energy voice you use when the telephone rings in the middle of the night and you roll over in bed, grab the phone, and say "hello." A "10" is when you're fully engaged, connected with the listener, and speaking with passion. Most people in business communicate at about a "5" most of the time. Maybe you only reach "10" when you're speaking with your spouse or a close friend. Maybe you need a couple of glasses of wine to get there. But watch for it. That "10" is "Maximum You."

(2) *Make a videotape.* Not a real videotape (although you can if you choose). Make a mental videotape of yourself when you've reached Maximum You. Remember how it feels. Replay it in your mind several times. What you should do is try to remember how it feels and recreate that feeling.

(3) *Rehearse presentations at a "10."* When you're practicing your presentation (you do practice your presentations, don't you?), close the door and try turning on the "10." No one is going to see you. Just let it all hang out. Now try really videotaping yourself to see how you look.

(4) *Deliver at a "10."* Once you're comfortable that you can turn on Maximum You in rehearsal, start giving your real presentations at Maximum You.

Fight the Legal Culture: Be Maximum You

Learning to communicate like Maximum You is not easy. It takes some practice and it's good to get some coaching. But finding Maximum You is not nearly as difficult as overcoming the cultural hesitancy in the legal world to "letting it all hang out" and being yourself. This takes some guts.

At the beginning of this section, I told you about a woman attorney who resisted speaking with passion because that's not the way most lawyers communicate. She was right. Most lawyers (and most people in business, for that matter) speak with a low-energy, overserious style. Don't you speak like that. Be one of the few. Be brave. Be Maximum You.

Elements of Maximum You

One way to approach Maximum You is to recognize when you've achieved your goal at least once, and then try to replicate your approach when it's time to speak. Another way to get there is to learn each separate element of what makes up compelling communication skills. The key elements include:

- ▶ Voice energy
- ▶ Facial energy
- ▶ Gestures and movement

Once you've mastered these things separately, you will be approaching Maximum You.

Keys to Voice Energy

Voice energy is about music in the voice. There is a story about Mark Twain when he lost a favorite pair of cufflinks. He was getting ready to give a speech (he made a lot of money speaking) and he was tearing his bedroom apart. As he searched his drawers, he was cursing a blue streak.

Meanwhile, his wife was in the other room, fuming over her husband's tirade. After all these years, she had decided it was finally time to do something about her husband's cursing.

So Olivia Langdon Clemens stood in the doorway of her bedroom, waiting patiently for her husband to finish swearing. And, according to the story, when he finished, she began to repeat back to him every curse word he had just said. *Except that she said the words in a flat monotone.*

Mark Twain listened with a bemused expression. And when she finished, he looked at his wife and said, "Darlin'. You've got the words, but you ain't got the *music.*"

Voice energy is about music in the voice. It's about speaking with the kind of energy that makes your words sing. It's about giving the listener the sense that you care passionately about what you're saying.

Indeed, we've repeatedly discussed how spoken communication is not very good at conveying complex ideas and data. *But spoken communication is great at conveying emotion.* And you do that largely with your vocal energy. To speak without energy is like driving a Porsche without ever putting it into overdrive. Sure, you might get where you're going. But you're failing to utilize the machine's full potential. It's a waste. Great communicators know how to take the machine on the road and open it up.

What Does Voice Energy Actually Do for You?

One famous piece of litigation wisdom goes something like this:

> *"If you don't have the facts on your side, you pound on the law. And if you don't have the law on your side, you pound on the facts. If you have neither on your side, you pound on the table."*

Well, I don't recommend pounding on the table. But I do believe that energy and emotion can be highly engaging and persuasive. That is exactly what voice energy can do. It can persuade and move your listeners. Voice energy sells.

Indeed, voice energy creates a force that pulls the listener in. We've all experienced this force. Several years ago I was at a friend's home with my wife and three kids for dinner and an evening with my friend, his wife, and his four kids. It was a wonderful evening of wine and conversation.

After a delicious steak dinner, my friend looked at me and said, "Hey Joey, would you like to go upstairs and see my stamp collection?" I'm not crazy about stamps. I never understood their attraction. But since I had eaten his steaks and drunk his wine, I decided to go upstairs and look at the stamp collection.

When we got upstairs, my friend took down an album and began to show me one of his prized stamps. As he was speaking, his voice was literally a roller coaster of excitement as he described the history and value of this stamp. In fact, he was so excited that I start to get a little excited myself. I actually started wondering if I might like to collect stamps.

That's what voice energy can do. It sweeps listeners up. It can sell ideas. It can make people believe you.

And great communicators know that every time they're speaking with a client or a colleague about some aspect of the law, they're selling stamps.

Make Your Voice Like a Roller Coaster

To add excitement to your voice, make your voice like a roller coaster, riding up and down and with interesting changes in cadence. Similarly, you need to make your voice do the same thing by varying speed and volume. Loud. Soft. Fast. Slow.

In our workshops, we have our clients stand to read the following sentences as directed. The more you try to ham it up, the more you accomplish.

READ LOUDLY.
Volume adds emphasis to an important word or phrase.
Read softly.
A whisper acts as a magnet and pulls the listener to you.
Read fast.
Speaking rapidly excites and energizes an audience.
Read slowly.
A slow rate of speech creates a mood of awe and wonder.

Tape record yourself and play it back. Or team up with a colleague and listen to each other. Many of our clients are stunned to learn that their "loud" voice doesn't sound very loud at all and their soft voice has the exact same volume as their usual speech.

The Contrast Is the Thing

Your voice shouldn't be just loud or soft. It should ride up and down, creating counterpoint and range. We have many clients who speak loudly all the time. Those clients often think that volume is energy, and they usually do sound enthusiastic at first. But after a few minutes, they just seem to be shouting as if the listeners were deaf.

The drama in your voice comes from speaking both loud and soft, fast and slow, all in the same thought.

To test your own sense of contrast, following is another exercise we do with our clients. Read the sentences as directed.

First, read the first half loudly and the second half softly, with a long pause in the middle:

ARE WE GOING TO TAKE ALL THIS WORK . . . *and throw it down the drain?*

Second, read the first half quickly and the second half slowly, with a long pause in the middle:

How long have you been working on this project? . . . H a s i t b e e n 2 5 w e e k s ?

Calibrating Your Instrument with a Tape Recorder

Your voice is your primary instrument for communication. Yet most of us have no idea how we sound to the outside world. For example, have you ever heard yourself on tape? Were you shocked at how you sounded? That's a common experience. But that *is* how you sound. Yet, you will have a difficult time showing passion if you don't know what your voice sounds like to others.

The great communicators play their voices like a finely calibrated instrument, using the full range of volume and cadences to create impressions.

You can calibrate your "instrument" by practicing your presentations with a tape recorder and listening to yourself. Try attempting various effects. For example, read the role-plays below. Then give yourself one minute to act out the role on videotape. Ham it up. On a scale of 1 to 10 (with "10" being Maximum You), shoot for a "12."

▶ *Used car salesman:* Try saying your presentation like you're a slick-talking salesman. Even if it "feels" wrong when you're doing it, listen to yourself, and you might be surprised at how good it sounds.

▶ *Angry boss:* This exercise should teach you how to express anger. You might find that soft can be just as angry as loud.

▶ *The dramatic closing argument:* Okay. So the dramatic closing argument (à la television's "The Practice") doesn't happen that often in real life. But use this exercise to learn how to add energy and drama to your voice.

▶ *The passionate politician:* Pick a political issue about which you feel passionately and imagine that you're giving a rousing stump speech. But don't just shout. Get loud and soft, fast and slow. Remember that it's the contrast that creates the drama.

▶ *The inspirational coach:* Coaches get paid a lot to speak at corporate events. That's because they're motivators. They understand that vocal energy is the key to moving listeners. Pretend that your team is losing and you want to get them fired up for the second half of the game.

If you can convey passion during these exercises, you should be able to do the same when you speak about your own business topics. Spoken communication is always something of a performance. Great communicators know that when it's show time, it's time to turn on the passion.

The Pause: Sign of a Master Communicator

Mark Twain said, "The right word may be effective, but no word was ever as effective as a rightly timed pause."[2]

And although Mark Twain wasn't a lawyer, he was certainly a master when it came to communication.

Pausing is an incredible tool for adding energy to the voice. A pause is so versatile, it is like the Swiss Army Knife of the

---

[2] A. B. Paine & W. D. Howells, eds., "Introduction," *Mark Twain's Speeches* (1923).

communicator's toolbox. How can a pause help lawyers communicate? Let us count the ways. Pausing helps you:

▶ Create a sense of drama by pulling the audience in.

▶ Gather your thoughts if you can't remember them (you look cool even if you're frantically trying to remember what to say next).

▶ Grab a chance to breathe.

▶ Replace filler phrases like "um" and "you know" (we lawyers have been known to lay an "uh" on a listener or two).

▶ Let listeners absorb your idea.

▶ Emphasize a key word or phrase.

The Key to Pausing? Hold It!

We've all heard the saying, "Silence is golden." Judging from many speakers' inability to pause during presentations, silence is also painful and terrifying.

My clients are often amazed at how difficult it is to hold a pause for the three or four seconds needed to have any impact. In our workshops, we do an exercise where we have participants read the following phrase, with long pauses:

A pause shows poise . . . control . . . confidence . . . use it . . . master it.

Without fail, we'll have people read the phrase as follows:

A pause shows poise, control, confidence, use it master it.

No pauses at all. "So how did those pauses feel," I will ask. The answer is always, "They felt fine." I will then turn to the other participants in the workshop. "Did he pause?" I'll ask.

When everyone shakes his head "No," the participant will look surprised. And I am certain that the surprise is sincere. That's because even a short pause can seem like an eternity if you're not used to pausing.

But, for a pause to have impact, you have to hold it . . . . for what seems like a long time!

How long? How about four seconds?

Try this: Call your voice mail and read the following sentence, tapping out four beats at the slash marks:

> *"In ten years of law practice // this is the worst case of attorney malfeasance // I have ever seen."*

If you're like many people, those four beats *felt* like a long time. Now listen to your voice mail. Chances are that those four beats don't sound as long as they felt. In fact, most people find that those four beats make them sound confident, even if they were cringing during the silence when they were leaving the message.

MASTERING FILLER WORDS

Probably no profession has uttered more "ums" or "uhs" than the legal profession. Such words are a clear indication that the speaker's style is halting and uncertain. Eliminate these filler words. The lack of "ums" and "uhs" alone can make you sound more confident.

And it's not hard to do. Just pause. Every time you feel that you're about to use a filler word, pause instead.

Easier said than done?

Maybe so. But I did it. And it wasn't that hard. I was a filler word addict. But early in my legal career I eliminated my filler words with a three-step process:

Four Weeks of Focus

I resolved to work on the problem for several weeks, And in fact this took about three weeks. Four should certainly be enough. Just pick a time period and stick with it.

Reticular Activation

In order to deal with my own "filler word" problem, I resolved several years ago to be conscious of the problem. I made a mental note that I was going to notice my "uhs" and "ums." This is not as hard as it seems when you rely on the psychological concept of "reticular activation." Reticular activation allows you to sensitize your mind to certain things.

For example, when I bought my 2004 Honda Accord, I suddenly started seeing lots of 2004 Accords. There wasn't an actual increase in the number of Accords on the road. I just started noticing them. My mind became sensitized to them, whereas previously I had screened out Accords while I thought of other things.

You can use the same concept of reticular activation to become conscious of your filler words. Just tell yourself that you're going to start noticing them and you'll be surprised. You'll notice every one.

Pausing

This is how I eliminated my filler words. Every time I felt like I was going to use a filler word, I would close my mouth and pause. It wasn't easy at first. It felt like I was always pausing. Before long, I started pausing automatically instead of using the filler words. I turned a liability (the filler word) into an asset (a cool pause). Eventually, I didn't have to pause nearly as much but, rather, was using the pause consciously as a tool for creating effect.

You Don't Speak Too Fast, but You Probably Don't Pause

In our workshops, we ask our clients if anyone has ever told them that they speak too fast. Invariably, some hands go up. But we always note that it's virtually impossible to talk too fast for someone to understand you. Even the fastest talkers speak no faster than 175 words a minute, and the human ear can perceive more than 300 words a minute. So you're not speaking too fast.

When people say that you speak too fast, they generally mean that they're hearing all the words, but need time to digest what you're saying. Your listeners require that you pause so that they can absorb your ideas.

Pause to Hide Your Nerves

Even great speakers get nervous at the beginning of a big presentation. But they don't show it. One way to look calm under pressure is to pause.

Suppose you've just been introduced and you walk up to the stage to begin your presentation. You're really feeling nervous.

Here's what to do: Take a moment to straighten your notes. Take a breath (not a heavy sigh that makes you look nervous, but a breath nonetheless). Then pause and look out at the audience for a moment with a smile. Wait about five seconds. Then begin.

You'll look confident even if you're scared to death.

EYE CONTACT

It's Critical!

Eye contact is obviously important (at least in American culture). But I'm always surprised at how many big firm lawyers don't make eye contact very well. A partner at a large firm was attending one of our two-day programs. He had been practicing law for about fifteen years and had established a nice niche for himself in the leasing of large equipment. Over the two days of the program, however, I noticed that he made terrible eye contact.

Not only did he have trouble making eye contact during presentations, he had trouble making eye contact during one-on-one conversations. I spoke with him privately and said, "Has anyone ever told you that you don't make very good eye contact?"

He was stunned. And at first he seemed a little offended. But then he said, "No. No one's ever mentioned it to me." After discussing it a while, he confessed that he knew he didn't make eye contact because he found it a little uncomfortable. But no one seemed alienated so he hadn't focused on this as a problem.

Unfortunately, it *is* a problem. People do notice. When we ask people in our programs if they know anyone who makes poor eye contact, some people always raise their hands.

We must stress that making eye contact is important. And if you're bad at it, it's a problem. The only reason you may not know it's a problem is because no one is going to tell you.

Eye Contact During Presentations: Banish the "Devil in the Paper"

The first step in improving your eye contact during presentations is to stop relying on your notes. Too many lawyers rely on detailed notes and usually appear to be reading a script. Overreliance on notes drains the energy from your voice. Instead, concentrate on rehearsing your presentation enough so that you speak with only occasional references to your notes.

In this regard, we could all take a lesson from former UN Ambassador Andrew Young. Although he is not a lawyer, the former civil rights leader, congressman, and Atlanta mayor is certainly a master communicator in his own right. No one gives a better speech than Ambassador Young.

But it wasn't always that way. Many years ago, when he was a young minister just out of the seminary, Reverend Young learned a lesson about the importance of eye contact.

He was invited to give a sermon at a small Baptist church in Beachton, Georgia. And when it was time to go up to the pulpit, he reached into his breast pocket to pull out his written sermon. As he walked to the front of the church, a deacon saw him with his written speech and pulled him aside and asked about the notes. When the twenty-one-year-old minister told the deacon that he was getting ready to go up and read his sermon, the deacon objected. "We worship with the Primitive Baptists," the deacon said. "They believe that if anything is on paper, then the devil has something to do with it. They want to know that whatever you say comes from your heart, not from a piece of paper."

With that, Young put away his notes and spoke from his heart. To this day Andrew Young uses no notes when he gives a presentation.

We should all follow Andrew Young's lead. Few things are more boring than having a person read a speech to you. Instead, you should rehearse your presentation until you know it perfectly and need your notes only as an occasional reminder. Then you can make great eye contact with the audience and speak from your heart.

Reading PowerPoint

Just as you shouldn't read your notes, you also shouldn't read PowerPoint slides when you show them. If you want to refer casually to your slides as they are being projected, that's fine. But too often lawyers with detailed PowerPoint presentations turn their backs to the audience and narrate their presentations as if the slides are just a glorified script.

There are few violations of communication etiquette worse than reading a presentation. Learn to speak without notes and you'll be on your way to stardom.

The Nature of Eye Contact: Random Mini-Conversations

To best understand how to make eye contact, don't think of your presentation as a speech to a group. Instead, think of it as a series of mini-conversations with all the individuals in the room. Make eye contact with a single person and speak to him for thirty seconds or so, long enough for you to feel that you've made a strong connection with that one person. Then move on to another person and do the same thing again.

It is counterproductive to "graze" with your eyes from person to person. Such extremely brief eye contact does not forge a good connection with the listener.

In our workshops, in order to illustrate how to avoid "grazing," we play a game where one person stands in front of the room and speaks about a hobby. Before the person starts to speak, the other workshop participants each raise a hand. The speaker then works his way around the room, making eye contact with everyone else.

Moreover, the listeners won't put their hands down until they feel that the speaker has made substantial eye contact, long enough for a nice connection. If the speaker just grazes by, the listener's hand stays in the air.

The speakers are almost always amazed at how long they have to hold eye contact to make the connection. That is, the connection is in the eye of the listener, not the speaker. Too often, speakers graze past listeners in the audience without making a connection.

Now It's Time to Smile; No, I'm Serious. It's Time to Smile!

For many lawyers, the most difficult thing this book recommends is that they must smile more when they communicate. Really. Smiling builds relationships. I fell in love with my wife because she smiled at me one day at a fraternity party. Smiling connects you with other people. It's simple and it works.

Yet as soon as I suggest smiling, many lawyers stop listening. Complaints about this suggestion arise all the time in our workshops:

> ▶ "This is a serious subject."
> ▶ "I don't feel comfortable smiling."
> ▶ "I don't want to look phony."
> ▶ "I'm not a used car salesman."
> ▶ "I never smile."

I understand all of these complaints and I'm sympathetic. The legal profession is not a smiley culture. But as a well-trained lawyer, I've got some pretty good rebuttals lined up:

> ▶ I know that the law is serious. But where is it written that smiling is inconsistent with seriousness?
> ▶ I know you don't feel comfortable. You're not used to smiling about the law. Why must you feel comfortable every time you try something new? Did you feel comfortable the first time someone taught you how to swing a golf club?
> ▶ I know you don't want to look phony. But you can't see yourself yet. Wait. And if you think you look phony when you see yourself smiling on camera, you'll never have to smile again.
> ▶ I know you don't want to seem like a used car salesman. But that's a little melodramatic, isn't it? (Not to mention a nasty thing to say about used car salesmen. How would you like it if someone made fun of your profession? Hmmmm?)
> ▶ You say you never smile. Really? That's your excuse? Really? Your daughter gives you a kiss on the cheek and you don't smile then? Your favorite sports team wins a big game and you don't smile then? You've never seen "The Simpsons"?

If you don't want to smile, fine. But I don't agree that smiling is not consistent with the practice of law. We all know lawyers (there aren't many of them) who smile a lot. They smile when they speak to their clients. They smile when they speak with their partners. To be sure, they don't walk around with stupid grins all the time. But they do smile.

Moreover, people tend to like these smiling lawyers. At least they like the ones I know. And that's why you should smile when you communicate. Smiling at people tends to make them like you.

Try Smiling: It's Instant Charisma

A lot of people ask me how they can acquire "charisma." Charisma is an attractive combination of many traits involving personality, style, and message. But there is one thing that can certainly make you more charismatic: smiling. Why do movies stars habitually smile? Because they know it makes them more attractive. I have found that for lawyers, a simple thing like smiling can have a major impact on how they connect with people.

A law firm associate was sent to us because he was considered to be a brilliant lawyer technically but was unable to get along with clients. The firm's partners thought that our training would be a sort of "charm school" for this lawyer. And, in fact, many firms send us lawyers that they want us to "fix."

I met with this lawyer and he immediately impressed me as very intelligent. I'm certain that he truly was a great lawyer. But he also had a certain patronizing manner. He never actually called you "stupid." But his blank expression and snobbish tone made you think that he considered you to be stupid.

One of the first things I suggested was that he should try smiling more as he spoke. "You've got to be kidding," he said. But I persisted and finally got him to try it on camera while we role-played a conversation. He had a very natural looking smile and did this quite easily. And when he saw himself, he had to admit that he looked pretty good. "It's not like I never smile," he said. "I just don't feel right smiling when we're talking about the law."

I got him to promise me that he'd try smiling more.

He and I worked together privately for several months. And he made substantial progress such that his job was no longer in jeopardy.

He admitted that he had tried smiling and it had helped him a lot. He admitted that he felt people warming up to him.

And it definitely changed the way that people perceived him. "One person even asked me if I'd lost weight," he said.

So if you want a simple way to change your image, try smiling. If it doesn't make you as charismatic as a movie star, it just might save your job.

You May Need to Develop Your Cheek Muscles

It can be challenging to start smiling in a business context. Even people who smile a lot during their leisure time say it feels strange to smile at work. But you can work at this. I know because I did it. Indeed, I developed a more positive facial expression over the course of a one-month smiling program.

I never actually noticed how I looked until I left the practice of law. But when I began teaching public speaking, I started to see myself on camera. "My goodness," I thought. "I look way too serious."

So I went on a smiling spree. For a month I made a conscious effort to smile (or at least have some active facial expression) all the time. When I was speaking on the telephone, I'd smile. When I'd walk down to the little news stand in my building, I'd smile when I bought the newspaper. I'd smile at the coffee drive-through and whenever I spoke in meetings.

At first my cheek muscles literally ached. But gradually, what felt unnatural at first started to feel fine. Now people ask me how I can have such a positive expression most of the time.

Here is my answer: "Practice."

If You Don't Smile, at Least Show Some Expression

Now even I will admit that you can't smile all the time. But even if you're not smiling, don't put your face in "park." Use a full range of facial expressions. Your face has seventy muscles and can make hundreds of expressions. Yet we lawyers tend to rely on only one expression: the "serious" mask.

Here's an exercise you can try. You'll need a mirror and you may want to lock the door so that no one will walk in and embarrass you. Read the following sentence five different times using your face to convey emotions of anger, sadness, frustration, gratitude, and happiness.

"As your attorney, I must inform you that this case is not going to be easy. In fact, we'll do very well if we obtain a good settlement."

Your face can have a major impact on how you appear. So use lots of facial expressions. The face is a wonderful communication tool.

GESTURES AND MOVEMENT

Gestures Aren't as Important as People Think

When I tell people that I teach professionals how to give presentations, one of the most common questions I am asked is, "What do I do with my hands?"

I don't really like the question although I can understand why it is so important. People feel uncomfortable standing in front of a group with these two long appendages hanging from their shoulders. "What do I do with these things?" we wonder.

But the question "What do I do with my hands?" is unfortunate because hands aren't nearly as important for communication as one's face, one's eyes, and especially one's voice.

So one of the first things I tell people when they ask me that question is, "Before you fix your hands, first fix your voice and your eyes."

Sometimes a Gesture Is Connected to the Voice and Eyes

Often we find that poor gestures reflect a presenter's poor eye contact and voice energy.

I was working with someone who was very concerned about his gestures. "I have no idea what to do with my hands," he said. Indeed, his gestures were terrible. He appeared to be constantly worrying about what to do with his hands. Sometimes he kept his hands clasped in front of him in a self-conscious, defensive, awkward pose. Other times he would cross his arms in front of him in an "I'm in charge" pose. Still other times he held his arms behind his back.

As he was speaking, however, the man's voice was flat, and his eye contact was wandering as if he were grazing the audience, looking at no one in particular.

"Forget about your hands," I told my client. "Instead, I want you to make eye contact with me and never break it. Also, I want you to speak with as much energy as possible. On a scale of 1 to 10, with 10 being Maximum You, I want you to hit a 15. Go way over the top."

After these instructions he started speaking like a highly engaged speaker. His eye contact stayed with me. His voice was highly energized although he only got up to about a 9. Meanwhile, the client's gestures were suddenly, magically integrated with his presentation. Without thinking about his gestures, he reached up and out to make points, and just let his hands rest at his sides during less charged portions of the presentation.

Clearly, once this client became more connected with his audience, his gestures became more integrated into his presentation.

Hence, sometimes, if you ignore your gestures, they'll just fix themselves.

Basics for Strong Gestures

Despite my protestations that gestures aren't that important, our clients almost always want guidance on how to gesture effectively. And gestures can make you look more confident. With that in mind, here are some basics to remember about gestures.

Your Gestures Should Not Distract

Since your gestures don't add much to your presentation relative to voice and facial energy, it's especially important that you do nothing with your hands that distracts from your message.

Perhaps the most distracting gestures I ever witnessed were made by magazine magnate Steve Forbes when he was running for president in 1996. That year he came to our law firm to raise money. And he spoke very well.

But he had an odd mannerism. He kept his hands cupped together in front of him as if he had just captured a lightening bug and he wanted to be careful to keep it from escaping.

And that wasn't all. Every time he made an important point, he would punctuate his point by opening up his hands as if he were releasing the bug. So he would say something like, "Let me next talk about my plan to lower taxes." And on the word "taxes" he would release the bug. He did this over and over again, and I started focusing on his hands and missing what he was saying.

That's the worst case scenario with gestures. You don't want people noticing your gestures to the exclusion of what you have to say.

There are other things to keep in mind:

Don't Jingle

Men, take your keys and change out of your pockets before you speak. Clicking coins can drive your audience crazy. Women, don't finger your jewelry.

Don't Pick

I've actually seen people pick their noses while speaking. Don't do that. Ever. I hesitate to even mention this. But it's far more common than I would ever have suspected.

Don't Scratch

You'd be amazed where people will scratch in front of a large group. Or maybe you wouldn't. But if you don't want to alienate your audience, be careful where you put your hands.

Don't Pop

Cracking knuckles drives some people crazy. As a lifelong knuckle cracker, I have to be careful about this one.

Don't Beg

Some well-trained dogs will sit on their hind legs and hold their forelegs in front in a classic begging stance. Unfortunately, I've seen presenters do the same thing, holding their arms in front of them like a dog begging for a biscuit. I think it's a distracting gesture. Am I supposed to say, "Nice presenter. Now roll over?" Drop your hands at your sides. Clasp them in front if you must. But whatever you do, don't beg like a dog.

Don't Flap Like a Penguin

Some people have their elbows "Velcroed" to their hips so that their arms flop around. This pose is so silly that people will actually start laughing, and they won't be laughing "with" you.

Characteristics of Strong Gestures: Big and Steady

Big

When it comes to gestures, bigger is usually better. Most people make gestures that are too small. But if you want to have big presence, you must make big gestures. That means extending your arms out and forward and then holding them through a thought.

Something about big gestures conveys confidence. My favorite example of this is derived not from any of my clients, but from a favorite book entitled, *The Worst-Case Scenario Survival Handbook.*[3] The book details what to do to survive various horrible circumstances, such as how to survive a gun fight, leap out of a moving car, and so forth.

One of the scenarios asks the question, "What should you do if you are in the woods and come across a mountain lion?" The book notes that you should not run because the mountain lion is faster than you and will catch you. (In one of my workshops one wag asked, "What if you're with someone else and you know that you can run faster than he can?") Instead, the book urges you to reach out your arms and make yourself look big. There is something about size that commands respect from the mountain lion.

Similarly, there is something about size that commands respect from an audience. So make big gestures by reaching out and forward with arms fully extended. If you're not a large or tall person, here is a chance to gain some of the communication advantage that naturally comes with size.

Steady

When your hands are moving a lot, chances are that your audience will start to notice them. If the audience is noticing your hands, then they're

---

[3] J. Piven & D. Borgenicht, *The Worst-Case Scenario Survival Handbook* (2001).

probably not noticing what you're saying. So size isn't the only thing that counts with gestures. You want your gestures to be steady as well.

We tell our clients to "hold the gesture through a thought." Too often we see people stabbing the air with their hands or doing something we call "apple picking," reaching out and pulling back quickly.

When You're Not Gesturing, Keep Your Hands Down

So what do you do with those hands when you're not gesturing? Let 'em hang at your sides like a bunch of bananas. That's right, just let them hang straight down. Do nothing with them at all.

"It doesn't feel natural." That's what we hear from a lot of clients when we ask them to drop their hands to what we call the "neutral stance." But the only reason this doesn't feel natural is because most people are used to clasping their hands together when they're not gesturing. With a little practice, hanging your hands straight down will feel natural as well.

And remember that the "clasped hands" position is not particularly neutral. The position is just not as open and approachable a look as having your hands hanging straight down. Give a short presentation on camera and compare how you look when your hands are clasped versus when they are hanging straight down. You decide which looks better for you.

A CONFIDENT PRESENCE: WEAR THOSE BOOTS AND SPURS

They say you can't judge a book by its cover. But we judge our lawyers by how they walk, i.e., their "struts." It's not too difficult to tell a confident partner from a beleaguered associate. The poor associate shuffles to the elevator like he's wearing bedroom slippers, hauling the entire Federal Supplement on his back. The partner walks the halls with confidence, like he's wearing boots and spurs.

When you're giving a presentation (or even walking the halls or entering the room for a meeting), you must walk confidently to the front of the room with those boots and spurs. Even if you're not a partner, you should act and look like one.

Pretend you're an actor and have just won an Academy Award. Head up. Look out at the audience. Look positive (don't grin if you don't feel comfortable). Too many people walk to the beginning of a presentation with shoulders bowed as if they're saying, "This is by far the worst experience of my life."

If you look confident, your audience will feel that confidence and you'll probably feel confident.

PICK A SKILL AND WORK ON IT FOR A MONTH

Books and workshops on communication skills can be overwhelming. There are so many things to remember. When should I smile? How should I gesture? And when I do gesture, I must remember to hold that gesture all the way through a thought. I must make my voice rise and fall like a roller coaster.

To be sure, it's a lot of advice. And you can end up learning nothing if you focus on everything.

To cut through the confusion, pick a single skill in which you're particularly weak and work on it for a month until you've substantially improved. In his great book *Mental Tennis*, Vic Braden gives a wonderful lesson in how to improve at tennis that applies equally well to presentation skills:

> "When it comes to improvement, most players start thinking in terms of thousands of changes, and of course the whole idea becomes overwhelming. But in fact, frequently all you have to do is solve one or two problems and you become a whole new tennis player. Think about that: if you straighten out one single stroke, you can improve your game enormously."[4]

As with tennis, you can improve your overall communication "game" by solving just one or two communication problems. Most lawyers will substantially improve their communication "games" by improving their voice and facial energy. So pick one or two

---

[4] Vic Braden, *Vic Braden's Mental Tennis: How to Psych Yourself to a Winning Game* (1993).

communication skills and be on your way toward becoming a great communicator.

REHEARSAL: IT'S THE KEY TO BEING GREAT

At a party not long ago, someone asked me, "Can you tell me in one sentence the best way for me to become a better speaker?"

"Who needs an entire sentence?" I said. "I can tell you in one word: rehearse."

The dirty little secret of the public speaking business is that most people can become effective speakers simply by rigorously rehearsing their presentations. This is even true if you tend to be overcome by nerves. Indeed, it's especially true with people who suffer from stage fright. That's because the number one way to deal with nerves is simply to practice, practice, practice.

An attorney whom I have known for many years (let's call her Claire) came to me when she was about to give her first big trade show presentation. She was terrified. "I'm a terrible presenter," Claire said. "I get so nervous that my mind literally blanks out. I can't remember anything. I just look like an idiot." But she added that this was an important opportunity and she wanted to do well.

When I asked her how much she usually practiced her presentations, she said, "I practice a lot."

When I asked her to describe how she practiced, she said, "In my office, I have a couch. And to practice, what I do is close the door and lie down on my couch. Then I think about my presentation."

Looking at her, I tried not to laugh. "That's not practicing," I said. "That sounds more like napping."

I instructed Claire to practice her presentation out loud, from beginning to end without stopping, at least twenty times. By the time Claire had completed this exercise, she knew her presentation so well that she could have made a splendid speech even if a bomb had exploded in the middle of it.

What happened? She nailed it. In fact, her presentation was rated one of the best presentations at the entire conference. She was invited back to deliver another presentation the following year. She is also now considered one of the best speakers at her firm.

Ahh, the power of rehearsal! It can turn a poor presenter into a confident communicator overnight.

Rehearsal Isn't "Going Over It" on the Plane

When I speak to large groups I often ask the attendees to raise their hands if they rehearse their presentations. Invariably, most of the hands in the room will go up.

But then I begin to probe for the "real story." "Keep your hands up in the air," I say, "if your rehearsal includes saying part of your presentation out loud."

Hands start to drop. Indeed, many people think rehearsal is merely reviewing the PowerPoint slides and "going over it in my head."

Next I say, "Keep your hands in the air if your rehearsal includes saying your *entire* presentation out loud."

More hands will drop.

"Keep your hands up if your rehearsal includes saying the entire presentation out loud *from beginning to end without stopping*."

Still more hands drop.

Finally I add, "From beginning to end without stopping *multiple times*." Rarely are more than a few hands left up in the air.

The reality is that people who are great public speakers rehearse their presentations quite a bit. They practice their speeches out loud many times without stopping.

Rehearsal Is a Spoken Art: You Must Rehearse Out Loud!

The fact is that public speaking is a *spoken art*. It's a verbal performance in front of an audience. To do well, you must practice out loud. So although the following may seem obvious, let's quickly review what rehearsing out loud does for you. Rehearsal will help you do the following.

You Will Learn Your Lines

Since you should never read a presentation, you're going to have to "learn it." That means fumbling through the best ways to express certain ideas, especially the complex ideas. For example, if you want to make the point that non-compete agreements are often disfavored by the courts, you must decide how best to express that idea. Does it sound better to say, "In general courts don't like non-compete agreements"? Or would it sound better to say, "While there are exceptions to the rule, most courts are going to find that a non-compete agreement is a bad idea." Who knows? But you're going to want to determine what sounds best before you deliver the actual presentation.

You Will Focus on the 93%

How you look and sound is easily as important as what you say. But you're not going to be able to focus on how you look and sound if you're not confident about what you have to say. That means practicing the content until you know it cold.

You Will Gauge Your Time Limit

Few sins in speaking are worse than running over your time limit. Because most people are too polite to walk out, running over your time limit is tantamount to kidnapping your audience. And it makes people angry. I heard a speaker address a convention hall of 3,000 people. He had one hour to speak. But he ran over by ten minutes. In other words, his poor preparation wasted ten minutes for every one of those 3,000 people. That adds up to almost three weeks of wasted time.

Conclusion

You can read twenty books on presentation skills, attend workshops, buy videotapes, and pay coaches to hold your hand. And all of those things will help you. But nothing will help you more than rehearsing your presentation until you know it cold.

Practice makes great communicators.

CHAPTER **17**

Dealing with Nerves

INTRODUCTION

Public speaking is the number one fear of the average person. This statistic is repeated constantly. But the question remains, "Why?"

Why do we fear standing in front of large groups and speaking?

Many psychologists will tell you their theories. And I'm neither a psychologist nor a social scientist. But I've worked with thousands of people on their communication skills. And this is my book. So here is my theory on why we fear public speaking.

I think we fear public speaking because it is an unnatural act for the human species. That is, human beings were not designed to appear before large groups and communicate verbally. As a result, most of us feel uncomfortable doing it.

If this were a court, I would prove my theory with a string of overwhelming instances of circumstantial evidence:

EXHIBIT A: *Our voices.* We have soft voices that generally cannot be heard by large groups of people. If we were intended to address large groups, wouldn't we have voices that didn't need amplification in large auditoriums?

EXHIBIT B: *Our stature.* We are not very tall. If we were intended to speak to large groups, we would be much taller. We wouldn't have to stand on platforms when we address large groups.

EXHIBIT C: *Our facial features.* We have tiny eyes and mouths even though our faces are very expressive. As a result, our facial expressions are only effective when we speak in intimate settings where listeners can easily read your face.

I rest my case. The good news is that most people can overcome their fear of public speaking with practice and by the use of some techniques.

PRACTICE, PRACTICE, PRACTICE

Books on public speaking will tell you many different tricks to overcome nerves. Some experts tell you to imagine that everyone in the audience is naked. Others suggest a form of self-hypnosis. One expert even recommended natural herbal remedies.

Here's my number one prescription: *Rehearse like hell.*

Nothing works better to deal with anxiety than to rehearse your presentation until you know it cold. This is because, in my experience, you can't really eliminate nerves. You can only deal with them. And the best way to deal with them is to go into the presentation feeling confident that you're going to do well despite the butterflies.

You must know your presentation so well that you could give it if a bomb went off behind you. Remember the words of one of our best lawyers, Abraham Lincoln: "If I had eight hours to cut down a tree, I'd spend six hours sharpening my ax."

Lincoln was one communicator who knew the value of practice and rehearsal.

Practice the First Few Lines Even More

If you're going to practice the entire presentation five times, practice the opening lines ten times. Anxiety ebbs and flows, and reaches its peak when you begin speaking. You should know those first few lines so well that no matter how anxious you feel, you are confident you will be able to speak those first lines well.

If you nail the first few lines, you're going to relax and things will go well. Nailing the first lines will also make your audience comfortable. And chances are that you'll sense that and relax even more. However, if you fumble the first few lines, you'll tense up and things will go downhill.

I was speaking to a section of the Atlanta Bar Association a couple of years ago and was particularly nervous. My opening line was:

> *"I want to start with a fun fact. There was a researcher who studied how we communicate. And he found out something very interesting. . . ."*

As I was waiting for my chance to speak, I repeated that line under my breath over and over again. When I stood up to speak, it rolled right out and I nailed it. I started to relax and the rest of the presentation went fine.

Get those first few minutes right and it's usually easy sailing from then on.

SOME PHYSICAL APPROACHES TO DEALING WITH NERVES

In addition to practice, the most effective means of dealing with nerves is to undertake physical activities to counter the physical phenomenon of stage fright. It helps to understand exactly what's going on in your body when you're nervous.

I asked a physician what causes stage fright.

"You recognize a situation, such as a presentation, as stressful," she said. "The brain sends a message to the adrenal glands to send out more adrenaline. The adrenaline makes your heart race faster. It makes you sweat. It puts you in a hyper-alert state."

In other words, you feel nervous.

Exercise helps, she added. "When the body is in this hyper-alert state, if you direct the energy in a focused manner, such as through exercise, you use up the excess neurotransmitters and you feel less nervous."

What can you do to rid yourself of those excess neurotransmitters?

> ▸ *Walk around the block:* Once when I was nervous before a presentation to a Rotary Club, I did several laps around the parking lot. Getting my heart beating made me feel better.
>
> ▸ *Do push-ups:* Billy Crystal, the comedian, gets nervous when he goes on stage live. He does push-ups. "I like to break a sweat," he says.
>
> ▸ *Do isometric exercises:* I know an author who becomes terrified every time he has to give a reading. He presses his hands together and tenses his legs in his seat. He says it works.

MENTAL TRICKS TO HELP YOU RELAX

There are many "home remedies." for stage fright. People use techniques that seem to work for them. Although some people apparently are helped if they imagine their audience members naked, this never worked for me. However, the breathing techniques from my wife's Lamaze childbirth classes work great for me.

Here are a few other tricks that seem to work:

Work the Room Before Your Speech

It's always a good idea to introduce yourself to as many people in the room as possible. Just work the room saying, "Hi. I'm [your name]. I'm going to be your speaker today." It breaks down barriers and makes everyone in the room seem friendlier. And if you get really nervous, it's better to talk to people than stewing in your anxiety as you wait to speak.

Arrive Early to Check the Equipment

Always arrive early before giving a speech so that you have time to inspect any visual aids and equipment you will be using. This is certainly a good practice even if you don't get nervous. And it also helps if you do get nervous. People can be unnerved by strange environments. So arrive early and check out the location and the setup. There is something soothing about feeling comfortable with the room and the equipment.

Talk to One Person at a Time

In our earlier discussion about eye contact, we indicated how important it is to make eye contact with one person at a time, rather than making "grazing" eye contact with many people. Holding eye contact with individuals also helps to deal with nerves. After all, compared with staring at an entire room of listeners, it's far less intimidating to speak to one person and have a "conversation." Just be sure to spread the eye contact around. Looking at only one person for too long could upset that person.

Speak a Lot

Speaking a lot is probably the biggest trick of all for dealing with nerves. Speaking is like golf. The more you practice, the better you'll be. So seek out opportunities to speak. Bar associations always need speakers at their section meetings. I also recommend finding a good Toastmasters club. If you really want to get good at speaking, you'll need to start giving lots of speeches.

GRAB YOUR COAT AND GET YOUR HAT, LEAVE YOUR WORRY ON THE DOORSTEP

Nervous is normal. I speak all the time and still get nervous. But I don't let it show. I just tell myself to be passionate and have fun. And whatever you do, don't let the audience know you're nervous.

Too often a speaker will approach the front of the room, shuffling papers, looking down at his feet. "I don't speak very often," he says in an apologetic tone. "So please bear with me. I'm a little nervous."

Then there might be a little titter of laughter, or a nervous clearing of the throat and a deep cleansing breath.

As a judge might say, "How is that relevant, counselor?"

These pleas for sympathy just don't work and they actually make the audience nervous. "Oh, no," the listeners think. "Another rotten speaker. Another half hour of my life that I won't get back. I can't believe I have to sit through this."

Meanwhile the speaker likely will sense the audience's anxiety and get even more nervous. Before long, there's a vicious death spiral of tension, and the presentation turns into a disaster.

However, if you work through the nerves, chances are that no one will notice. Indeed, whenever I work with someone who gets very nervous, I videotape them and then ask if they think they look anxious. Rarely do the nerves actually show.

So rehearse. Do some push-ups or walk around the block. (Or imagine the audience naked.)

If you're still a little nervous (and you probably will be), just push yourself forward. Think good thoughts and follow all that positive thinking advice. One of my favorite bits of wisdom is from the Bible: "Act as if you have faith and faith will be given to you."

Or, put another way, "Fake it until you make it."

CHAPTER **18**

Going Interactive:
A Paradigm Shift

INTRODUCTION

The best way to make an audience love you is to deliver an interactive presentation. I don't care if you are the dullest tax lawyer in Washington, D.C. I don't care if the very thought of getting in front of an audience gives you hives. I don't care if you're already a great presenter. Going interactive with your presentations is a terrific way to ensure a great presentation.

Interactive makes almost anything exciting, regardless of topic or speaker:

▶ Are you speaking on administrative motion practice? Sounds dull. Not if you lay out a few basic rules and then let your audience gather in discussion groups to solve hypothetical problems where they have to apply the new administrative rules.

▶ Trying to get your client to understand how to comply with trade secret disclosure regulations? It's not hard if you lay out the three or four major rules to remember and then let the client work through typical examples in a discussion format.

To be sure, interactive presenting means rethinking your "public speaking" paradigm. The "stand and deliver" model is out. The "conversation with the audience" model is in. As the people at Apple Computers might say, interactive presenters "Think Different."

But interactive presentations are so effective and easy to create that I can't understand why everyone doesn't deliver them as often as possible, especially when the purpose of the presentation is to instruct the audience about some area of the law.

I worked recently with a patent lawyer who gave a continuing legal education presentation on how to draft an agreement that licenses the use of patent rights. Even my client had to admit that the presentation promised to be dull. But she made it interactive by keeping the lecture to a minimum. Instead, she allowed the audience to take a crack at drafting critical key contract provisions. Much of the time was spent discussing the audience's work.

And everyone loved it. The presenter told me, "Somebody came in just as I was wrapping up and the person next to her said, 'You just missed all the fun!'"

Now tell me the truth. When was the last time someone called a presentation on drafting licensing agreements "fun"?

That's the awesome power of interactive.

What Is an Interactive Presentation?

In an interactive presentation, audience participation is a planned, integral part of the program and not merely an afterthought.

Interactive presentations do the following:

▶ They plan for and encourage questions from the audience.
▶ They allow the audience to brainstorm answers to questions from the presenter.
▶ They present the audience with problems to be solved using principles discussed by the presenter.
▶ They give the audience exercises that illustrate the speaker's points.

Why Do Interactive Presentations Work So Well?

They Are a Welcome Relief from the Usual Drivel

Most people come to lawyer presentations with very low expectations. Conferences on legal issues are usually snooze-fests. So when the audience is suddenly participating, doing interesting activities and discussing interesting issues, they feel like death-row prisoners with an emergency stay from the governor. Ah, freedom! Hot dog!

Nothing pleases me more than to see that I'm to speak along with other lawyers. I know that my presentation will be considered great, even if I'm having an off-day. My presentations are always interactive. And when my speech is compared to one on the revisions to the Uniform Commercial Code, I can't help but appear to be the most dynamic communicator since John F. Kennedy.

Interactive Is Consistent with How Humans Were Intended to Communicate

Previously I theorized that nervousness prior to presentations occurs because standing up and speaking before large audiences is an "unnatural" act. If people were intended to speak to large crowds, why don't we have louder voices and bigger heads?

Similarly, standing up and speaking without getting a response from your audience is an unnatural way to communicate. If communication were intended to be only one way, then why do we have ears?

One of the reasons why people feel nervous when they speak is because they worry about other people's opinions of them. That concern vanishes with interactive presentations because the interactive presentation has a built-in audience feedback mechanism.

Interactive Ensures Audience Satisfaction

Recently, a company developed a new technology that was supposed to revolutionize business presentations. The technology consisted of a system wherein listeners could be quizzed and polled during the course of a presentation. Using this expensive instant feedback device, the presenter could gauge in real time whether the message was getting through.

The device received a lot of press and no doubt had some devotees, but it really is simply an expensive high-tech novelty. A highly effective *low-tech* method for gauging audience reaction—interactive presentations—already exists.

The best interactive presentations are conversations between the speaker and the audience with each asking the other questions and listening to the responses.

For example, if you're giving a presentation on how to comply with sex discrimination laws, it is easy to ensure that you focus on the most important concerns and questions of your audience. Start the presentation by asking the audience to divide into small groups and "list five questions you have about sexual harassment in the workplace." Then go around the room and take a sampling of the questions from each group and write them down.

As you go through your presentation, refer back to the list as you come to each question. And if, at the end of your presentation, you haven't answered all the questions, then answer the ones that you've missed.

Now that's responding to the needs of an audience. Great communicators do that without a high-tech polling device.

Interactive Is More Persuasive

When it comes to persuasion, we lawyers place a lot of emphasis on logic and precedent. In order to persuade a judge, you certainly need carefully honed arguments. But when it comes to persuading audiences, lawyers and others in business often overlook something that is far more persuasive than cases, statutes, or logic: *the audience itself.*

Bob Pike, a training guru and author, once said, "People don't argue with their own data."[1]

That statement has an important implication for presenters. It means that sometimes your audience can be the source of your most persuasive evidence. You just have to ask for it.

For example, let's say that you're trying to persuade an audience of utility workers of the value of complying with safety regulations. You can easily list all the legal arguments and business risks. But suppose you simply looked at the audience and said, "There are a lot of reasons why we need to comply with these regulations. Let's come up with a list of five." Then you pick up a marker and walk over to a flip chart and start listening and writing.

Chances are that the participants will compile almost exactly the same list that you would have compiled on your own. But which is more persuasive? *Their* list! The fact that the participants proposed the content of the list inhibits them from disagreeing with that list.

Interactive Has More Educational Impact

Confucius said, "What I hear, I forget. What I see, I remember. What I do, I understand." In other words, we learn through experience.

To understand the truth of this statement, you need venture no further than a kindergarten classroom. How are the children learning? Are they sitting at desks carefully lined up in rows with a lecturer at the front of the room? Of course not! They're sitting on floor mats and playing games with math, telling stories, and reading simple books to each other. In the education field, this is called "experiential learning," or more simply, "learning by doing."

When it comes to learning, adults are babies with big bodies. We too learn best by doing. So if you're trying to get an audience to learn something and retain it, give them something to do. Not only will they learn more, they'll have more fun.

Fortunately for us lawyers, it turns out that the law lends itself wonderfully to this type of learning. That's how we all learned in law school, through discussion of hypotheticals and actual cases. We should use the same process to teach our clients and colleagues.

---

[1] B. Pike, *Creative Training Techniques*, 2d ed. (1994), available at www.bobpikegroup.com.

Let's say that you are talking about antitrust regulations, and you can tell your client to avoid tying arrangements and then give him some examples. And that will have *some* impact. But if you really want to make an impression, try a second approach: You can give your audience members a problem to solve that involves tying arrangements. For example, you could describe two deals with customers and let the audience members determine which is illegal and which is not. Then ask the audience to discuss among themselves how to fix the illegal deal. Then debrief the group.

As Confucius suggested, the best way to learn is through experience. But sometimes obtaining real experience isn't possible or (in the case of antitrust violations) advisable. An interactive presentation has impact because it simulates experience.

Interactive Is Easier on the Speaker and More Fun for the Audience

Whenever I work with clients preparing them for interactive presentations, at the end of the session they look at me a little bewildered. They realize that they aren't going to have to do a lot of rehearsal for the presentation. That's because interactive presentations are almost always easier to deliver and prepare.

Think about it. Much of your preparation time is taken up with creating exercises and discussion topics. Once you've done that, you don't have to prepare much in terms of what you're going to say because the audience will be doing exercises and discussing issues with you much of the time.

To be sure, what you do say you have to say very well. Whenever you make interactive presentations, it is critical that all your instructions be crystal clear. You can't expect the audience to participate if they don't know exactly what they're supposed to do.

THE INTERACTIVE FORMULA

Preview

To create an interactive presentation, use the same formula that was detailed in Chapter 15. Your presentation should have a Hook, an MO, three points, and a recap and wrap. The only addition is that you bring each section to life with interactive exercises as well as stories, personal examples, and expert testimony.

Suppose we want to take the antitrust presentation that we discussed earlier and make it interactive. It might look like the following:

Hook (Attention Grabber)

"This presentation is about how to comply with antitrust laws. And to get started, I'd like to ask you to help me make up a list. I want you to help me identify ten different ways that people in this room have come into contact with their competitors. It could be anything from trade associations, e-mail, contract negotiations, industry conferences, social settings, anything."

Write down the list on a flip chart.

"Well, I have news for you. In every situation that you've named, someone in this country has done or said things that constitute violations of antitrust laws. In addition, they have gone to jail and cost their companies millions of dollars in penalties. You'd be surprised how simple it is to violate these laws."

Message Objective ("If/Then" Statement)

"Now, my purpose today is not to frighten you. But I have been asked to discuss with you the essentials of antitrust law. And if you follow the guidelines I give you today, you will stay out of jail and avoid the possibility that your company will be assessed millions of dollars in penalties."

Three Points

"I'm going to talk to you today about three things:

- ▸ *"Dealing with competitors.*
- ▸ *"Factors to consider when you're doing something that will seriously harm a competitor.*
- ▸ *"Issues regarding the content of your documents."*

BODY OF THE PRESENTATION

POINT 1: *Dealing with Competitors*

Subjects to Avoid during Discussions:

▸ Price, bids, volumes, plans for customers.

▸ Stories about Archer Daniels Midland. Managers and officers of ADM met with competitors in hotel rooms and conference rooms around the world to divide the market in detail. They were caught by the FBI on videotape and prosecuted. People went to jail.

▸ Trade association concerns. When you belong to associations where you meet with competitors, you must be careful. Discussions of certain topics such as lobbying and industry legislation at trade associations are, of course, legitimate.

▸ Seemingly unimportant pronouncements. A "conspiracy" can be implied from small things, even if there is no formal agreement with competitors. So be careful. One ADM executive wrote, "The competitor is our friend. The customer is our enemy." That statement was characterized as evidence of a conspiracy.

Interactive Exercise: Create two fact patterns where executives from competing businesses are hobnobbing at various business and social events. Include lines of dialogue where it is difficult to determine whether there is antitrust activity occurring. Have groups decide whether the dialogue rises to the level of antitrust activity. Require the groups to state reasons to support their positions. Then have them rewrite the dialogue to eliminate any possibility of being charged with antitrust activity.

Debrief: As the facilitator, ask each group to discuss their fact patterns. After listening to each rationale, give your view of the problem.

POINT 2: *Actions That Have Adverse Impact On Competition*

There is nothing inherently wrong with competing vigorously in the marketplace. That's what businesses are supposed to do. But certain activities require consultation with counsel:

▶ *Predatory pricing.* If you're planning to sell a product at below cost, that could suggest antitrust activity. So before you do that, call the lawyers in for consultation.

▶ *Exclusivity agreements.* If you're about to enter into a major contract with a customer that will displace a rival, be careful. Consult with the lawyers. Remember that Microsoft tried to get computer makers to include Microsoft Explorer pre-installed on computers instead of Netscape, and that this was one of the activities that led to the big antitrust case against Microsoft.

▶ *Tying arrangements.* Avoid requiring a customer to buy a second product as a condition of obtaining a first product. Example: If Microsoft prohibited you from buying Windows unless you also bought PowerPoint, that could be tying.

Interactive Exercise: Play "Antitrust Jeopardy." Describe antitrust actions undertaken and deals entered into by a company that is remarkably similar to your client. Divide the group into teams of three or four. You read each clue (answer) out loud and the group leader rings a bell when he thinks he knows the question to that answer. The response must take the form of a question such as, "What is a tying arrangement?" or "What is predatory pricing?" Prizes are given for the best responses.

Debrief: Discussion and question and answer after each question.

POINT 3: *Issues Affecting What You Put In Documents*

Remember that everything you say or write can come back to haunt you. But what you write can be especially troublesome. So be careful.

> ▸ Be cautious what you write in e-mail. An e-mail that said "We're going to cut off their oxygen" might sound like a monopoly engaging in unfair trade practices.
> ▸ Avoid inflammatory phrases such as:
>
> "We're going to dominate."
> "Squish the competition like a bug."
> "Put a lid on the competition."
> "Squeeze them until they scream."

Interactive Exercise: Pass out e-mail with language that is vague but which arguably could imply antitrust activity. Have groups propose a circumstance in which the language could indeed be found to imply antitrust activity.

Debrief: Discuss each e-mail to emphasize how easy it is to cross over the line into antitrust activity.

Recap and Wrap

"If you follow these basic guidelines, you will stay out of trouble and keep your business out of trouble.

> ▸ "When dealing with competitors, avoid talk about prices, dividing up the market, what your plans are, etc.
> ▸ "When you're considering undertaking activities that might be construed as predatory pricing, tying, or exclusivity agreements, be careful. Call the lawyers before completing the deal.
> ▸ "And be careful what you put in documents.

"So keep these basics in mind and you'll keep the company out of trouble. And you'll keep yourself out of jail."

KEYS TO A GREAT INTERACTIVE PRESENTATION

Focus on Two or Three Points

Focusing on just two or three points in interactive presentations ensures that your presentation will pass the "lapel test." The lapel test occurs when one of your audience members leaves your presentation only to be confronted in the hall, grabbed by the lapels, and asked to name the three most important things that he or she learned in that presentation. Your presentation passes the lapel test if that audience member answers correctly.

Well-crafted interactive presentations always pass the lapel test by focusing on two or three main ideas and making sure that the audience doesn't leave without a thorough understanding of those ideas.

To make sure that your interactive presentation passes, the first step is to focus on two or three key principles. Then do interactive exercises to ensure that the audience understands those principles.

For example, a patent lawyer who gave an interactive presentation on contracts to license the use of patents decided that the presentation would be a success if the audience left with a strong understanding of two major points:

POINT 1. The contract must clearly define the patent rights at issue. Specifically, these contracts should define those rights broadly and inclusively.

She discussed the relevant laws and gave examples of good and bad contract definitions of patent rights. Then she instructed the participants to gather into small groups and handed each group a sheet of paper with the following problem:

"You are negotiating a License Agreement on behalf of a licensee. How would you amend the following definition of patent rights?

"Article 1: Definition

"1.1. 'Patent Rights' shall mean the U.S. patent applications listed on Exhibit A attached to this Agreement and made a part thereof."

Each group was asked to describe what was wrong with the definition and to try to draft a better definition.

POINT 2. The license must not last beyond expiration of patent rights. To license beyond the patent's term raises antitrust concerns.

Once again, she discussed the important law involved and gave examples of good and bad contract language surrounding the term of the license of the patent rights. The attorney then had the groups deal with the following problem:

"You are negotiating a License Agreement on behalf of a licensor. How would you amend the following section regarding the duration of the License Agreement?

"Article 8: Terms and Terminations

"8.1. Term. The term of this Agreement shall commence on the Effective Date and shall continue in full force and effect for 20 years."

After each problem, the attorney debriefed the groups and discussed how she would have dealt with each hypothetical.

By focusing on fewer points and doing interactive exercises for each, she ensured that her audience actually learned something, rather than just hearing a smattering of things that would soon be forgotten.

Four Steps for Every Interactive Exercise

Before having your participants undertake an interactive exercise, it's critical that you properly prepare them to succeed. There is a four-step process you should follow:

STEP 1: *Give participants the tools to succeed.* Giving participants the necessary tools to succeed means making sure that you clearly explain the law that they must apply. In the prior example, the patent lawyer started each section by carefully explaining the law that was applicable.

STEP 2: *Demonstrate how to use the tools.* With law presentations, explaining how to use tools means demonstrating the law's application with a hypothetical case that is similar to the one that the group will solve on its own. In the example of the patent lawyer discussed above, she was careful to review specifically how to correct bad contract language before asking the audience to correct the language on their own.

STEP 3: *Let participants play with the tools.* Once you've laid the groundwork by discussing and demonstrating the law, the audience is now ready to try to resolve a problem on their own. Give them the opportunity by allowing enough time to resolve the problem.

STEP 4: *Listen and debrief.* Debrief by asking individual participants to tell you what they've concluded. Listen carefully. Question their reasoning. Don't be too quick to correct. Let another group or person respond first. Remember, this is supposed to be a conversation, not a lecture. Do not criticize or critique an answer until you have received plenty of input from the audience.

Rehearse the Interactive Exercises Carefully

One of the big dangers with interactive presentations is what I call the "Thunderdome effect." Remember the old "Mad Max" movies where the highest form of entertainment was a professional wrestling style form of chaos called "Thunderdome"? In an interactive presentation, if you fail to explain your exercises properly or if the exercises are not properly constructed, you can end up with a form of chaos that's not quite Thunderdome but will be pretty unpleasant as you watch your presentation crash and burn.

One prescription for Thunderdome is faulty or unclear instructions. Take extreme care in explaining each exercise. The instructions should be very simple. For example:

> ▸ *"First, I want you to break into small groups of three of four. Just turn your chairs around and get into small groups.*
> ▸ *"Then I want you to read the hypothetical.*
> ▸ *"Then I want you to discuss and answer three questions."*

If the exercise is a little complex, consider putting the instructions on a slide and projecting it in the front of the room during the exercise.

Once you've created simple instructions, you should test them with your colleagues. Try giving them the instructions and note whether they ask you any questions. If they aren't sure what to do, you must rework the instructions to make them simpler and clearer.

The easiest way to ruin an interactive presentation is to give unclear instructions. So it is important that you prepare wording that works and stick with it.

Rehearsal is important for any presentation. But when you're relying on the audience to help make your presentation work, it's even more important to anticipate how the participants will react. The only way to do that effectively is with a dry run.

INTERACTIVE IS POSSIBLE WITH LARGE AUDIENCES

To some degree, interactive presentations are about managing crowd behavior. The larger the crowd, the more difficult it is to manage. Fortunately, in my experience most audiences are no larger than fifty people, and interactive presentations are relatively simple for groups of that size.

But I've seen and done interactive presentations with much larger groups that include as many as 300 people. The key is in the rehearsal. With large crowds, people can't really ask you what to do if they don't understand the instructions. So you must be very precise when you describe what to do. The explanations should be simple and clear. Moreover, once you've developed a good explanation that works, stick with it and don't vary the wording.

With large groups, it's also advisable to put the instructions on a PowerPoint slide and project it in front of the room.

WHAT IF INTERACTIVE IS NOT PRACTICAL?

At the beginning of this chapter I said that the best way to ensure a great presentation is to go interactive. Unfortunately, sometimes that's not practical. If you're speaking to the board of directors of a client, the board members might resent being asked to do exercises (even if they might find this valuable, depending on the circumstances).

But you can make your presentation as interactive as possible by leaving time for questions and actively seeking feedback during the presentation. For example, when you finish a point, you can ask whether there are any questions. You can even solicit the audience's opinion, e.g., "Does anyone here have anything to add on this particular issue?"

GET COMFORTABLE GIVING UP CONTROL

Even though interactive presentations aren't always possible, they are still the best way to ensure that you really connect with the audience. Nevertheless, many people resist them. What causes this resistance?

The answer is simple: Control.

Interactive means interacting with the audience. Interaction can be unpredictable. Who knows what questions might arise?

Great communicators understand that the best presentations are more like conversations. They are not afraid of unanticipated questions.

We worked with the head of a law school library who had a great presentation style. But she never made her presentations interactive. "I'm afraid," she admitted. "I don't want to lose control."

A year later, we heard her again and she started the presentation by asking the audience to respond to some questions. She had also cut back her remarks substantially. When we complimented her, she said, "I'm working at it and the audiences seem more captivated."

CHAPTER **19**

How to Think Fast on Your Feet: Communicating Impromptu

INTRODUCTION

Few skills say that you're a great communicator more convincingly than the ability to speak simply, persuasively, and confidently about the law *off the cuff*.

When I was practicing law, I would attend client meetings with one of the top partners in the firm. He was a terrific lawyer for many reasons. He understood the client's business. He understood the law. He was unflappable when he spoke before regulators.

But what I envied most was how this partner handled himself in meetings. We'd be at the client's offices in a conference room. Gathered around the table would be half a dozen assorted managers, vice-presidents, and directors. And in discussing a client issue, someone would turn to the partner and say, "Jack [not his real name], what do you think we need to do to make sure that the regulator is satisfied that we're in compliance?"

Now, Jack would have had no time to think. He would have had no formal presentation prepared. And although he certainly knew the law and regulations in question, it is doubtful that he had made a detailed review of the relevant law in preparation for the meeting.

But he almost always delivered a great answer. Where I might have stumbled through the regulatory complexities of the situation, Jack would deliver an answer that was short, simple, and most of all, convincing.

The client ate it up. I was usually in awe.

SPEAKING OFF THE CUFF

Many lawyers consider the ability to speak "off the cuff" as something of a Holy Grail of law practice. When lawyers ask me to help them achieve this skill, they often will ascribe the skill to one of the firm's senior, most powerful partners.

I met recently with a partner in a major law firm who told me that he wanted to improve his "presence" in meetings with partners. When I asked what he meant by "presence," he said, "I want to sound smooth like Bob Jennings, our managing partner [not his real name]. You should hear him in our partnership meetings. When he speaks up, it's totally spontaneous. But he sounds so smooth, so focused and organized. And people believe everything he says. Can you help me sound like him? You know, smooth in meetings?"

The answer to his question is "No" and Yes." "No," I can't help you sound like someone else. No matter how good a model "Bob Jennings" may be, you're going to have to find a way to sound good with your own style and voice. You're going to have to learn how to communicate like "Maximum You." With that in mind, however, "Yes," you can learn to sound persuasive and focused off the cuff. The key is to focus on two areas:

> ▸ How to quickly organize your thoughts; and
> ▸ How to speak with a confident style.

You must focus on both elements if you want to be perceived as a great impromptu communicator.

The Off the Cuff Formula (PV + 3Q): Organizing Your Thoughts in Real Time

My clients often admit to me that, "In meetings with clients, I'm terrible when I have to speak impromptu. I usually ramble on and on. If I'm not prepared, I just can't seem to sound focused and organized."

Occasionally we're all asked to make off the cuff remarks. Maybe a client asks us to describe the problems with a new law. Maybe we must describe the risks of a new deal. Maybe we have to describe the challenges associated with complying with a new tax law. Any time we're called upon to give impromptu remarks—in client meetings or before a larger group—this is a challenge.

And most people find this type of communication very difficult. For most lawyers, the most daunting part of sounding good "off the cuff" is being able to organize their thoughts quickly, simply, and in a way that is immediately relevant to the client's needs.

We have found that the best way to quickly organize your thoughts is with a template, a simple Formula that you can use with little preparation in real time. This "Off the Cuff Formula" is as follows:

$$PV + 3Q$$

where:

PV = Primary Value or Main Idea (i.e., "The primary value for you here is" or, "The main idea I want to get across is. . . ."), and

3Q = "Three Questions" (i.e., "The three main questions you may wonder about here are. . . ." or, "The three most important things to remember here are. . . .").

Why Does This Formula Work?

You may recall that I said that spoken communication was like a bridge with a posted weight limit. If you overload the bridge with too much detail and complex explanations, it will collapse. But if you keep your ideas simple and focused on listener needs, your message will cross the bridge easily and connect with the listener.

The Off the Cuff Formula works because it keeps you from overburdening the bridge of communication. That is, it keeps you from violating the first principle of effective spoken communication:

Spoken communication is a limited medium that does some things well and other things badly.

How Does This Formula Work?

Whether you have to unexpectedly speak to a large group, or a client asks you during a meeting to summarize the latest tax law, use the Off the Cuff Formula to gather your thoughts. It's a three-step process:

STEP 1: *Establish a single main idea for what you want to say.* Establish a single main idea by completing one of the following statements:

▶ "The primary value for you here is _____."
▶ "The main idea here is _____."
▶ "The key thing we need to accomplish here is _____."

Note that this part of the process is consistent with one of the core principles of great spoken communication: That spoken communication is good at focusing on big picture ideas and listener values.

STEP 2: *Briefly preview what you're going to say.* You accomplish the preview with a quick three-point statement, usually by asking three questions that the listener most likely will want to know. It will sound something like the following:

"The three main questions that people ask are:

▶ *"*How much will it cost?
▶ *"*When is the deadline?
▶ *"*What happens if we miss the deadline?*"*

Of course, you don't have to use three questions. You can use any simple, three-point organizational structure that sounds good. How about the following?

"The three main concerns you may have are:

▶ *"*Cost
▶ *"*Deadline
▶ *"*Penalties*"*

Or how about this example?

"Let's focus on three things:

▶ *"*The law
▶ *"*Whom the law applies to
▶ *"*The penalties*"*

This preview will help you avoid rambling and sounding disjointed. Instead, the three-point preview makes you seem organized. The three-point structure is always easy for the listener to follow.

Note that this preview is also consistent with one of the principles of effective spoken communication, i.e., that spoken communication isn't generally effective at transmitting more than two or three points.

STEP 3: *Answer the three questions that you raised in the preview.* Your preview is essentially a road map that you follow to keep on track. Don't deviate from your road map and you'll never ramble again.

Your "road map" will sound something like this:

▶ *"*First, let me address the first question: How much will it cost?" Then answer the question.

> ▸ "Next, let's talk about the second question: When is the deadline?" Answer the question.

> ▸ "Finally, let's talk about what might happen if we miss the deadline." Answer the question.

In answering your questions, try to use stories that bring your ideas to life. Usually, stories are the evidence that is most readily available off the cuff. And, as already discussed, spoken communication is a wonderful medium for stories.

Learning to Use PV + 3Q in Real Time: Developing a Mental Habit

So imagine the situation. You're at a meeting with a client and she asks you to summarize the current negotiations about a big contract. You respond, "Hold on a moment, let me think about the three-step Formula that I just read through."

Obviously, that won't work.

Using the Off the Cuff Formula PV + 3Q will take some practice. But it's not as difficult as it may seem. Most important, you must develop the *mental habit* of focusing first on the main idea or the primary value and then going to a three-point preview.

Developing new communication habits generally is not as difficult or unusual as this might seem. There are many kinds of communication where we are programmed to think and respond in a certain way. For example:

> ▸ Most of our customary exchanges are pre-programmed: We automatically say "please" and "thank you" in response to dozens of everyday scenarios.

> ▸ Ordering food at a restaurant, we can get in the habit of asking for the salad first and then the entrée.

> ▸ Customer service representatives learn a typical script for answering telephone complaints that is based on the most helpful, expeditious model. I called AAA for roadside assistance recently, and the telephone representative started by saying, "Are you calling from a safe place? . . . What is wrong with the car? . . . Have you tried jumpstarting the battery?"

Obviously, we constantly speak in patterns. PV + 3Q is just another pattern to learn.

For many people this change in discipline is a real challenge. Most of us speak poorly off the cuff because we usually respond to inquiries by focusing on what's most important to us and then going through a logical argument that tracks the state of our knowledge.

But great communicators develop the mental habit of focusing on what's important to the listener. That's what the Off the Cuff Formula is designed to help you accomplish.

PV + 3Q Shticks *That Help the Learning Process*

Even if you don't learn how to respond in the PV + 3Q format every time you must "think on your feet," after a while you should develop a few standard *shticks* that you can use repeatedly in response to most common scenarios.

Who Is Covered? What Does the Law Require? What Are the Penalties?

Variations on this *schtick* are common in the legal profession. The client turns to you and says that he's read about a new law and wants to know more about it. "Can you summarize it for me?"

PV: You start by describing the "main idea behind the law," such as what the law is generally trying to accomplish in relation to the client's business. Then you say:

3Q: *There are three main things to think about here:*

> ▸ "Who in our business is covered by this law?" Or perhaps, "What activity is covered by the law?"
> ▸ "What does the law require?"
> ▸ "What are the penalties?"

That *shtick* will cover many issues raised by clients.

What Do You Have to Do? What Are the Downsides? What Are the Upsides?

This is a slight variation on the first shtick. I worked with a healthcare lawyer who had to summarize how a new law impacted a heavily regulated healthcare client. Here's the pattern he developed:

PV: The main thrust of this new law is to standardize how we file reports with insurance carriers.

3Q: *There are three main things to think about:*

> ▸ "What does the law require of us?"
> ▸ "What are the downsides [disadvantages]?"
> ▸ "What are the upsides [advantages]?"

What Stage Are Negotiations in Now? What Are the Sticking Points? When Will the Deal Close?

I worked with a client whose primary job was to negotiate deals with clients' business partners. He was constantly being asked by clients for updates on contract negotiations. Unfortunately, his answers tended to be rambling. After we role-played several of these meetings, the client could answer update questions, with some variation, as follows:

PV: The main objective of this deal is _____. Or, the deal is going well/badly.

3Q: *Let me focus on three things:*

> ▸ "Where are negotiations now?"
> ▸ "What are the sticking points in the negotiations?"
> ▸ "When can we close the deal?"

Control? Remaining Interest? Limits on Owner's Rights?

I worked with a lawyer who helps business owners in closely held companies acquire junior partners as minority owners. This can be sticky because the owner must relinquish enough of the business to interest the junior partner in participating. And, unfortunately, the business owner usually wants to retain control for himself or herself.

Hence, the issue that generally arises in meetings of the owner with clients is how to quickly explain all the options to business owner clients. The lawyer proposed the following:

PV: The main idea here is to determine how much control you're going to retain over the business.

3Q: *There are three issues:*

▸ "What voting rights do you relinquish?"

▸ "What *other* rights do you want to relinquish as the owner?"

▸ "What happens to the minority owner's interest if he leaves, dies, or is disabled?"

Who Will You Sue? If No One, What Funds Can Be Pursued?

I worked with a real estate lawyer who helps clients buy property from real estate developers. A key problem with these deals is that once a deal closes, the former owner's corporate entity often ceases to exist because the developer dissolves that entity upon sale. For the buyer, the problem then is what happens if something goes wrong and he wants to sue someone once the deal has been completed? There are of course many legal solutions to this problem. But I wanted to help this client discuss those solutions without sounding like a legal nerd.

When this client summarizes the issue for his clients, following is what he says:

PV: The main concern we must address is, what will you do if something goes wrong after the deal closes?

3Q: *There are two issues here:*

▸ "Who are you going to sue?"

▸ "If the answer is no one, can we guarantee that there are funds somewhere for you to claim if you're damaged?"

ANSWERING QUESTIONS

Know the Questions

There's a famous story about Henry Kissinger when he was Secretary of State during the Nixon administration. During a press conference he had just given some brief remarks and was about to take questions when he said, "Does anyone have questions for the answers I've prepared?"

Kissinger knew one of the real keys to handling questions effectively: Think long and hard about what the questions are going to be and prepare the answers.

A little effort goes a long way. Whenever you will be subject to questioning by a client, you should take some time to think about the questions you might be asked.

This shouldn't surprise anyone who has gone to law school or argued before a judge. The students who do best on law school exams are often the ones who are best at "psyching out" the exam. That means they've guessed the questions in advance. And anyone who has prepared for an oral argument in court knows that the best way to prepare is by correctly anticipating all the questions the judge might ask.

Similarly, you should prepare for meetings with clients by thinking about all the questions they might ask during the meetings.

Lessons in Watch Building

"Why is this contract invalid?"

"Let me see if I can explain the elements required to form a binding contract. . . ."

Five minutes later, the client is ready to hang himself.

This scenario is not far-fetched. Many lawyers answer a simple question like a detailed law seminar. And, of course, that's the entirely wrong approach. Instead, you should assume that the questioner wants the simplest answer possible. Clients are smart. If they want to know more, they'll ask.

I learned this lesson the hard way when I was a second-year associate working on my first big case. I was a neophyte electric utility lawyer involved in what we used to call "customer choice" cases. That is, in certain circumstances in the state of Georgia, owners of large new buildings would have the chance to make a one-time choice of power supplier.

Since it was a *one-time* choice (the electric utility that wins the competition gets to supply power to the building forever or until the law changes), you can imagine how fierce the competition became. Once in a while the losing utility would claim the right to serve the new building regardless of the customer's choice. In those cases, there would usually be a lawsuit that we would call a "customer choice" case.

Because the cases weren't too complex and the amount of money in issue was usually modest by utility standards, less-experienced lawyers like me would sometimes get the chance to try a case. Of course, I was excited about the chance to try my first case even if (as it turned out) the case was something of a loser.

So one day I was in my office, drafting testimony for the case, when a top lawyer in my firm (let's call him Vic) telephoned me to discuss the case. Nervously, I reported to his office.

"Joey, how's the case going?" he asked.

I began telling Vic everything I knew about the case. I told him about our facts and the opponent's facts. I told him about details I had discovered that might be of help. I also told Vic some of the things our client had done that weren't helpful. I began telling Vic in detail about the brief I had written (and of which I was very proud).

To all of this Vic just sat quietly with his arms crossed.

Finally, he interrupted. "Joey!" he barked. Then he paused.

His sharp voice pulled me out of "brain dump" mode.

"I've asked you the time of day," he said. "But you're telling me how to build a fucking watch."

And that's pretty much how most lawyers go wrong when they are asked questions. Rather than start with the simple answer, we interpret the question as a license to regurgitate everything we know about the subject into the questioner's lap.

Going APE: Handling Questions Effectively in a Meeting

Imagine a training room filled with lawyers. I stand at the head of the room answering questions on how to answer questions. I'm trying to explain that the best way to answer questions is to give a simple answer, pause and wait for a response, and then evaluate whether the client wants or needs more information.

Here's how the dialogue might go:

Trainer: "Just as I did in my young associate days, many lawyers tend to use a simple question as an excuse for a 'brain dump,' a chance to show off knowledge, to describe how to 'build the watch.' Unfortunately, this is not what the person asking the question wants. We tend to start talking as soon as the question is asked, losing contact with the listener and disregarding the clear intent of the question.

"To handle questions well, we must learn to answer them simply and briefly."

Great Communicator in Training (GCIT): "What if the client wants to know more? What if the client wants a longer answer?"

Trainer: "Just because you've given a short answer doesn't mean the conversation is over. We humans are pretty remarkable in that we know how to communicate our needs. If the clients feel they need more information, then you'll know that when they ask follow-up questions. It's a beautiful thing."

GCIT: "But what if the client doesn't know he needs more information?"

Trainer: "This is the great excuse for brain dumping. We want to tell a client everything we know because we assume that he doesn't know what he wants to find out. Certainly, you must understand your client. And you need to advise him thoroughly, using your best judgment. But most clients are pretty sophisticated about what they need. Usually, if they want to know something, they'll ask."

GCIT: "So, what do you recommend?"

Trainer: "I'm glad you asked. The key is answering simply while staying in close touch with whether your answer has satisfied the client. We say that you should go APE."

GCIT: "APE?"

Trainer: "That's right. **A-P-E.** *Answer. Pause. Evaluate. Answer. Pause. Evaluate.* It's a cycle that you repeat over and over. For example:

"Answer: Deliver a short simple answer. Two to four sentences is usually fine. It's probably what the client wants.

"Pause: Once you've answered, pause (or just slow down) and look at your listener. This doesn't have to take long. It can be for a fleeting moment. Simply observe your listener and determine how he's responding to your answer. Does he look puzzled? Does it seem that your brief response is long enough? Does he ask any questions? It is most important not to lose touch with the questioner.

"Evaluate: Then you must evaluate whether the client wants to know more."

GCIT: "How do I evaluate?"

Trainer: "Look and listen. If the client wants to know more, he might look puzzled. Or he might ask a follow-up question. Either indicates that you must deliver more information. Remember, you should stay close to the questioner and make sure you're closely attuned to his needs. If he looks satisfied or bored, move on."

GCIT: "So you're saying that I need to answer briefly and simply, but also listen and pay close attention to the client who is asking the question. Otherwise I might become mired in a long answer that doesn't interest the client."

Trainer: "My work here is done."

COMBINING THINKING ON YOUR FEET AND Q&A

Thriving in Thunderdome

So far we've discussed how to deliver impromptu remarks as well as how to answer questions effectively in meetings. The problem is that in business meetings, neither situation happens in a vacuum. Most likely, you'll be asked to deliver impromptu remarks and at the same time you'll be interrupted with questions before you have a chance to get to your second point.

These free-for-all meetings, what I call "Thunderdome Meetings" after the old Mad Max slug fest movies, are increasingly common in business, especially with more entrepreneurial fast-growth businesses where young executives with big egos are running the show.

These meetings can be very challenging and frustrating for poor communicators. I was working with one lawyer who told me that he hated going to meetings with one client because he was constantly being interrupted and challenged when he was called on to speak.

"I think it's rude," he said. "They'll ask you a question and before you have a chance to say anything, they're interrupting, asking questions, challenging your assumptions. They should have the courtesy to let you finish talking."

Thriving in Thunderdome meetings is a skill. It takes a combination of three things to seem knowledgeable and proficient in such meetings:

(1) *Attitude*: To do well in these meetings, you must understand that these intensive interactive meetings are not mere rude ego-fests, but rather are fast-paced, interactive team events.

(2) *Organization*: You need to rely on the PV + 3Q Formula to quickly organize your thoughts into a short, simple statement.

(3) *Connected style*: How you look and sound is critical in these meetings. You must connect with the audience.

Attitude: The Heart of a Servant

People don't like being interrupted. It can seem rude. But I suspect that we lawyers find it more troublesome than people in business who are used to working on teams where ideas are flowing and energy is high. These high energy meetings usually involve creative people working together with excitement.

You will be happier in these Thunderdome meetings if you adopt the right attitude. I call this attitude "the heart of a servant." The only reason you exist as a lawyer is to be a servant to your client's needs. You must put your client's needs first.

Therefore, when a client interrupts you with a question, you shouldn't get angry or frustrated. Rather, you should think, "I am here to serve you. If you have a question that you feel is so important you need to interrupt me, I'm going to assume that you have a good faith reason for asking. And I'm going to drop everything to serve you with the best answer I can think of."

At the heart of every great lawyer and communicator is the heart of a servant.

Organization: Using a PV + 3Q Bullet to Keep the Wolves at Bay

Speaking up in a Thunderdome is a lot like walking into the middle of a hungry wolf pack. The wolf pack circles with dripping jaws. Its members look for weakness. If they see you limp or if you otherwise falter, the wolves pounce, teeth bared, aggressively questioning, undermining your assumptions. Because of the nature of Thunderdome meetings, it's impossible to hold off the wolves forever. But if you have your thoughts well-organized, you won't look weak. You'll look confident and strong. As a result, the wolves will show restraint while you explain your position.

Organize your thoughts and hold the wolves at bay with a PV + 3Q Bullet—a tightly organized nugget of thought that explodes when it's your turn to talk.

Here's how it works. When you go to a meeting, you should have a pretty good idea of what will be discussed. For example, if you're helping a client implement a new tax strategy, the client might ask you, "Tell us how the new strategy implementation is coming." With that in mind, you go to the meeting prepared with your "PV + 3Q bullet" ready to fire off quickly and confidently when it is your turn to talk. It might sound like this:

PV: The main thing we're trying to achieve with this strategy is lowering the company's effective tax rate by 5%.

3Q: *Now the three main ideas here are:*

> ▶ "Exactly how much money can we expect to save this year?"
> ▶ "Does this change how we account for our revenues?"
> ▶ "And has the IRS addressed our situation directly?"

Why does the PV + 3Q bullet hold the wolves at bay?

The wolves respect strength and pounce on weakness. If you fire off your bullet cleanly, you're going to sound strong, like you have your thoughts organized. The wolves will sense no weakness. They're going to want to hear what you have to say rather than pouncing at once. Indeed, when the wolves hear the bullet, they will stand back and listen.

Of course, the bullet doesn't allow you to speak indefinitely. The wolves will still pounce, asking questions to meet their needs. But if you have the Heart of a Servant, you're going to welcome those questions. And if you confidently deliver your bullet, chances are the wolves won't pounce with teeth bared. Instead, they'll leap on you gently you like happy puppies, gathering information from a confident servant rather than devouring weak prey.

Confident Style: Mesmerizing the Wild Things

No one offers a better lesson in how to tame the wolves in a wild business meeting than the little boy Max in Maurice Sendak's famous children's book *Where the Wild Things Are*. In the book, Max found himself in a Thunderdome Meeting with "Wild Things" that "roared their terrible roars and gnashed their terrible teeth and rolled their terrible eyes."

But Max quickly learned that a little style went a long way toward calming the Wild Things. Indeed, Max "tamed them with the magic trick of staring into all their yellow eyes without blinking once."

Although it may be foolish to get into staring contests with clients, Max understood that confident style commands respect.

What's true for Max is true for you too in your wild business meetings. Flash some confidence and the wolves in your meetings are going to respect you and give you a little space. In other words, rather than speaking in a flat monotone, speak with energy. Be "Maximum You." Lose the dull business mask that most people wear all day and present an animated positive face. Of course, like Max, you should make strong eye contact.

In our workshops, we role-play Thunderdome Meetings with participants sitting around a conference table like a real meeting. We instruct the participants to jump in with aggressive questions in as soon as they want. I often time the exercise to see when the first questions begin. It's amazing to see how the participants with the strongest style almost always get thirty seconds more than the ones with flat voices and facial expressions.

You want to thrive in Thunderdome? Be like Max. Tame the wolves with great style.

Handling Questions in Presentations: Some Tips for Crowd Control

Just as in meetings, you should give simple answers when you make presentations. However, presentations present some important issues of crowd management.

To Get Questions, Train the Audience to Ask

Some people hesitate to leave time for questions because they fear there won't be any questions and the ensuing silence will be embarrassing. Usually, however, the number of questions has as much to do with the speaker as it does with the audience. Whether a speaker is asked questions is usually a function of whether the audience senses that questions may indeed be asked.

In fact, you can actually train your audience to ask questions just as comedians train their audiences to laugh. Several years ago I even took a two-month course in stand-up comedy just to see how the process works. I wasn't particularly funny. But I learned something about audiences: You can train them!

Instructor Jeff Justice, a wonderful comic and teacher, explained how great comedians see the audience as a group of people that must be trained to laugh. This is not simple. But one absolutely essential element is to tell the punch line and then *wait for the laugh*. You must stop talking and let the audience laugh. If you don't wait after the punch line, you'll train the audience *not to laugh* because they will be listening for the next punch line.

I have found that something similar occurs when you speak to audiences in business. You can actually train the audience to ask questions or, conversely, train them never to ask a question.

To train the audience to ask questions, it is necessary to create an environment in which they feel comfortable asking questions. You can create such an environment by:

(1) *Allowing at least one-third of the presentation time for questions.* If you try to cram sixty minutes of information into a fifty-minute presentation, the audience will sense that you don't have time for questions and will not ask any.

(2) *Periodically asking the audience for input.* If you start asking for input early in the presentation, the audience will understand that they are expected to contribute, and they will start asking questions.

(3) *Waiting for questions when you ask for them.* Too often speakers will say, "Any questions?" And then they will move on if a hand doesn't shoot up instantly. When you ask for questions, you must wait a while for someone to raise his hand. If you don't wait, your audience will probably assume that your call for questions wasn't sincere and may never ask another question during the rest of the presentation. If you wait patiently for questions every time you ask, you'll find

that the audience will become more forthcoming with questions as the presentation proceeds.

(4) *Rewarding the questioner by taking the question seriously.* This is the equivalent of rewarding your dog when he heels or sits on cue. The best way to get more questions is to convey the sense that people who ask questions are "good." The way to convey that sentiment is not to say, "good question." Rather, how you act and respond should be the equivalent of saying, "good question." Look the questioner in the eye and respond seriously. I've seen presenters respond to questions with annoyed expressions, with a smirk, or worse, a jibe aimed at the questioner. If you seem to like questions, your audience will respond with more of them.

Of course, audiences differ. But a good speaker can usually persuade the audience to start asking questions. You must train your audience to do your bidding.

Repeating Questions to Handle Hostile Questioners

With larger groups, it's a good idea if you repeat a question after it is asked. Repeating ensures that everyone else has heard the question and will give you time to gather your thoughts. Moreover, you will have a chance to rephrase a hostile question if necessary.

Suppose you are advocating for a new tax policy. You might get the question, "Isn't this new tax policy a waste of money?" This "stick-in-the-eye" question can be rephrased to, "The question is: How much will the new policy cost?"

Great communicators are never thrown by hostile questions. But they don't let the questioners push them around either.

Avoid Complimenting the Questioners

"Can you tell me the policy behind the law?"

"That's a great question!"

You hear presenters compliment questioners all the time. The problem is that you can't compliment every questioner without seeming insincere.

Instead of saying, "Great question!" simply treat every question as if it were great. You do that by maintaining great eye contact, smiling, and taking every question seriously.

Respond to Multi-Faceted Questions in Segments

"I have a question about how the OSHA regulation applies to me and when I have to begin implementing it in my office." That's a compound question. Don't try to answer all parts at once. Preface your response by saying, "You've asked me two questions. I'll take the 'how' question first and then I'll address the 'implementation' issue."

Cut Off Showboaters

Sometimes a participant will try to take over the presentation with many questions and with grandstanding statements. There's a trick to handling these folks and it takes a little psychology.

When someone is showboating and asking never-ending questions, make good strong eye contact until he's done. Then give a good strong answer to the others in the crowd, but move your eye contact away from the questioner. When you've finished, add "Does anyone else have a question?"

By ending eye contact with the showboater and asking the audience for another question, you've cut off the nuisance questioner without humiliating him. If you handle these folks gently, the crowd will be appreciative. Remember, no matter how nasty the showboater gets, never be nasty in return. If you're polite, you'll win over the rest of the audience with your kindness.

End with a Recap of Your Presentation Points

Once you've finished answering questions, return to the main idea of your presentation by recapping your Message Objective and Three Main Points.

For example: "So, let me recap my main messages here today. The central thing you should do is keep the antitrust laws in mind if you want to keep yourself out of trouble. Be careful about what you discuss with the competition. Keep the law department apprised of any programs that will cause severe damage to a competitor. And be careful about what you write in memos and e-mails."

By recapping at the end, you ensure that you end the program with your points foremost in the audience's mind, rather than other matters that may have been raised by questioners.

CHAPTER **20**

Visuals: What's the Point
of PowerPoint?

THE POWERPOINT REBELLION

EFFECTIVE USE OF SLIDES: ONE PRINCIPLE AND FOUR RULES
  Principle: You Are the Most Important Visual
  Rule 1: Use Fewer Visuals
  Rule 2: Use Simple Slides
  Rule 3: Keep Sentences Short
  Rule 4: Pictures Work

USING THE FORMULA TO GUIDE YOUR SLIDES

ALWAYS MAINTAIN CONNECTION WITH THE AUDIENCE

THE POWERPOINT REBELLION

This could be a very short chapter. If I had the full courage of my convictions (and was a tad glib), I would write, "Great communicators don't use PowerPoint." And I would move on with a self-righteous sniff. That's all. Don't like it? Get another book.

Pound sand, Bill Gates!

Indeed, if there is any doubt that the business world is swinging away from PowerPoint, consider that, as I write these words, I'm on an airplane traveling to work with an important client on a series of presentations for a conference. The group leader has decreed that none of the presentations shall include PowerPoint. "I hate watching PowerPoint presentations," he says. "And so does everyone else."

Although you may not agree that PowerPoint is evil (and I don't think it's evil either), based on my experience working with lawyers and executives, there is definitely an anti-PowerPoint rebellion afoot.

There is a pretty good rule of thumb in the communication and selling skills business that *the rank of the presenter is inversely proportional to the number of slides in his presentation*. That's because true leaders know that communication is not about how much data can be crowded onto a slide. Rather, good communication should connect with the audience, make them understand, and move them.

Remember the most basic principles of this book: spoken communication only does certain things well. It communicates big ideas and a limited number of points. The best way to make those points memorable is by using stories and personal anecdotes. But most people use PowerPoint to try and crowd a lot of data into a presentation. Somehow, they believe, putting data in bullet points and graphs is going to make the listeners remember it better. But PowerPoint's bullet points don't allow for a ringing narrative.

Remember also that spoken communication is wonderful for using the force of your personal style (your personality) to persuade. PowerPoint actually undermines your ability to connect with personality by shifting attention away from the presenter to a slide show. Indeed, it's almost commonplace for presenters to narrate their presentations while staring at their slides. You will be unable to connect with the audience if your back is facing them.

EFFECTIVE USE OF SLIDES: ONE PRINCIPLE AND FOUR RULES

Let us not lose sight of the fact that PowerPoint and other types of visuals can be helpful in some circumstances. However, when you use visuals for any presentation, you must remember one principle and four rules.

Principle: You Are the Most Important Visual

You cannot move an audience if you're not connecting with them. And you won't connect if your listeners are sitting in the dark watching a slide show.

Rule 1: Use Fewer Visuals

Fewer slides allow you to be more engaging and persuasive, which is not possible if you're simply narrating a slide show. In a thirty-minute presentation, you should project no more than ten slides. Eight is better.

Rule 2: Use Simple Slides

Too often, audiences are faced with slides that look like complex puzzles with shapes and arrows and flow charts. These charts are almost always too complicated to have any impact during the one minute or so that the audience sees them. Simplify so that fewer ideas are included in any one slide.

Rule 3: Keep Sentences Short

PowerPoint is actually good for reinforcing the main ideas that you are trying to make. Reinforce those big ideas with short "headline style" sentences that the audience can quickly read. Too often, slides include considerable text in small type. Do we really expect the audience to read that? If not, then why present the slides?

Rule 4: Pictures Work

Photographs and pictures are quickly understood without much effort. The right picture can make a point memorably.

Keep this rule in mind as you create slides for presentations, and you'll be viewed as a great communicator rather than a corporate toad who has no better sense than to slavishly read slides.

USING THE FORMULA TO GUIDE YOUR SLIDES

If it is too broad to say, "Great Communicators don't use PowerPoint," I certainly can insist that "Great Communicators never use fifty slides." We frequently endure presentations in which the speaker has one hour and has so crammed his time with slides that the listeners' eyes glaze over and the audience ceases paying attention.

Meanwhile, the presenter rushes through the presentation trying desperately to cover all the information when, if he'd only look at the audience, he would quickly realize that they are at best confused and at worst totally disengaged.

Use the Formula to make sure that you don't overwhelm your listeners with slides.

Let's go back to the antitrust presentation that we discussed in Chapter 18.

Slide 1: Hook

Show the recent *New Yorker Magazine* cover that features businessmen in a tony men's club, smoking cigars, drinking martinis, and wearing handcuffs. If you don't want to pay *The New Yorker* for reprint rights, then spend ten minutes on the internet to find a public domain photograph of businessmen being led away in handcuffs. Professional business people don't expect to be defendants in criminal prosecutions; reminding them of this possibility can be a potent warning against illegal business activities.

Slide 2: MO and Three-Point Preview

Be sure to prepare an agenda slide to precede one of the most important parts of your presentation: the MO and the preview. The agenda slide sets up what you're planning to say and makes sure that your audience actually gets where you want

Stay Out of Jail and Avoid Fines

- Deal with competitors legally.
- Take care when harming a competitor.
- Watch your documents.

them to go. In the following case, the agenda slide consists of your three points in headline form:

▶ "Dealing with competitors."

▸ "Factors to consider when harming a competitor."
▸ What to put in documents."

Slide 3: Point 1

Deal with Competitors Legally

- Price
- Bid-Volumes
- Strategic Plans
- Plans for Dealing with Competition

Determining how many slides will be prepared for each major point depends on what you want to say and whether the slides will enhance that message. You should not include slides simply because you wish to make a point.

In the antitrust presentation, the most important point is determining which topics to avoid discussing with competition. In order to support your point, you might simply include a slide with a heading as follows:

POINT 1: *Things To Avoid Talking About With Competitors*

▸ Price
▸ Bid-Volumes
▸ Strategic Plans
▸ Plans for Dealing with Competition

Slide 4: Reinforcing Point 1

In the fourth slide, the presenter explains how the Archer Daniels Midland executives were tape-recorded as they conspired to divide the market. For your next slide, you might want show photographs taken by the FBI of the conspirators in the Archer Daniels Midland case.

Stay Out of Jail and Avoid Fines

- Deal with competitors legally.
- Take care when harming a competitor.
- Watch your documents.

Slide 5: Point 2

POINT 2: *Factors To Consider When Harming A Competitor*

In this section, the presenter talks about how to proceed when your actions have adverse consequences on your competition. The main idea is to be aware of certain potentially legitimate business activities that raise antitrust concerns.

Take Care When Harming a Competitor

- Tying
- Predatory Pricing
- Exclusivity Arrangements

You might prepare a slide that lists key activities such as tying, predatory pricing, and exclusivity arrangements.

Moreover, if you relate how Microsoft was accused of antitrust activity, you might simply project on the screen the Microsoft logo with the Internet Explorer logo overriding the Netscape logo.

Slide 6: Point 3

POINT 3: *What To Avoid Putting In Documents*

This is a point that doesn't need much visual support. Do you really believe that the audience is helped by a slide that says, "Be careful what you put in documents"? A better strategy is to copy an e-mail with language that implies anti-trust activity and project it on the screen.

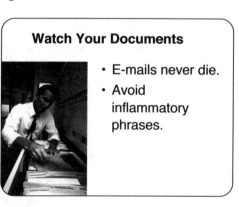

Watch Your Documents

- E-mails never die.
- Avoid inflammatory phrases.

Slide 7: Agenda Slide Again

Usually you will want to end the presentation with a recap of your main points. The easiest way to recap is to project your agenda slide again. No, it's not flashy. But it serves your purpose of making sure that the listeners internalize your main three points.

ALWAYS MAINTAIN CONNECTION WITH THE AUDIENCE

I went to a CLE presentation once where the presenter began his entire presentation with the following words: "Can someone turn off the lights?"

From there, he went on to give his presentation in the dark, clicking through the slides for an hour, never connecting with the audience.

The resulting boredom was excruciating.

When you're using slides for your presentation, don't forget to connect with the audience. Don't turn off the lights. Instead, make sure that your projector is powerful enough to work well with the lights on.

And most important, don't read your slides. One of the greatest crimes against audiences is turning your back to the audience while you narrate slides. Instead, make your point and then refer back to the slide.

Great communicators sometimes use PowerPoint. But when they do, they don't lose their connection with the audience.

CONCLUSION:

Great Selling and Communicating Is Helping Clients Succeed

Lawyers tend to be better at keeping clients than winning new ones. But I believe that if you can make clients love you, you should be able to win new clients as well. That's because at the heart of both winning and keeping clients is the same skill: the ability to understand the company's perspective and communicate in terms of business success.

When it comes to *communicating* with existing clients effectively, lawyers must remember that most clients don't care much about the technical part of the practice of law. That's what they've hired you for. So when you speak to them about their business, you need to speak in terms of business solutions, not legal technicalities. Don't talk in terms of what the tax code says. Talk in terms of how you can help them make money.

And when it comes to winning new clients, lawyers must remember that clients hire new lawyers for the same reason they fall in love with existing lawyers. Clients want lawyers who understand their business and can help them succeed. Technical expertise is important, but not primary. So, business development is nothing more than an extended process of making decision-makers believe that you can help their business succeed. If you want to get a business to hire you as their tax lawyer, try to understand their business and then communicate how you can help them save money on their taxes.

Great selling and communication for lawyers is simple. Understand your client's business. Then help the client. Do that consistently and you'll have a terrific, highly profitable legal career.

JOEY ASHER is an attorney and President of Speechworks, a selling and communication skills coaching company in Atlanta that has been helping lawyers grow their businesses and connect with clients since 1986. He has worked with hundreds of lawyers in dozens of law firms with offices across the country. Speechworks offers workshops and seminars that help lawyers learn to sell and communicate more effectively. He can be reached at (404) 266-0888. To learn more about Speechworks, go to *www.speechworks.net.*

ALSO FROM **ALM PUBLISHING:**

Inside/Outside: How Businesses Buy Legal Services
by Larry Smith

Game, Set, Match: Winning the Negotiations Game
by Henry S. Kramer

The Essential Guide to the Best (and Worst) Legal Sites on the Web
by Robert J. Ambrogi, Esq.

Full Disclosure: The New Lawyer's Must-Read Career Guide
by Christen Civiletto Carey, Esq.

On Trial: Lessons from a Lifetime in the Courtroom
by Henry G. Miller, Esq.

Negotiating and Drafting Contract Boilerplate
by Tina L. Stark, Esq.

Other publications available from ALM:

LAW JOURNAL PRESS professional legal treatises—over 100 titles available

Legal newspapers and magazines—over 20 national and regional titles available, including:

The American Lawyer
The National Law Journal
New York Law Journal

Visit us at our websites:
www.alm.com
www.law.com